Non-Aristotelian Drama in Eigtheenth Century Germany

European University Studies

Europäische Hochschulschriften
Publications Universitaires Européennes

Series I
German Language and Literature
Reihe I   Série I

Deutsche Sprache und Literatur
Langue et littérature allemandes

Vol./Band 621

PETER LANG
Berne and Frankfurt/Main

Helga Stipa Madland

Non-Aristotelian Drama in Eighteenth Century Germany and its Modernity: J.M.R. Lenz

PETER LANG
Berne and Frankfurt/Main

CIP-Kurztitelaufnahme der Deutschen Bibliothek

Madland, Helga Stipa:
Non-Aristotelian drama in eighteenth century
Germany and its modernity: J.M.R. Lenz /
Helga Stipa Madland. – Bern; Frankfurt am Main:
Lang, 1982
   (European university studies: Ser. 1, German
   language and literature; Vol. 621)
   ISBN 3-261-05079-9

NE: Europäische Hochschulschriften / 01

For my parents, Ann and Hubert Stipa

Acknowledgments

I wish to express my thanks to Professor Gunter H.
Hertling for his considerate support and unfailing assistance
and advice. I am also greatly indebted to Professors Diana
Behler, William H. Rey and Hellmut Ammerlahn.

I express my continued admiration and appreciation to
my parents, Ann and Hubert Stipa, and my sister and brother,
Ingrid and Michael, for their moral support. A special word
of thanks I reserve for my children, Kathryn, Michael and
Patrick, for the love, patience and support they have given
me during the months of researching and writing this study.
Michael deserves my final thank you for his assistance in
preparing the bibliography.

Seattle, Washington

December, 1981

TABLE OF CONTENTS

Jemehr ich in mir selbst forsche und über
mich nachdenke, destomehr finde ich Gründe zu
zweifeln, ob ich auch wirklich ein selb-
ständiges von niemand abhängendes Wesen sei,
wie ich doch den brennenden Wunsch in mir
fühle.

(J. M. R. Lenz--"Über die Natur
unsers Geistes")

CHAPTER I

INTRODUCTION

The 1774 appearance of Jakob Michael Reinhold Lenz's
poetological essay "Anmerkungen übers Theater," and his
"comedy" <u>Der Hofmeister</u> of the same year was greeted with
applause and enthusiasm in contemporary literary journals.
Both the essay and the play were erroneously attributed to
Goethe. In rapturous tones the <u>Frankfurter gelehrte
Anzeigen</u>, a mouthpiece for Storm and Stress, called Lenz's
anonymous essay: "einen sehr vollwichtigen Beytrag zur
Dramaturgie!--tiefdurchdachte Einsichten in die Kunst!
ächtes warmes Gefühl des Schönen! anschauend dargestellt!
in jedem Zuge die Hand eines Meisters kennbar!"[1] Wieland's
<u>Teutscher Merkur</u> joined the encomium, albeit in less ardent
language: "Sein dramatisches Glaubensbekenntnis hat uns Hr.
Goethe in einigen Anmerkungen über das Theater vorgelegt,
worinnen er alle Regeln der Bühne darauf reducirt, worauf
man die ganze Poesie zurückführen sollte, auf die <u>Darstellung
des Menschen</u>."[2] When the identity of the author was soon
revealed, the <u>Merkur</u> continued to support Lenz's dramatic
theories and suggested that contemporary dramatists follow
his advice; however, the author formerly praised as a genius

now became a <u>Bilderstürmer</u> who possessed no original talent
but simply jumped on Lessing's bandwagon of protest against
the influence of the French theater.[3] The publisher of the
journal, Wieland himself, took pen in hand. Using Nicolai's
phrase satirizing Goethe in his <u>Leiden</u> <u>und</u> <u>Freuden</u> <u>Werthers</u>
<u>des</u> <u>Mannes</u>, "Traun der Kerl ist 'n Genie,"[4] Wieland suggested
that Lenz was indeed a genius, however, one who wrote for
geniuses like himself in a language neither Wieland nor
anyone else could understand. He called Lenz's language
"ein wunderbares Rothwelsch"[5] and pointed out that Lenz's
attempt to acquaint the Germans with Shakespeare's superiority
as a dramatist was not original, for it had already been
accomplished a year ago--in 1773--in his <u>Merkur</u> by Wieland
himself.[6] Wieland's contradictory reaction to Lenz's
dramatic theory and practice proved to be prophetic. His
oeuvre has continued to evoke similar responses, a fact
which can only be attributed to the intensely paradoxical
nature of his writings.

In a compendium to <u>J</u>. <u>M</u>. <u>R</u>. <u>Lenz</u>: <u>The</u> <u>Renunciation</u> <u>of</u>
<u>Heroism</u>, John Osborne makes the following observation:

> Nach den grossen Zeitgenossen Goethe und Herder
> ist Lenz wohl der bedeutendste und interessanteste
> Dichter der Sturm-und-Drang-Epoche. Aber trotz
> der zunehmenden Beachtung, die sein Werk in der
> neueren deutschen und ausländischen Forschung
> erfahren hat, ist es als ganzes und in seiner
> Vielseitigkeit noch verhältnismässig unbekannt;
> einzelne, für das Verständnis des Werkes und des
> Menschen wichtige Schriften sind bislang sogar
> Neuland geblieben.[7]

Osborne could not have been more correct in his conclusion
that much needs to be done to place Lenz's oeuvre in the
proper perspective. It is a diverse body of work consisting
of poetry, prose pieces, theoretical writings, dramas, frag-
ments of dramas, and letters. For our purposes, we shall
concentrate on Lenz's dramatic theories postulated in the
"Anmerkungen übers Theater" and other pertinent essays and
on his dramas Der Hofmeister and Die Soldaten.

Lenz's dramas cannot be regarded as an extension of the
bourgeois drama of the Enlightenment nor as typical examples
of Storm and Stress dramaturgy. In order to shed light on
the genesis of a concept of the drama which is reflected in
his theories, we must initially turn to the Non-Aristotelian
dramatic trend opposing Gottsched which originated in the 18th
century with the theories of Johann Jakob Bodmer and Johann
Jakob Breitinger. The Non-Aristotelian undercurrents preceding
Storm and Stress are also visible in the dramatic theories
of Gellert, J. E. Schlegel, Gerstenberg, and in the poetics
of Klopstock, all of which are examined in this study.

An analysis and reassessment of the dramatic theories of
Lessing is not included. While Lessing's thought shares many
of the characteristics we identify as Non-Aristotelian--he
advocates both the primacy of character and the mixed character,
for example--his views differ from those concepts which form
the basis of this study in several important particulars.

Lessing adheres to a major principle of classicistic structure--unity of action. For Lessing a drama must be an harmonious entity, a "chain of causes and events. It must not exhibit the episodic structure which is an hallmark of Non-Aristotelian drama. In addition, Lessing does not place the same emphasis on psychological realism as Gerstenberg and Lenz do. He includes psychologically motivated aspects in the depiction of his dramatic figures, but the psychological portrayal of characters and their "inner experience" does not occupy a central position in his dramas. In contrast to Lessing, the intense exploration of the human psyche in order to determine the causes of man's actions and understand the individual in his totality is one of the major orientations of Non-Aristotelian drama in the 18th century.

Non-Aristotelian drama is a movement toward an ever greater realism on the stage. It focuses on character rather than on plot and seeks to depict and comprehend the individual in the multiple situations which constitute his life. The new character preferred by Non-Aristotelian dramatists is multi-faceted; he is not the one-dimensional type advocated by Enlightenment dramatists. Dramatic discourse no longer consists of formal stage language but becomes less stylized and more natural. And the plot is not a unified whole, but it contains numerous sub-plots. In the 18th

century these tendencies are apparent in German dramatic
theory as early as Bodmer and Breitinger. Lenz's concept
of the drama therefore does not represent a sudden and
drastic caesura with the dramatic literature of German
Enlightenment, nor are his theories and practice a continuation of the dramatic art of that epoch. Instead, Lenz's
perception of the drama is at the same time the culmination
and extension of a Non-Aristotelian dramatic trend which
coexisted with those dramatic forms which more precisely
followed classicistic precepts. This study focuses on
the evolution of the concept of mimesis from "imitation"
to "creation" and the effect of the new understanding of
mimesis on dramatic character, language and structure from
Bodmer and Breitinger to Lenz.

* * *

"Ich denke, es wird doch für mich auch ein Herbst einmal kommen, wo diese innere Pein ein Ende nehmen wird.
Abzusterben für die Welt, die mich so wenig kannte, als ich
sie zu kennen wünschte--o welche schwermütige Wollust liegt
in dem Gedanken!"[9] These are the words of Herz, the main
character of Lenz's largely autobiographical epistolary
novel Der Waldbruder. For some time it looked as if Herz's

wish had become true for Lenz. The 20th century, however, shows a new appreciation for the work of a man for whom it experiences considerable affinity. With this study we hope to illuminate the development of Non-Aristotelian dramatic theory during the 18th century and to add another segment to understanding the mosaic of Lenz's oeuvre.

CHAPTER II

NON-ARISTOTELIAN UNDERCURRENTS PRECEDING STORM AND STRESS:
THE CHANGING CONCEPT OF MIMESIS AND ITS
EFFECT ON DRAMATIC CHARACTER, LANGUAGE AND STRUCTURE

1. Bodmer and Breitinger--Toward a New Realism

Today's student of 18th century German drama, having at
his disposal a myriad of literary histories which essentially
agree in their portrayal of the German stage at that time,
emerges with the following picture: In the early decades of
the 18th century, the state of the German theater was a dismal
one. Theatrical fare consisted primarily of frivolous enter-
tainment appealing only to the uneducated and the insensitive.
(Hettner condemns the repertoire of the average theater as
consisting of "Lauter schwülstige und mit Harlekinslustbar-
keiten untermengte Haupt- und Staatsactionen, lauter unnatür-
liche Romanstreiche und Liebeswirrungen, lauter pöbelhafte
Fratzen und Zoten... .")[1] Into the arena strode Johann
Christoph Gottsched. Armed with orthodox convictions derived
from classical authorities, Gottsched effectively and thoroughly
cleared the stage of all former excesses and abuses and
succeeded in imposing his vision of classicism upon German
literature and the German drama in particular, a feat described

by Hettner as an unprecedented dictatorship.[2] Gottsched's
reign was of limited duration and his attempted reforms soon
met with opposition, particularly in the work of Bodmer and
Breitinger, whose primary objections to Gottsched were directed
toward his denial of the rights of the poetic imagination.
Gottsched's eventual public ridicule and literary rejection
were reactions against his excessive rigidity and didacticism,
but not against the classical tradition itself. Lessing, his
most formidable opponent, disagreed with the French interpretation of Aristotle which Gottsched advocated, but his
reinterpretation of Aristotle and repeated return to Aristotelian principles in his own dramas is, to a considerable
degree, a reiteration of the classical doctrine. The classicistic orientation dominating the 18th century was briefly
disrupted by the Storm and Stress movement, a disorder
successfully suppressed by the rebellion's most eminent
authors, and classicism reached a golden zenith in Weimar.

According to this prevailing view, the 18th century
emerges as an era in which the general and predominant
movememt is toward an ever more stringent and pervasive
classicism. This is an accepted but inaccurate assessment
of the complexities of German thought, life, and literature
in the 18th century.

Gottsched's rejection of the last traces of baroque
mannerism exhibited by the poets of the second Silesian

school Lohenstein and Hofmannswaldau, indicates that he,
like others, experienced the need for a literary form which
would more accurately express the spirit of the times.
Gottsched believed that an age which prided itself in its
reliance on reason would naturally be attracted toward
simplicity and naturalness of form and expression, which
he missed in baroque literature and sought to find in French
classicism. But Gottsched did not understand the complexity of
the era and opposition to his traditional dramatic concepts
surfaced quickly. In its infancy, the banner for independence
from classicistic rules was carried by the Swiss critics
Bodmer and Breitinger.

Lesser known than the Swiss critics, and a fiery
adversary of Gottsched, was the North German Jakob Immanuel
Pyra, who in his <u>Erweis</u> <u>dass</u> <u>die</u> <u>Gottschedianische</u> <u>Sekte</u> <u>den</u>
<u>Geschmack</u> <u>verderbe</u>, 1743, accused the Leipzig professor of
a lack of originality and creativity and labelled him a
literary historian, not an innovative thinker.[3] For Bodmer
and Breitinger, however, Pyra has the highest praise, and in
his two part treatise, he becomes their dedicated champion.

Pyra recognized that among the Swiss critics' major
contribution to literary theory was their contention that
the marvelous--<u>das</u> <u>Wunderbare</u>--is a proper concern of
poetry, a view in opposition to Gottsched's dictum that in
an enlightened age the marvelous must be de-emphasized.[4]
Bodmer and Breitinger's heralded "freeing of the imagina-

tion" is well known and needs no elaboration here. In-
frequently mentioned, however, are their thoughts on
dramatic theory. Although the drama or the renewal of the
stage was not their major focus, they did comment on the
nature of tragedy in the Critische Briefe, 1746, and their
views on mimesis and characterization, scattered throughout
their writings, suggest the dawning of a new era for the
German theater.

That differences existed between the Swiss critics and
Gottsched as early as 1725 is evidenced by a Bodmer essay
of that year entitled "Anklagung des verderbten Geschmacks
oder Anmerkungen über den Hamburger Patrioten und die
Halleschen Tadlerinnen." In this treatise the question of
literary taste is deliberated, an issue which is significant
to literary theory because the discussion of aesthetics
suggests that literary form does not have to be determined
by tradition, but is subject to national and personal preference. This document, which was not published until 1727,
is the first major record of the Swiss opposition to Gottsched and his views as expressed in his weekly Die ver-
nünftigen Tadlerinnen.

There seems to be some doubt in the minds of their contemporaries what the prolonged Literaturfehde between
Gottsched and Bodmer and Breitinger was all about. Thus,
it is noted in the prologue to the Hallischen Bemühungen zur

Aufnahme der Critic, that "...die schweizerischen
Schriften von der Poesie mit der Gottschedschen Dichtkunst
in einem Schranke hätten beysammen stehen können, ohne dass
eine Schlacht unter ihnen würde vorgefallen seyn."[5]   Certainly there were many points in which Gottsched and the
Swiss were in agreement. Both rejected what they termed
"den barocken Schwulst" in German literature. They also
shared an admiration for Opitz, compared him with Homer,
and using his own words, called him "Bruder der Natur."[6]
As a whole, they relie upon established authorities in
formulating their own critical views: Gottsched prefers
Horace and Boileau, while Bodmer and Breitinger turn towards Quintilian and DuBos. Clearly, both Gottsched and
the Swiss critics look back toward tradition in an attempt
to evolve a critical poetics for German literature. The
major difference lies in the fact that Gottsched looks
only towards the past and tradition, whereas Bodmer and
Breitinger also open a window toward the new and fresh
ideas which were regenerating the literature of Europe.
This is particularly evident in their views on mimesis.

   Breitinger discusses his concept of mimesis in the
first volume of Critische Dichtkunst, 1740. Like
Gottsched, Breitinger declares that the true artist is an
imitator of nature, including, however, the plastic arts in
his discussion.

> Die beyden Künste, des Mahlers und des Poeten,
> bestehen angeregter Massen in einer geschickten
> Nachahmung der Natur. Die Natur ist die weise
> Lehrmeisterin, bey welcher diese Künstler in die
> Schule gehen; sie legt ihnen eine unzählbare
> Menge der vortrefflichsten Urbilder zur Be-
> wunderung und Nachahmung vor, woran sie das
> Vermögen ihrer Kunst versuchen, und auf die
> Probe setzen können.7

But as he develops his thoughts, he evolves a new interpretation of the nature of imitation.

Primary to Breitinger's concept of mimesis is his
division of reality, or nature, into two worlds--the real
or visible world, die wirkliche Welt and the possible or invisible world--die mögliche Welt. The true artist concerns
himself with the representation of not just one or the other
of these worlds, but with both of them, for both have equal
validity and truth value. Breitinger distinguishes between
the quality of the representation of these two realities.
The poet who confines himself to the representation of the
visible world, as Gottsched demands, is seen by Breitinger as a
mere imitator or copier--"ein guter Abdrücker" (Breitinger, C.D.,
I, 55)--whose work differs only in purpose from that of the
historian. The one, however, who expands his vision to include
the invisible world reaches a new and heretofore discouraged
dimension. The tool the poet must use to represent the
invisible world is his imagination. Through the powers
of his imagination he is capable of giving form to objects
and events which he has not actually observed and for which

nature provides no patterns. Breitinger has given the
poet an important freedom--the freedom to invent. No
longer is the poet a mere imitator, but he becomes an
active creator and innovator. Breitinger qualifies his
remarks; by no means does he veer as far from the old
masters as contemporary artists have done. For Breitinger,
the "possible" is just as much a part of nature as the "real."
Since nature can produce nothing that is "unnatural," portrayals from the possible world must remain within the realm
of reason.

> Denn es giebt zwo Gattungen des Wahren in der
> Natur, eines hat alleine in der gegenwärtigen
> Welt Platz, das andere aber findet sich nur in
> der Welt der möglichen Dinge; (Breitinger, C.D.
> I, 63)...und die Natur kan nichts wider-
> sprechendes hervorbringen; folglich hat auch
> das unnatürliche weder in der Würklichen noch in
> der möglichen Welt einiges Original, sondern es
> ist eine blosse Würckung des blinden und
> unverständigen Zufalles.(Breitinger, C.D. I,
> 63)

But the implications for literary theory are enormous. The
artist is not urged to copy the tried and true classical
forms, be it the literature of Greece or 17th century
France, but he is encouraged to experiment and take a fresh
look at nature.

In addition to poetic theory, Bodmer and Breitinger
investigated an area which had heretofore not been of
concern to literary critics and theoreticians-- the
psychology of poetics. Their psychological probing,

"die Regeln der Poesie aus der innern Natur des Menschen zu erweisen,"[8] their interest in not only the psychology of the creative process, but also the effect of literature on the emotions of the reader, is revealed in their concept of poetic language and of dramatic character.

The prevailing character on the German stage during the first half of the eighteenth century was not the mixed character, but the "typical" character or type. The type characters were divided into two categories, the Standestypen and the Moraltypen. The former are identified by outer characteristics, such as age, occupation or sex, the miles glorioso or the senex of the commedia d'ell arte for example. The latter represent an inner trait--greed, pride, obedience--portray either good or evil qualities, and are, in a sense, the personification of a moral idea. These characters are not allegorical figures, but appear on the stage as humans who possess certain qualities in an extreme degree. Bodmer and Breitinger concur in the acceptance of types as proper characterizations, but Bodmer, in particular, discusses a further element involved in the creation of a dramatic character. Bodmer observed that the climate, the educational system, and the state has a definite impact on the character formation of the individual. Therefore the dramatist must take into account national differences in the creation of a dramatic character,

differences which must be clearly noticeable, particularly
in the dialogue, in "charaktermässigen Reden." [9] In this
concept of characterization, Bodmer sees characters as
nationally and historically individualistic and complex;
he is no longer speaking of types, but rather of "mixed"
characters in the sense of Lessing and other later dramatists. The movement is clearly one toward a more realistic
and natural portrayal of character. Bodmer explains the
difference between what he calls "personal" characters and
type characters, revealing considerable psychological
insight.

> Sie sind von den moralischen Charakteren
> darinnen unterschieden, dass sie nicht so
> abgezogen sind wie dieselben, denn sie geben
> uns den Menschen nicht in einer eintzigen
> absonderlichen Gemüthes-Beschaffenheit
> zu sehen, welche ihn zu einer gewissen Tugend
> oder einem Laster lencket..., sie sind viel
> vermengter und aus mehreren Gemüths-Eigenschaften
> zusammengesetzt; sie begreifen in ihrem Umfange
> den gantzen Menschen mit allen seinen Tugenden,
> Neigungen und Gebrechen, welche sie auseinander
> lesen und einer jeden ihren Grad von Stärcke
> anweisen. [10]

Bodmer goes on to say that because the "personal" or
"historical" character is an attempt to portray the individual
in the multiple aspects of his personality, he does not
rise to extreme heights, nor does he fall to great depths,
a notion which anticipates the dramatic hero of the later
middle class drama.

Bodmer, however, could not completely accept the

mixed character as the preferred characterization and
suggested instead that the mixed character should approach
the type character as closely as possible. On the other
hand, he could not heap enough praise on the individual
characterizations of Homer, the manner in which courage
and caution are united in Odysseus, for example, and the
fact that the quality of courage appears in different
forms in the various characters. It seems that in Bodmer's
and also in Breitinger's thinking, their concept of beauty
generated a conflict with their psychological insights.
They attempted to come to terms with both, the classical
view that beauty is portrayed through unity conquering
adversity, a thought largely represented by Boileau, and the
viewpoint which preferred diversity to unity resulting in
greater "naturalness" advocated by Fontenelle and La
Motte.[11] Their interest in the nature of both poetry and
the poet, their aesthetic-psychological approach to
literary theory, would naturally cause them to vacillate;
on the one hand, they were influenced by classical aesthetics; on the other, they could not help but take delight in
the multiplicity of phenomena confronting the artist in
nature and in man.

Indicative of further new considerations in dramatic
theory is Bodmer's view of the importance of character
versus action. Traditionally, Aristotle has maintained

that the "plot is the principle and the soul of tragedy,
while characters are second" (Poetics, Chapter 6).
Gottsched holds similar views: "Die Fabel ist haupt-
sächlich dasjenige, was der Ursprung und die Seele der
ganzen Dichtkunst ist." (C. D. I, 202). This position
is reiterated by Pietro dei Conti di Calepio, with whom
Bodmer was engaged in an active correspondence between
1728-31, discussing the question of poetic taste and the
nature of tragedy. Bodmer's objections to Calepio's views
are related in a later, fictitious letter published in
Critische Briefe, 1746.

Calepio upholds the Enlightenment view that the final
purpose of tragedy is a didactic one, namely, the improvement of public virtue--"Seine eigene Absicht [that of
tragedy] kan keine andere seyn als die Fehler der gemeinsten
Leidenschaften zu verbessern, solche Misstritte welche von
den mehresten Leuten begangen werden... ."[12] The ideal
character to convey "gute Lebens-Regeln" (Critische Briefe,
p. 11) is a tragic hero who is virtuous and honest and has
only made one fatal mistake, "der rechtschaffen tugendhafte
Mensch der nur einen Fehler begangen hat" (Critische
Briefe, p. 4). Calepio disapproves of Corneille's more
complex characterizations and his suggestion that the
character of the dramatic persona (rather than the dramatic
event) might serve as an example, thus exercising a moral

influence on the audience.[13] Instead, Calepio asserts that the
moral lesson is best taught through the action, thus subjecting
character to action (Critische Briefe, p. 47). He contends
that a too powerfully drawn character would only cause
amazement in the audience, a reaction not leading to moral
improvements. His primarily didactic orientation is further
revealed by his assertion that the pleasure or enjoyment
experienced by the spectator, "das Ergetzen," a factor which
is one of the major points discussed by Bodmer and Calepio,
can only be appropriate if it is related to the useful,
"... weil die rechtschaffene Poesie sich nur das Ergetzen
gefallen lässt, welches mit dem Nützlichen und Lehrreichen
verbunden ist..." (Critische Briefe, p. 49).

Bodmer disagrees.[14] Of course he is enough of a son
of the Enlightenment not to disregard the didactic purposes
of tragedy; but he clearly rejects the Aristotelian dictum
upheld by Calepio that action is superior to characterization,
a notion later developed by Lessing and by Lenz.

As he develops his argument, Bodmer tries to answer the
question of what causes pleasure when viewing a tragedy.
He seeks to locate the experience of pleasure in the characterization.

> So angenehm uns auch eine wohlabgefasste Fabel
> einmal durch ihre Neuigkeit die Zeit kürzen kan,
> so werden wir doch ein weit dauerhafteres
> Ergetzen empfangen, wenn die Gesinnungen, die
> Sitten und Charakter, der Menschen geschickt
> auseinander gesetzt sind.(Critische Briefe, p. 74)

Bodmer's emphasis on character reflects a growing belief that events do not occur at the whim of the gods, but that man can influence and manage his affairs.

In addition, Bodmer extends the commonly held precept that the conveyance of a single moral lesson should be the final purpose of tragedy.

> Jetzo stelle ich ihrer Beurtheilung anheim,
> welches System des Trauerspieles sich einen
> edlern Nutzen zum Endzweck setze, ob dasjenige
> nach welchem der Poet sich nichts weiter
> vornimmt, als irgend eine einzelne Lehre zur
> Besserung des menschlichen Lebens in einem
> langen Exempel anzubringen, oder dasjenige, wo
> er das weitere Vorhaben fasset, eine
> vollständige Schilderey des menschlichen Lebens
> zu liefern, in welcher man nicht allein die
> natürlichen Folgen der menschlichen Hand-
> lungen, sondern die Temperamente, und die
> Neigungen der Menschen zu sehen bekömmt, mit
> den innerlichen Beweggründen zu guten Hand-
> lungen und zu Abweichungen von den allgemeinen
> Grundregeln der Tugend. (Critische Briefe, p. 76)

Of course the emphasis in this evaluation is still on the didactic value, on Nutzen, Horace's prodesse, as the final purpose of tragedy. But Bodmer is concerned about showing not only the error committed by the tragic hero, for which punishment must be meted out in order to re-establish the lost harmony. He also wants to know and show what inner compulsions caused the actions of the tragic hero. What

does the emphasis on the motivation of the tragic hero
mean? It indicates that there is a shift from the mere
teaching of a moral lesson, with its implication that the
individual is dependent and subject to direction from
without, towards an attempt to understand the intricacies
of human nature and find therein the cause for events.
This concept is further explored by Lenz in his "Anmerkungen
übers Theater."

It had been Gottsched's acknowledged aim to rid poetic
language of excessive adornment and introduce it to Nüchtern-
heit and Verständigkeit. Similarly, the Swiss theoreticians
devoted much of their efforts to the examination and analysis
of language. Because of their speculations on the impact of
the emotions upon the creative process, they did not share
Gottsched's preference for linguistic sobriety and rationality,
but followed a much different course.

As early as 1723 in the Discourse der Mahlern, they
discuss the affective quality of language, although at this
early point they focus on actual linguistic encounters rather
than on literary language. In the eighth discourse of the
fourth part, which by now had attained the more specific title
Die Mahler oder Discourse von den Sitten der Menschen, the
following observation is made in reference to language
supposedly spoken by women:

> Ihr redet allezeit mit einer Passion, die euch
> fürchten machet, dass die Sprache der Worten
> zu schwach seye, eure Gedancken auszudrücken;
> ihr bedienet euch neben der selben der Sprache
> der Gebehrden. ... also sind die Grimatzen eine
> gewisse Sprache, durch welche sich die Passionen
> ausdrücken. Die Natur selbst hat den Menschen
> die Sprache der Grimatzen gelehrt, und er weiss
> dieselbe zu reden, bevor er noch die Sprache der
> Worten, oder der Gedancken verstehet.[15]

By Grimatzen the two commentators mean, of course, gestures, a means of expression which requires neither logic nor learning, but comes natural. In their view, the most profound nuances of feeling can be more powerfully expressed through gestures than through words. This is perhaps a first indication of future doubts that language is not fitting or sufficient to express all, that something exists, "das Unsagbare," which cannot be confined by words. This early emphasis on gestures also foreshadows the Non-Aristotelian dramatist's extensive reliance on gestures to speak truth when language fails, a factor which plays an important role in the dramas of J. M. R. Lenz.

But literature can, of course, not exist without words, and eventually the theoretician must come to terms with language. This Breitinger does extensively in Part II of his Critische Dichtkunst, 1740, which consists exclusively of his concept of poetic language.

Of primary importance to our investigation are his thoughts on language and the emotions. Breitinger believes that in order to move the reader, which he regards as one

of the major goals of literature, the poet must use
language which comes straight from the heart. The poet,
however, is not capable of writing in this manner unless he
himself experiences the passion he wishes to express, a
condition which is achieved through the imagination. En-
larging on the assumptions expressed in the Discourse, he
maintains that like gestures, the language of passion does
not have to be learned, but occurs naturally.

> Die bewegliche and hertzrührende Schreibart ist
> nichts anders, als eine ungezwungene Nachahmung
> derjenigen Sprache oder Art zu reden, welche die
> Natur einem jeden, der von einer Leidenschaft
> aufgebracht ist, selbst in den Mund leget.
> (Breitinger, C. D., II, 354)

Characteristic of the language of passion is its lack of
logic and disregard for syntax; the intensity of the
emotion is expressed in the dynamic movement of the
language itself (Breitinger, C. D., II, 355)

Breitinger advocates not only a natural, non-stilted,
non-declamatory literary and dramatic language, but also
suggests that not only the connotation, but the structure
of the language itself becomes a tool for the exploration
of character and situation. Much later he is echoed by
Lessing who, axing the pompous quality of contemporary
dramatists' dialogues, writes in the Hamburgische Dramaturgie
that every passion has its own eloquence, an eloquence which
is inspired by nature and is learned in no school.

2. Klopstock - The Neglected Theoretician

Although Klopstock is fervently lauded as a poetic
genius and renovator of the German language, his theory of
poetics as a whole has been generally ignored. Schleiden
mentions several comprehensive histories of poetics which
have completely excluded Klopstock's theoretical writings.[16]
Partially responsible for this omission is the fragmentary
nature of his theory, together with the inaccessibility and
political focus of his more extensive theoretical work,
Die Gelehrtenrepublik, 1774. Because of its rather intense
nationalism and problematical style (it consists of epi-
grams, aphoristic vignettes, and verse) the book was
panned by many of Klopstock's contemporaries, including
Wieland and Lessing. A few, however, recognized that
among the Teutonic zeal and linguistic acrobatics lay concealed isolated gems of literary theory. Gerhard
Koziełek maintains that for the young Goethe and his
generation the book was as meaningful as Opitz's Buch von
der deutschen Poeterei was for the 17th century and
Gottsched's Critische Dichtkunst for the Enlightenment.[17]
Gervinus recognized its shortcomings, but evaluates the
work positively.

> Dieses Werk stellte sich wie ein Banner der
> republikanischen Freiheit unserer Literatur auf
> gegen allen Druck des Königtums und der
> Hierarchie, gegen alle französichen Diktaturen

> und Mäcenatischen Joche, gegen den Druck der
> blinden Verehrung der Alten, gegen das
> 'Regelbuch' der Ästhetiker, gegen alle Kritik,
> die nicht auf Natur, Erfahrung und Seelenkunde
> ruht. Wäre das Buch nicht von Grillen und
> anfangenden Altersschwächen, durch wunderliche
> Formen und Formeln entstellt und verdunkelt,
> und wäre der Sinn fasslich, klar, durch
> Beispiele und Geschichte verständlich, durch
> Satire und Tadel lebendig gemacht, so würde es
> für die spätere Literaturgeschichte eine
> Fundgrube, für die damalige Kritik ein
> epochenmachendes Werk geworden sein.[18]

Gervinus was one of the few 19th century literary historians and aestheticians who recognized that Klopstock constitutes another link in the chain of those who were struggling to formulate a new and relevant poetics.

Klopstock, whose poetry had been applauded by Bodmer and Breitinger, but who later had an unfortunate quarrel with Bodmer (caused by personal rather than aesthetic differences), holds views on mimesis which very much resemble those of the Swiss. Klopstock rejects pure imitation. In his view, "Das Urbild ist der Baum, die Nachahmung sein Schatten; und dieser ist immer bald zu lang, und bald zu kurz, nie die wahre Gestalt des Baums."[19] Imitation is "Schatten ohne Saft und Kraft, Bildung ohne Schönheit." (Gelehrtenrepublik, p. 117) Instead of following established and spelled out rules of poetics, Klopstock urges the poet to turn inward and listen to the spirit within.

> Lass du dich durch kein Regelbuch irren, wie
> dick es auch sei, und was die Vorred auch davon
> bemelde, dass ohne solchen Wegweiser keiner,
> der da dichtet, könne auch nur einen sichern
> Schritt tun. Frag du den Geist der in dir ist,
> und die Dinge, die du um dich siehst and hörest,
> und die Beschaffenheit des, wovon du vor hast zu
> dichten; und was die dir antworten, dem folge.[20]

Klopstock's disdain for rules and regulations as expressed
here is undoubtedly responsible for the esoteric style of
his Gelehrtenrepublik, in which he consciously avoided
formulating a poetics in pragmatic or even scholarly
language. He proposes the creation of a poetics based on
experience and asserts that because of the complexity of
human nature there can be no absolutely binding rules:
"Wir werden die Natur unsrer Seele nie so tief ergründen,
um mit Gewissenheit sagen zu können, diese oder jene poetische
Schönheit muss diese oder eine andre Wirkung...nothwendig
hervorbringen" (Gelehrtenrepublik, p. 313). For Klopstock,
the "human factor" is beginning to play an increasingly
important role. He is conscious of the part nationality
and personality play in the creative process and is eager to
be flexible and experiment with new forms, as the freie
Rhythmen he utilizes in much of his own poetry demonstrate.

Like the Swiss critics, Klopstock no longer regards
imitation as the unconditional essence of poetry.

> Das Wesen der Poesie besteht darin, dass sie,
> durch die Hülfe der Sprache, eine <u>gewisse Anzahl</u>
> von Gegenständen die wir <u>kennen</u>, oder deren
> Dasein wir <u>vermuten</u>, von <u>einer</u> Seite zeigt,
> welche die <u>vohrnehmsten</u> Kräfte unserer Seele
> in einem so <u>hohen Grade beschäftigt</u>, dass eine
> auf die andere wirkt, und <u>dadurch die ganze</u>
> Seele in Bewegung setzt. (<u>Werke</u>, p. 295)

Klopstock was no realist! Inspired by Longinus' <u>Peri
Hypsus</u>, he held only the sublime worthy of literature, for
it alone could occupy the most noble aspects of man's soul.
But if not in the imitation of antiquity, where was the
sublime to be found? Certainly not in 18th century
Germany! Instead of the imitation and glorification of
Greece, Klopstock therefore advocated the literary representation of the Germanic and turned to Teutonic mythology
and to biblical themes as the major focus of his literary
endeavors. However, in spite of his disavowal of tradition, he did not completely reject Greek skill, as his
essay "Von der Nachahmung des Griechischen Silbenmasses im
Deutschen" indicates. He had no intention of ignoring
formalistic devices from which German poetry could benefit.
His call for renewal is primarily aimed at the rejuvenation
of poetic language and a redirection of literature to more
genuinely express the concerns of the time. However, he
was not yet prepared to come to terms with his century
realistically, as was attempted by the writers of the
Storm and Stress movement, but instead chose the Bible and

Teutonic mythology as his substitute.

Klopstock was primarily a poet; he has little to say
about the drama, although he did write several dramas of
his own. Only cursorily does he refer to the drama in the
Gelehrtenrepublik, where he determines that the only
difference in epic and dramatic action lies in the fact
that dramatic action must be vorstellbar, (p. 310). He
offers no theoretical insights that contributed to the
development of the German drama toward realism. But his
rejection of the imitation of antiquity and plea for a
poetics based on experience suggest that mimesis means the
representation of reality as perceived by the poet, and that
there is more than one reality to portray--in Klopstock's case,
the replacement of a Greek concept of reality with a Germanic one.

Klopstock was convinced that "something new" was
necessary to vitalize literature because merely maintaining
the literary heritage without contributing something original or novel was a sign of stagnation, and in Klopstock's
eyes, the saddest occurrence which could befall a nation.
In a three-line paragraph of the Gelehrtenrepublik entitled
"Vom Neuen," Klopstock writes: "Kein Buch, dessen Inhalt
oder Ausführung nicht wenigstens in einigen Stücken neu
ist, wird hinter den goldenen Vorhang gestellt" (p. 92).
By the golden curtain Klopstock means the literary heritage
which a nation produces and passes on to its descendants.

According to him, it is not necessary to regulate the new, important is only that it is new; future generations will determine what is worth keeping and what is not.

For Klopstock, there are two means of introducing the new, Entdeckung and Erfindung. His definitions of the two terms are brief and self-explanatory.

> Wer entdecken will, siehet sich gar genau um
> in dem Gewimmel der Dinge, so um ihn her sind;
> und siehet er darin etwas, das sonst noch
> Niemand hatte gesehn; so hat er entdeckt. Wer
> erfindet, setzt Vorhandnes auf neue Art und
> Weise zusammen. (Gelehrtenrepublik, p. 116)

According to Klopstock, then, there is room for the new in both content and form. The poet is no longer bound by old rules. He is more or less free to choose and to create in a manner that will affect and move his readers. Similar thoughts are expressed by Breitinger in the Critische Dichtkunst. In his chapter entitled "Von dem Neuen," he argues that familiarity breeds contempt.

> Dass nicht alles, was natürlich und wahr ist,
> die Kraft habe, die Sinnen und das Gemüthe auf
> eine angenehm-ergetzende Weise zu rühren und
> einzunehmen, sondern dass diese Gabe alleine
> dem Neuen, Ungewohnten, Seltsamen, und
> Ausserordentlichen zukomme .... (p. 110)

Breitinger believes that not even the beautiful and noble can move the reader if it becomes habitual, for habit deadens the spirit. No one, says Breitinger, likes to be continuously told that the sun gives light, that man must

die, and so forth. Instead, a moral truth is best clothed
in a sprightly fable. And there is no danger of running
out, for nature (life) is inexhaustible.

The "new" which the two theoreticians are urging must
be found outside of tradition. Mimesis interpreted as
strict imitation no longer suffices. The time is ripe for
new visions and new forms. Clearly, both Breitinger and
Klopstock are encouraging the poet to invent, and not to
imitate.

Klopstock's primary focus for the renewal of literature is language. He encourages the poet to master
language thoroughly and hone his sensitivity to it. He
himself is conscious of language as an expression of
culture and character. Therefore, the writer must be pru-
dent in his choice of words and phrases, so that they will
reflect his thoughts and emotions as accurately as possible.
The problematical relationship of the thought-word transition did not remain unrecognized by Klopstock and occupied
him during a good portion of his life. He writes, "Wie dem
Mädchen, das aus dem Bade steigt, das Gewand anliegt, so
sollt es die Sprache dem Gedanken, und gleichwohl immer
noch zehn Röcke übereinander und ein Wulst darunter"
(Gelehrtenrepublik, p. 116). Although the thought should
emerge cleanly and simply, it often remains hidden under
layers of ten skirts. For Klopstock, this seems to be

primarily the fault of the incorrect use of language--the
selection of ineffective words, or even minor linguistic
errors, such as improper choice or position of particles
and interjections. Although he believes this could be
remedied through learning, he is aware of the fragility of
language as an instrument to express feelings and ideas.
Again, a hint of language scepticism is present here, an
experience which emerges more fully in the letters of
Klopstock's correspondent, Friedrich Leopold Stolberg. For
Stolberg, poetry is only an attempt to give verbal shape to
pure feeling, an effort which can never completely succeed,
for the poem must always remain a pale imitation of the
original emotion. [21]

Although Klopstock investigated primarily the language
of poetry and infused a new vitality into poetic diction,
his linguistic insights are also applicable to the drama.
He reiterates the Swiss' argument that poetic language
must move the reader (or spectator). In his own dramas,
both the biblical cycle, Tod Adams (1757), Salomo (1764),
and David (1772), and the Hermann-Trilogy, Hermanns
Schlacht (1769), Hermann und die Fürsten (1784), and
Hermanns Tod (1787), Klopstock utilizes an emotionally
charged language: "Du rasest, sage ich! Katwald ist mein
Freund!" Hermann tells his fellow soldier, Horst, who
answers, "War dein Freund!" "Ist mein Freund!" Hermann

insists, and Horst answers, "Verfluch ihn! War es nie,
weil er es nicht geblieben ist!" (Hermanns Tod, Act I,
Scene 2). Gerhard Kaiser calls it "eine Sprache des
Gefühls, der Ausdrücke und Ausrufungen."[22] It is characterized by exclamation points, question marks, ellipsis, and
repetition of significant words: "Erbarmung Gottes,
Erbarmung, / Vom Herrn, vom Herrn, Erbarmung..."[23]
(emphasis mine). In this respect, Klopstock's diction is
related to the dramatic language of Storm and Stress and of
Expressionism. However, as a whole, he preferred a far
more convoluted sentence structure than was favored by the
expressionists and the writers of Storm and Stress. Klopstock's language is innovative, in that it emphasizes feeling and emotion. While it is not yet the cry or emotional
outburst of his heirs, even his earliest dramas are much
less formalistic than was the norm. His language cannot be
called realistic; nevertheless, it is a step toward exploring the human psyche, which trend is the major thrust of
the evolving, Non-Aristotelian drama.

3. Sulzer's Allgemeine Theorie der schönen Künste

Sulzer, the erstwhile student of Bodmer, was more intent upon cataloguing the particulars of aesthetics than in
formulating his own comprehensive theory of aesthetics. The

fragmented nature of his thought, collected alphabetically in essays of varying lengths in his <u>Allgemeine</u> <u>Theorie</u> <u>der</u> <u>schönen Künste</u>, 1771, is largely responsible for its contradictory reception and his controversial position within the history of aesthetic theory. Goethe rejected him as asensual and coldly pragmatic, while for Kant, he was the "fortreffliche Sulzer."[24]

Sulzer's work does contain contradictions. Nivelle blames them on the fact that his opus was produced over an extended period of time and that many of his judgments were dictated by convictions based on his readings of the moment.[25] On the one hand, Sulzer views art as the servant of morality, a notion which links him to the Enlightenment and which earned Goethe's disdain; on the other, he extolls the effect of art upon the emotions, which suggests an affinity to Storm and Stress. This is expressed particularly in his interpretation of mimesis. Sulzer does not regard the imitation of nature, or man's propensity to imitate, as the essence of poetry, but rather presumes man's innate drive to give expression to his feelings and emotions to be the motor of creativity.

> Die zeichnenden Künste scheinen die einzigen
> zu seyn, die aus Nachahmung der Natur entstanden
> sind. Aber Beredsamkeit, Dichtkunst, Musik und
> Tanz sind offenbar aus der Fülle lebhafter
> Empfindungen entstanden, und der Begierde sich
> zu äussern, sich selbst und andere darin zu
> unterhalten.[26]

The priority given the emotions is indicative of a leaning toward a more anthropomorphically oriented literature as opposed to a formalistic one, a trend that is also apparent in the writings of Klopstock and Bodmer and Breitinger, and becomes of course more pronounced during Storm and Stress.

Robert Sommer states Sulzer's view of the active role played by the emotions in the creative process as follows: for Sulzer, "[ist] die menschliche Seele der Mittelpunkt der Kunst. Aus ihrer Beschaffenheit müssen die speziellen Kunstregeln abgeleitet werden."[27]

Sulzer, however, is no rebel. Many of his pronouncements reveal the traditionalist and advocate of classical norms. He rejects the mixture of the comic and the tragic, or what Auerbach calls the elevated and the low style and which he regards as one of the earmarks of Realism.[28]

> Es ist also kein guter Rath, den Voltaire giebt, in einem rührenden Drama auch lächerliche Scenen nicht zu verwerfen, aus dem Grunde, weil dergleichen Vermischung bisweilen in der Natur vorkomme. (Allgemeine Theorie, III, 489)

For Sulzer, a tragedy must consist of a whole and complete action, the geschlossene Form, to use Klotz' terminology. "Die Handlung muss volständig und ganz seyn, das ist, man muss ihren Anfang und ihr Ende sehen" (Allgemeine Theorie, IV, 562). He concludes: "Indessen wollen wir gar nicht behaupten dass nur das Trauerspiel gut sey, das nach

den Regeln der Alten behandelt wird: aber diese Behand-
lung halten wir überhaupt für die beste" (_Allgemeine_
Theorie, IV, 564).

In view of these assertions, he cannot wholeheartedly
approve of Shakespeare, although he recognizes him as the
greatest of the new dramatists.

> Dass Shakespear, der grösste tragische Dichter
> unter den Neuern, sowohl diese [the unity of
> time], als manch andre Regel übertreten, und
> doch gewusst hat, zu gefallen, beweist nichts
> dagegen. Wenn er zu dem grossen Verdienst
> das er würklich hat, noch die Beobachtung der
> Regeln auch hinzugethan hätte, so wäre er noch
> grösser, und würde noch mehr gefallen. (_Allgemeine_
> _Theorie_, IV, 564)

It did not occur to Sulzer that Shakespeare's greatness and
ability to evoke pleasure in the audience stems from the
very fact that he _did_ disregard the three unities and thus
produce a dramatic form that is more representative of
modern reality and provides the spectator with a greater
opportunity for identification and exploration of his
world.

In one respect Sulzer ventures to disagree with
Aristotle--in the time-honored precept of the superiority
of action over character. "Wenn der Philosoph, wie es
scheint, die Fabel würklich für das wichtigste Stück des
Trauerspiels gehalten hat, so können wir nicht seiner
Meynung seyn, weil es uns ausser Zweifel scheint, dass die
Sitten [characters] ein wichtigerer Theil seyen" (_Allge-_

meine Theorie, IV, 565). Sulzer'reason for the eleva-
tion of character is that although one can see from the
fable (Sulzer uses Oedipus as an example) that man cannot
escape his fate and that misfortune can strike even pru-
dent individuals, this is not as important as "die Empfindungen und die Aeusserung der Leidenschaften und des
Betragens der interessirten Personen bey solchen Umständen"
(Allgemeine Theorie, IV, 565). According to Sulzer,
the audience is interested in the smallest detail of the
characters' thoughts, emotions, and reactions. We witness
here, as is the case with Bodmer, Breitinger, and Klopstock,
an increasing interest in the psychology of the character,
a desire to portray and understand the motivations and
secret stirrings of the soul. This is one of the major
characteristics of Non-Aristotelian drama.

Sulzer's essay on language is cursory; he writes that
it is intended to serve as an impetus to others and does
not present an extensive study of the characteristics and
function of poetic language. For him, language does not
naturally well up from within the poetic temperament, a
notion posited by the genius generation; but his linguistic
gift must be carefully nurtured and cultivated by the poet.
Sulzer is sensitive to the sensual quality of language, a
quality which he considers essential to poetry and sees en-
dangered by excessive abstraction, a view also held by

Hamann and Herder. He is conscious of the individualistic
and characteristic aspects of language, warns against the
artificiality resulting from imitation, and favors multiplicity, variety, and individuality of expression. Sulzer
stresses independence of thought and action and relates
them to linguistic versatility. Imitation stultifies the
language and reduces it to monotony and mediocrity: "Denn
wo die Menge sich nach wenigen, die den Ton angeben, richtet,
da verschwindet auch die Mannichfaltigkeit des Charakteris-
tischen an der Sprache" (<u>Allgemeine</u> <u>Theorie</u>, IV, 449).

Sulzer also treats the topic of dramatic language
in his essay on tragedy--"...Ton und Ausdruk müssen
für jeden Charakter und für jede Leidenschaft besonders
abgepasst sein" (<u>Allgemeine</u> <u>Theorie</u>, IV, 570)
again, a more realistic dialogue on the stage--and
in an essay entitled "Leidenschaften." Sulzer upholds
the Swiss critics' view that one of the artist's major
purposes is to affect the emotions: "Es gehöret unmittelbar
zum Zwek des Künstlers, dass er Leidenschaften erweke, oder
besänftige" (<u>Allgemeine</u> <u>Theorie</u>, III, 223). This is
accomplished through lively language which excites the
imagination: "Nämlich es geschiehet durch eine lebhafte
Schilderung leidenschaftlicher Gegenstände, besonders wenn
die Phantasie dabey erhitzt wird" (<u>Allgemeine</u> <u>Theorie</u>,

III, 224). The artist must therefore not only study
and adhere to the rules, he must also be a student of mankind: "Der Künstler muss ein Kenner der Menschen seyn,..."
(Allgemeine Theorie, III, 226). This is a demand
which had not been stressed before the reaction against
Gottsched had set in.

It is apparent that Sulzer assumes an intermediary
point of view in literary theory, one which situates him
somewhere between tradition and modernity. On the one
hand, he reiterates many of Gottsched's precepts, i.e.,
moral betterment as the primary purpose of art, separation of style and genre, and adherence to the three unities;
he does, on the other hand, broaden the definition of
mimesis, recognize the power of the emotions and the affective qualities of poetry, and affirm the importance of
characterization in drama as a tool to better understand
man. After Gottsched, the tendency toward the representation of internal and not just external nature in the drama
and in literature as a whole becomes an increasingly significant factor.

4. J. E. Schlegel--Fresh Insights from the North

For the urbane and scholarly Johann Elias Schlegel, the
extradition from the shadow cast by Gottsched became final

when he moved to Denmark in 1743. According to his
brother, Johann Adolph Schlegel, both he and Johann Elias
had evaded direct association and confrontation with the
literary mogul of the decade by avoiding his lectures from
the moment they enrolled at the University of Leipzig in
1739. This assertion, made thirty years after the event,
may reveal Johann Adolph to be suffering from a faulty
memory, for history attests to a working relationship between Gottsched and J. E. Schlegel, albeit brief and primarily devoted to publication.[29] But it also testifies to
the early and substantial variance between Gottsched's and
J.E. Schlegel's aesthetic theories.

   The earliest indication of J. E. Schlegel's independence from Gottsched is his decision to translate
Sophocles' Electra into rhymed verse in opposition to
Gottsched's request for an unrhymed version.[30] A fundamental difference in their perception of mimesis and the
nature and function of art lies at the heart of Schlegel's
decision to disregard Gottsched's recommendation.
Schlegel, whose poetic theories resemble those of the
Swiss in many aspects, first formulates his interpretation
of mimesis in an essay entitled "Schreiben an den Herrn
N. über die Comödie in Versen," 1740.[31]

   Central to Schlegel's thought is the promulgation that
art is not nature, and that instead of being a copy of

nature, it must at times be <u>unlike</u> nature: "Man soll,
nämlich, zuweilen die Nachahmung der Sache, der man
nachahmet, unähnlich machen" (<u>Werke</u>, p. 97). This is an
assertion in direct opposition to Gottsched, who stresses
the similarity, and not the difference between art and
nature. The implications of Schlegel's thought for the
creative artist are profound. During Schlegel's time, the
artist was limited by demands for authenticity which required an exact likeness between his creation and its origin in reality, and as E. Wilkinson points out, even today
the public mind is still obsessed with art as imitation of
nature. By asserting that sometimes the object created
must be unlike rather than like nature, Schlegel attempts
to show that imaginative or "abstract" art can be even
more convincing and aesthetically pleasing than an
authentic and concrete representation of reality. Ultimately, the broadening interpretation of mimesis to which
he contributed would lead to the abstractions of the ex-
pressionist drama and to surrealism on the stage and in
literature as a whole.

   This undoubtedly makes J. E. Schlegel a pioneer in the
forward thrust of the development of German drama and
artistic theory. That he does not completely reject
adherence to rules, however, particularly in his practice, is revealed in a question he raises in his essay

"Abhandlung dass die Nachahmung der Sache, der man nachahmet, zuweilen unähnlich werden müsse" when he states: "Aber habe ich dadurch [his assertion that art may be unlike nature] auch vielleicht der Unähnlichkeit zu einer zügellosen Herrschaft verholfen? Habe ich dadurch vielleicht ein Feld geöffnet, wo man ohne Regel herumirren, und seine Hirngespinste für Nachahmungen verkaufen wird?" (Werke, p. 104). But he quickly and confidently adds, "Nichts weniger, als dieses" (Werke, p. 104), and goes on to explain that an artist's decision to differentiate the "Abbild" from the "Vorbild" must be based on a good reason and that the artist is still bound by rules in cases where the rules enhance the work of art.

A "good reason" for Schlegel is always and foremost the artistic quality of a work of art. Thus he argues that although it is unlikely that the common folk portrayed in comedy would speak in verse (Gottsched's reason for advocating the use of prose in that genre), verse enhances the artistry, and therefore the pleasure experienced by the spectator, of comedy. Schlegel considers meter ("das Silbenmass") to be the medium ("die Materie") used by the writer and upholds the writer's right to choose his own medium. He is, in fact, granting art and the artist a new autonomy, rather than requiring him to be the slave to classicistic law. In his later writings, Schlegel somewhat

alters his views to admit that the informality of prose does
add a certain necessary lightness to comedy and thus provides the spectator with greater pleasure. This Schlegel
regards as the final purpose of a work of art. But never
could he concur with Gottsched, who based all of his opin-
ions and advocacy of the rules on the principle of proba-
bility.

At no time does Schlegel reject the Aristotelian precept that mimesis represents the nature of art; but he does
succeed in breaking through the confining barriers resulting from its too narrow interpretation. According to Schlegel,
the poet does not imitate an object or event which actually
exists in nature, but rather the public's (or artist's)
"idea" of that object or event. Indeed, Schlegel maintains,
the public compares the similarity of the artistic creation
with its own image or idea of an object. If the artist's
conception of an object agrees with that of the public,
the artist is praised; if not he is condemned and scorned
(Werke, p. 99).

Imitating the "idea" of an object, argues Schlegel, is
an entirely different matter than copying something that
actually exists; and many events and characters, historical
and mythological, for example, must by necessity arise out of
the imagination, for truthful observation is an impossibility. To
illustrate the absurdity of the total agreement of artistic and

empirical reality, Schlegel says:

> Wie kann man diese Unähnlichkeit tadeln; ... da
> wir, wenn entweder die Comödie dem gemeinen
> Leben, oder das gemeine Leben der Comödie voll-
> kommen ähnlich seyn sollte, entweder in der
> Comödie einschlafen, oder im gemeinen Leben uns
> beständig aus dem Athem lachen müssten
> (<u>Werke</u>, p. 102). 32

Because of his tolerance and open-mindedness to new
artistic possibilities, Johann Elias Schlegel becomes the
first German critic to recognize the merits of Shakespeare
and thus introduce a major new dimension into the development of German drama. He first brought Shakespeare to the
attention of his contemporaries in an essay entitled "Vergleichung Shakespears und Andreas Gryphs," 1741 (<u>Werke</u>,
p. 71). Schlegel does not reject the French theater in
favor of the English, but rather accepts the merits of
both. In a later essay, "Gedanken zur Aufnahme des
dänischen Theaters," 1747 (<u>Werke</u>, p. 193), he recognizes
the national character of the theater and regards preference
to be a matter of national taste rather than superiority.
In Schlegel's opinion, nations evolve dramatic rules
arising out of their particular customs and taste, and
for that reason the theater pleasing to one nation may not
be so to another. He cites the difference between the
French and English theaters as an example, and concludes that
although both possess definite appeal, one cannot expect that
the English be completely comfortable with the French theater,

nor that the French prefer the English theater to their own
(Werke, p. 194).

In the former essay, Schlegel is generous in his
praise of Shakespeare, but does not hesitate to reprimand
what he considers to be his faults--primarily his irregularity and disregard of the unities. He does not, however,
advocate a mechanical adherence to the unities, and without
naming him, in the latter essay criticizes Gottsched's
interpretation of the unities of time and place. This is
an indication that Schlegel's attitude is gradually shifting toward a loosening of the requirements of the rules.
In his own dramas, such as Die stumme Schönheit and Canut,
Schlegel does not dispense with the unities. The scene of
the former is a house in the country, while the latter
takes place in a chamber of the king's residence, without a
shift of scene occurring in either play. Schlegel also observes the unity of time, the unity of action, and the
traditional five-act division, although Die stumme Schönheit
consists of one act. This is a dramatic structure which
Kleist uses in Der zerbrochene Krug, but which did not
really become conventional until later in the nineteenth
century. It is significant that Schlegel utilizes the
unities, as he uses verse in his comedies, for aesthetic
and not imitative purposes. For Schlegel, all rules have
relative value only; they are merely an external feature

and do not assure that if properly followed great drama
results. Schlegel contends that it is not his intention to
scorn the three unities under all circumstances, but he is
highly critical of those who judge a drama only by its outer
form. He declares that the "äusserliche Form" is not the
appropriate criterion to evaluate the "innerliche Schönheit"
of a dramatic work (Werke, p. 224).

It is clear that Schlegel maintained a less rigid
stance toward the compulsory application of dramatic rules
than was demonstrated by many of his contemporaries. This
enabled him to recognize the validity of the non-traditional
drama of the English, a drama which dispensed with the
unities and stressed character over action. The relaxation
of Schlegel's attitude is a significant step in opening the
door toward new dramatic forms on the German stage.

Schlegel's willingness to consider other dramatic
possibilities than those prescribed by Gottsched and the
French classical theater is also evident in both, his
theoretical discussion of characterization and its practical application in his own dramas. For Schlegel, who regards "das Vergnügen" (Werke, p. 202) rather than the
teaching of a moral lesson as the major purpose of theater,
aesthetic satisfaction is achieved through the realistic
and natural portrayal of character. It is precisely in this
sense that he foreshadows Lessing. In an essay which com-

pares antique and modern tragedy, Schlegel is critical of
modern dramatists because they have the tendency to portray
their "eigene Gemüthsbeschaffenheit" (Werke, p. 7) rather
than create believable and well-rounded characters.[33]
Schlegel does not say that the characters in a drama are
more important than the action, but he mentions more than
once that the action arises out of the "character" of the
acting individuals: "Ein Stück ohne Charaktere ist ein
Stück ohne alle Wahrscheinlichkeit, weil die Ursache,
warum ein Mensch so oder so handelt, eben in seinem
Charakter liegt" (Werke, p. 214).

It is now obvious that Schlegel's appraisal of the
role and function of character within the structure of the
drama stresses a shift away from the assignation of responsibility for events to the gods, toward an emphasis on
the individual and an attempt to understand to what degree
the causes of events lie within man's nature.

Because of his fascination with realistic and
theatrically effective characters, Schlegel praises Shakespeare's grand and vital characterizations. He quotes an
anonymous critic who is said to have written, "Der Himmel
habe die Helden Johnsons gemacht, Shakespear aber habe
seine eignen gemacht" (Werke, p. 80). He attributes an
even deeper knowledge of men to Shakespeare than to
Gryphius, whom, contrary to the criticism of the time, he

views favorably because he too created powerful characters (Werke, p. 87) such as Schach Abbas in Catharina von
Georgien. Schlegel considers Shakespeare's ability to
create viable and dynamic characters his greatest asset and
is willing to overlook his "weaknesses," his irregularity
and disregard of the rules.

In his own dramas, such as Hermann and Canut, which
are tightly structured according to classicistic precepts,
Schlegel's success with vivid, colorful characterizations
is conspicuous. While the main characters in his historical drama Hermann, Hermann and Thusnelde, represent
specific attitudes and must be classified as types, they
are surrounded by an array of individualistic, rounded
characters. These characters are not the product of convention, but rather resemble flesh and blood human beings
whose inner struggles are revealed by their words and
actions. In addition, Schlegel utilizes character development, an impossibility in a theater which prefers types to
mixed characters. Both Flavius and Siegmund in Hermann
change from vacillation at the beginning of the drama,
through disillusionment, to chastened understanding at the
end.[34] Much before Lessing, Schlegel has succeeded in
creating realistic, life-like, and psychologically penetrating characters. These characters have shed the one-
dimensional and didactic quality of their fictional peers

and are instead probing studies of human nature capable of
providing aesthetic pleasure through their dramatic totality.

In a number of aspects, Schlegel's views on characterization resemble those of Bodmer. According to Bodmer, the
poet must not merely imitate nature, but rather improve upon nature and create a character who embodies his grand and
noble vision.

> Alleine da die Natur in ihrem gewöhnlichen
> Laufe insgemeine nur mittelmässige Dinge
> hervorbringt, trift man dergleichen
> vollkomene Character in der Historie überaus
> selten an, und muss sich darum des eigenen
> Rechts der Poesie, die eine Schöpferinn ist,
> bedienen, und die unvollkommenen Character,
> die man in der Historie findet, mittelst
> Zusätzen, Abziehungen und Zusammensetzungen
> seiner Absicht gemäss ausarbeiten.[35]

Schlegel also urges the poet to come to the aid of history,
but cautions against an overly zealous approach.

> Man kann den Charakter einer Person, die in der
> Historie bekannt ist, zwar in etwas ändern, und
> entweder höher treiben, oder etwas weniger von
> seinen Tugenden und Lastern in ihm abbilden als
> die Geschichte ihm zuschreibet. (Werke, p. 82-83)

> Wenn man eine Fabel nach seiner eigenen
> Freyheit ausschmücken will, so ist es nicht
> gut, sich an der wahren Historie, besonders
> der neuern, zu vergreifen. Und sich bloss an
> die Geschichte zu halten, ist gleichfalls nicht
> rathsam, weil diess eine gewisse Trockenheit
> verursacht. (Werke, p. 216)

Thus, both Bodmer and Schlegel are clearly encouraging the poet to invent and create his own characters. To a

48

degree, the result of following such a course would be the
creation of an idealized character, rather than a realistic
one, and it could be argued that in this sense both theoreticians seem to be advocating "idealism" rather than moving
closer toward realism. But it must be remembered that unlike Gottsched, who only urged imitation of "die schöne
Natur," they also considered the "unpleasant" to be a proper subject for art. Convention required that a death, for
instance, or a horrifying scene, such as Oedipus' self-
mutilation, does not occur on stage, but rather be conveyed
to the spectator through the technique of <u>teichoskopia</u>.
According to Schlegel, however, "man kann sie [the portrayal
of a death scene] nicht hinweglassen ohne den Menschen die
lebhaftesten Vorstellungen zu rauben" (<u>Werke</u>, p. 103).
Bodmer also argues for the inclusion of the unpleasant in
literature.

> Eine gute Beschreibung eines unglückseligen,
> abgearbeiteten Mannes mit holen Augen und
> abgefleischten, eingesunkenen Wangen, einem
> schwartzen und schmutzigen Angesicht, zottigen
> Bart und schimmlichten aufgestraubten Haare,
> das er nicht gewohnt weder zu scheeren noch zu
> kämmen, mit geschwollenen Händen, die sich in
> der Asche gebrannt haben, und unflättigen
> Fingern die mit langen Nägeln gespitzt sind,
> um gantz bequeme die Speisen zu zerreissen:
> eine solche Beschreibung ergötzet uns so wohl,
> als eine andere von Venerischen Cupidons,
> Adonen, Anacreons und Floren.[36]

Important for Both Schlegel and Bodmer is that the unpleasant scene must be portrayed in an aesthetically and artistically pleasing manner (eine _gute_ Beschreibung), not necessarily in an idealized fashion. In that sense, Schlegel is advocating a new realism for the German stage, a realism that includes the entire spectrum of human experience, unlike Gottsched's artificial realism, which concentrates on verisimilitude but excludes the portrayal of the unpleasant. The significant factor in Schlegel's contribution to the development of dramatic theory is the recognition that the dramatist can _alter_ nature without _idealizing_ it, a notion which represents a major thrust toward new dramatic possibilities on the German stage and a step towards modernity in literature and art.

It is common knowledge that Johann Elias Schlegel's discussions of poetic language are indeed dispersed throughout his theoretical essays, although he treats the topic in greater detail in his essay "Von der Würde und Majestät des Ausdrucks im Trauerspiele," 1747 (_Werke_, p. 167), which was published as a forward to his _Theatralische Werke_. In concurrence with Longinus, Schlegel favors an elevated and sublime language for tragedy. Yet in his discussion of dramatic language, Schlegel is far less cognizant of the difference between art and nature than he is in his other essays. Schlegel argues that a noble and cultured individual would under no circumstances resort to

ordinary and inelegant language, and therefore the tragic
hero is bound by similar requirements. One would expect
Schlegel to defend an elevated language on aesthetic
grounds and is surprised to read arguments that are reminiscent of Gottsched! Nevertheless, in spite of his
temporary lapse into confusion between art and nature,
Schlegel offers significant insights into the nature of
dramatic language. He is conscious of language as a
rhetorical device, of the power of language to persuade.

> Aus der Art des Ausdruckes machen wir die aller-
> meisten Schlüsse einen Menschen entweder hoch-
> zuachten oder zu verachten; und ein Mensch, der
> die allerniederträchtigsten Gedanken und
> Empfindungen auf eine edle Art einzukleiden und
> vorzustellen weiss, hat das Glück unsere
> Hochachtung zu erschleichen, die ein anderer
> nicht erhalten kann, der auf eine plumpe Art
> spricht, ob er gleich dabey noch so aufrichtig
> und redlich, das ist, wahrhaftig edel denkt.
> (Werke, p. 174)

Johann Elias Schlegel is exhibiting a language awareness which recognizes the various levels on which dramatic
language functions. Not only is language a tool for communication, a means whereby information is conveyed, it
also has aesthetic and emotional impact. Schlegel sees the
primary function of dramatic language in the arousal of the
emotions. He permits the dramatist to employ monologues
and asides, a technique which Gottsched had eschewed, because it allows a dramatic character to reveal his
thoughts and emotions to the audience. The language in

Schlegel's own dramas is forceful and vital in direct contrast to the generally stilted stage language of the era.
It is particularly apparent in his charming comedy Die
stumme Schönheit, in which the art of conversation and
language itself become the central issue[37] Wolf calls it a
language which is "von sprudelnder Lebendigkeit und
Natürlichkeit."[38] The alexandrine utilized by Schlegel,
which from a less talented pen can sound monotonous and
grandiloquent, is sprightly and retains a light, conversational tone throughout the play. Schlegel frequently
divides a line among speakers: Jungwitz: "Dann redt man
desto mehr." Praatgern: "Mich dünkt ja, dass ich rede."
Jungwitz: "Dann kriegt man auch Verstand." Praatgern:
"Itzt bin ich gar nicht blöde."[39] He uses both hemisticho-
mythia and stichomythia, techniques intended to create
linguistic liveliness and rapid movement within a drama.
Questions, exclamations, and ellipsis occur frequently;
lengthy monologues are avoided. The result is a witty and
spirited comedy, one which has probably been unduly relegated to the back shelves of Germany's dramatic canon.

Schlegel's recognition of the affective power of
language, his awareness of the aesthetic and realistic
rather than didactic function of literature, and his respect for non-traditional dramatic forms testify to the
advent of a new era in German drama.

5. <u>Christian Fürchtegott Gellert--Merely a Dramatic</u>
    <u>Sentimentalist?</u>

A small number of authors seem to have personality or
character traits which invite comment throughout the centuries. Unfortunately, their artistic <u>oeuvre</u> is frequently
judged in relation to and as the result of certain characteristics attributed to them. Thus, literary history
abounds with references to Gellert's equanimity and gentle,
indeed at times maudlin nature. Accordingly, he is all too
quickly dismissed as a mere sentimental dramatist embodying
the spirit of a peculiarly subjective and soulful period of
time, the Age of Sentimentality.[40]

The nineteenth century had a different view of
Gellert's contribution to literature and literary theory.
Hettner judges Gellert to be the first original German
writer, "ein wahrhaft erweckender und befreiender Schriftsteller.[41] Braitmaier is equally effusive in his <u>laudatio</u>
and posits that Gellert's theory is:

> ein entschiedener Fortschritt nicht bloss
> über Gottsched, sondern auch über die Zürcher
> ja über die beiden Schlegel hinaus in dem
> resoluten Bruch mit der Regel in Sachen der
> Empfindung und in der Betonung des Genies
> gegenüber der Routine.[42]

Although Gellert did not write as extensively about the
nature of poetry as some of his contemporaries, he--like

they--makes it clear that he regards the imitation of
nature as central to the creative process, but--like his
predecessors--he qualifies his definition of mimesis. He
is particularly conscious of the ancients' affinity to
nature and lauds their artistic supremacy in a lecture
"Von den Ursachen des Vorzugs der Alten vor den Neuern
in den schönen Wissenschaften besonders in der Poesie und
Beredsamkeit." Gellert observes: "Sie [the ancients]
bildeten die Natur mit einer liebenswürdigen Leichtigkeit
und sorgfältigen Genauigkeit nach."[43] His analysis of the
superiority of the ancients concludes that the charmed
relationship with nature attributed to classical poets
has been lost, a nostalgic view prefiguring Schiller and
later the romantic lament decrying man's separation from
nature. Gellert insists that the apparent lack of vitality
and inferiority of modern literature is not the result of
copying nature, but rather of too stubborn an adherence
to the rules. Nature has been and must continue to be
the great teacher: "Die Natur war ihre [that of the
ancients] Lehrmeisterin; und so soll sie auch die unsrige
seyn!" (Werke, V, 278). According to Gellert, modern
poets are in error, however, if they too slavishly follow
the rules of the ancients. Gellert calls an excessively
devoted follower of classicistic rules a "verblendeter
und sklavischer Anbeter der Regeln" (Werke, V, 166),

and warns that such a poet is doing himself and his time
an injustice. "Wir können ungerecht gegen die Natur, gegen
uns selbst werden, wenn wir unsern eignen Geist verdrängen,
um den ihrigen mit ungeschickter Hand an seine Stelle zu
setzen" (Werke, V, 278). Gellert does not express it as
forcefully as later theoreticians, particularly as some
exponents of Storm and Stress, but his thoughts reveal his
intimation that literature must express and evolve out of
the spirit of its specific time; if it is an imitation of
another literature, it is stilted, lifeless, artificial.
Gellert is particularly critical of the work of contemporary
dramatists and castigates their superficial adherence to
rules. Although technically flawless, the plays written
by them are "leer und ohne Leben." They lack the ability
to create "eine grosse, sonderbare, anziehende Handlung,
heroische Charaktere, starke Leidenschaften, Reden, die
der Würde der Personen, der Sache, der Poesie gemäss waren
..." (Werke, V, 169). Gellert recognizes that merely
obeying rules and copying traditional dramatic techniques
does not produce dramas which can compete with those of the
ancients. An essential element is missing in these dramas
written by misguided epigones: they do not have the power
to move the spectator as did the tragedians of classical
Greece.

Gellert shares Bodmer's and Breitinger's, Klopstock's and
Schlegel's insight that literature must touch the reader,
that it must appeal to his passions and stir him. This
conviction does not arise out of an excessive tendency toward sentimentality, as Gellert's emphasis on the emotions
in his own plays has been interpreted, but rather of the
recognition that the dramas presented on the German stage
are unsatisfactory. Therefore Gellert, even more poignantly than Schlegel, proposes a new kind of drama for
Germany, one that teaches and pleases, demonstrates a
fresher realism and thereby amuses and moves the audience--
the comédie larmoyante. In his lecture "De comoedia
commovente," 1751, Gellert defends his introduction of the
serious comedy to the German stage: "Warum sollte man denn
nicht auch dann und wann der Komödie einen ernsthaften,
seiner Natur nach aber angenehmen Inhalt, geben dürfen?"[44]
Gellert suggests here that the "serious comedy," a genre
inspired by the Frenchmen Marivaux, Destouches, and Nivelle
de la Chaussée, is the genre which most aptly reflects the
conditions of his era and is therefore the most appropriate
dramatic form. In formulating his views, he proceeds from
the classical concept which holds that tragedy imitates a
noble action, whereas comedy imitates a common or ordinary
action. It is common knowledge that the traditional view
of the Enlightenment was that it is the intent of comedy to

give pleasure and to teach a moral lesson through the ridicule of a vice as personified by the characters. Gellert,
on the other hand, argues that enjoyment or pleasure, "die
ausgelassene und heftige Freude," is not the only emotion
experienced by the spectator, but that it is also appropriate
for comedy to induce a bitter-sweet emotion, "eine Art von
Gemüthsbewegung...welche zwar den Schein der Traurigkeit
hat, an und für sich aber ungemein süsse ist" ("Abhandlung,"
pp. 50-51). Gellert divides comedy into two types: the
lasterhafte comedy, depicting a vice, as advocated by
Gottsched; and the tugendhafte comedy, portraying a virtue,
which Gellert consideres to be a suitable theme for serious
comedy.[45] He defines the "new comedy" introduced to the
German stage as

> ein dramatisches Gedicht, welches Abschilderungen
> von dem gemeinen Privatleben enthalte, die Tugend
> anpreise, und verschiedene Laster und Ungereimt-
> heiten der Menschen, auf eine scherzhafte und feine
> Art durchziehe.("Abhandlung," p. 52)

In other words, Gellert combines the depiction of vice and
virtue in one play and advocates a less severe approach to
the portrayal of human foibles.

It is significant that Gellert chose to call the dramas
he wrote depicting ordinary life "comedies" rather than
"tragedies." On the one hand it is indicative of his
inability to break away from the classical tradition.
He recognizes that ordinary life deserves to be treated

in a more serious vein, and that because of the
bourgeoisie's demand to be taken seriously, the time is
ripe for a new dramatic form. But let us note that he uses
traditional genre denominations! On the other hand, the
first seeds of today's controversy over whether or not
tragedy is possible in the modern world may be present here.
Perhaps Gellert would not have shared Dürrenmatt's scepti-
cal views of modern life as black comedy, but his "serious
comedy" is a first step in that direction.

It is specifically in his characterizations that
Gellert, like Schlegel, distances himself from his contemporaries. In his 22d essay of the <u>Hamburgische Drama-</u>
<u>turgie</u>, Lessing writes the following about Gellert's
characters:

> es sind wahre Familiengemälde in denen man
> sogleich zu Hause ist; jeder Zuschauer glaubt einen
> Vetter, einen Schwager, ein Mühmchen aus seiner
> eigenen Verwandtschaft darin zu erkennen.[46]

One is inclined to agree with Lessing's assessment when
analyzing the character of Julchen in <u>Die zärtlichen</u>
<u>Schwestern</u>. That Julchen is a complex and not a one-
sided character is immediately apparent. According to her
father, Cleon, she harbors peculiar notions with which he
finds it impossible to deal: "Ich weiss nicht, wer ihr
den wunderlichen Gedanken von der Freiheit in den Kopf ge-
setzt hat."[47] Indeed, Julchen continues to refer to her

much cherished freedom throughout the marital manipulations
which constitute the plot of the drama. The question of
Julchen's personal freedom, which she considers threatened
by her proposed marriage to Damis, recurs so frequently
throughout the drama that it must be seen as a major component of Julchen's psychic profile. Gellert does not
develop the problem posed by personal freedom versus the
traditional expectations of a young woman, but rather
treats it as somewhat of a peculiarity of Julchen's
character, which is resolved by her recognition of her love
for Damis. But the complexities of her character are
demonstrated in other ways: she is dubious of the ameni-
ties of love, "Es kann seyn, dass die Liebe viel Annehm-
lichkeiten hat; aber das traurige und eingeschränkte
Wesen, das man dabey annimmt, verderbt ihren Werth, und
wenn er noch so gross wäre" (Lustspiele, p. 14); she
struggles with her emotions, "Bald hätte ich sie [her
sister, Lottchen] beneidet; aber verwünscht sey diese
Regung!" (Lustspiele, p. 91); she ponders the nature of
contentment, "Ich habe eine so reiche Erbschaft gethan, und
gleichwohl bin ich nicht zufriedner. Ob ich etwan gar
krank werde?" (Lustspiele, p. 71); and she admits that she
is troubled, "es ist mir alles so ängstlich" (Lustspiele,
p. 40). Although Gellert writes, "Ein geiziger Orgon, eine
eitle und verleumderische Clelia, und ein unerträglicher

und grossprecherischer Damon auf dem Theater, sind nichts, als der Geiz, die Verleumdung und Grossprecherey selbst,"[48] Julchen does not fit into that mold. She is clearly not a "type" but a mixed character in the mode advocated by the Swiss critics, by Schlegel, and later by Lessing.

There is also evidence in Gellert's dramas of an attempt to explore the intricacies of his characters' souls. He therefore repeatedly uses the monologue as a technical device to reveal his characters' emotions and thoughts. The language Gellert uses is graceful and natural. In his "Vorbericht zum Bande" he writes of the language spoken by the characters in the pastoral, "wenn ihre Sprache zwar leicht und ungekünstelt, aber doch die Sprache der feinern Empfindungen seyn muss" (Werke, III, 437) and "von der Sprache habe ich schon geredt. Sie ist, wie der Charakter, nur gar zu natürlich" (Werke, III, 439). True to his theory, his characters express themselves in a language much more appealing to the theatergoer than the formal stage language which was the norm.

Gellert's dramatic dialogue obviously reflects a rejection of artificial and academic language and represents a movement toward the language spoken by the members of the social strata he chose to portray, the Umgangssprache of the middle class. Well known is the episode of the

famous interview between Gellert and Frederick the Great,
during which the king exclaimed after hearing Gellert read
one of his fables, "Das verstehe ich alles!" This in
direct contrast to his experience with Gottsched, whose
translation of Racine's Iphigenie he did not understand, in
spite of having had the French original in front of him!
G. Merkel says of Gellert: "Er ist seit Luther der erste
grosse Erzieher und Schriftsteller in Deutschland, der es
verstand, zum ganzen Volke, jung und alt, arm und reich,
klug und einfältig, Mann und Frau zu sprechen und gehört
zu werden."[49] Gellert created a literary language which
was democratic in nature and served to give the middle
class a desperately longed-for identity. Gellert certainly
is not naively sentimental in his concepts of language and
interested only in using a language which the people can
understand, but seems to be aware of the potential of
language as a tool for wielding power, and the necessity
of mastering language in order to render ideas fruitful and
influence the environment: "Wer seine Gedanken gut aus-
drücken will, muss die Sprache in der Gewalt haben."[50] The
language spoken by the aristocrats and the Latin of the
academics had been inaccessible to the middle class. In
spite of Gottsched's attempts at language reform, no adequate written language existed which the middle class
could assimilate and employ in its efforts to gain some

influence. By eliminating baroque, foreign, and archaic
elements from the language he used in his dramas and in his
prose, Gellert made language accessible to the ordinary
citizen.

Although language seems to flow naturally and easily
for Gellert, he is conscious of the elastic elusiveness of
language and the poet's difficulty in choosing the right
words. It is a dilemma which causes Cleon to exclaim,
"dass die Welt die Sprache immer ändert, dafür kann ich
nicht" (Lustspiele, p. 37), and the author to muse:

> Ist diess die rechte Schreibart, die sich für
> meine Materie schickt? An jenem Orte durfte ich
> nur deutlich seyn, aber werde ich hier nicht zu
> lebhaft? Verschwende ich die Figuren? Verlangt
> die Sache nicht einen gelindern Ton? Wähle ich
> die Sprache zu wenig, oder zu sehr? Bin ich
> richtig und genau in meinem Ausdrucke, ohne karg
> und dürftig zu seyn? Bin ich lebhaft und
> prächtig, ohne üppig und pralerisch zu seyn?
> (Werke, V, 173-174)

Gellert's language may appear to be natural and informal, but his thoughts reveal that he carefully and
consciously chose his words. That same apparent simplicity
permeates his dramas. It may detract from, but does not
negate, his major role as an innovative dramatist--one who
anticipated new trends in the drama and in dramatic theory.

At least a partial rejection of convention is also
evident in his dramatic structure. While he retains the
unities of time and place and divides his dramas into

three acts, those acts consist of a great number of often
brief individual scenes. Some of the scenes appear to be
superfluous to the main action, others are interchangeable.
His arrangement of scenes reveals a tendency toward an
epic structure, which is one of the chief characteristics
of Non-Aristotelian drama.

CHAPTER III

THE CRITIQUE OF THE CLASSICISTIC TRADITION INTENSIFIES:
GERSTENBERG, THEORETICIAN AND DRAMATIST

1. From Mimesis to Poiesis

A tendency in literary history has been to categorize
Heinrich Wilhelm von Gerstenberg as either a transitional
figure between the German Enlightenment and Storm and Stress
or as one of the primary founders of the Storm and Stress
movement.[1] While both arguments are valid to a degree,
Gerstenberg's contributions to dramatic theory and the
evolution of the German drama toward today's predominant
Non-Aristotelian structure has not been sufficiently
examined. An analysis of Gerstenberg's interpretation
of mimesis, his theories of dramatic structure and
characterization, and his drama Ugolino demonstrates
that his views, like those of Lenz, do not represent a
radically new beginning, nor are they a transition, but
rather they constitute a continuation of the poetics of
Bodmer, Breitinger, Klopstock, Schlegel, and Gellert.

The rapid and profound changes in dramatic theory
occurring in the period immediately preceding and during

the Storm and Stress movement are inextricably interwoven with the dramatic works of William Shakespeare. From Wilhelm Meister's confrontation with Hamlet in the Theatralische Sendung to Goethe's and Herder's laudatory essays, from Lessing's Literaturbriefe to Gerstenberg's Briefe über die Merkwürdigkeiten der Literatur and Lenz's "Anmerkungen übers Theater," Shakespeare dominated and preoccupied the minds and writings of German authors.[2]

Gerstenberg's letters concerning literature were published between 1766-1767, one year after Lessing's six-year barrage castigating the efforts of those writers who were too eagerly following in the footsteps of Gottsched. Although Lessing had already brought the monumental Briton to the attention of the German literary public--his irrepressible 17th letter has made history--Gerstenberg formulated in his letters a more novel concept of the nature of drama in general and Shakespearian drama in particular. According to A. M. Wagner, Gerstenberg's letters are "das bedeutsamste Zeugnis für Shakespeare, das die deutsche Kritik des 18. Jahrhunderts hervorzubringen wusste."[3]

Gerstenberg's theories of the drama are intensely opposed to those of Gottsched. Between 1756 and 1759 he participated, as one of its major contributors, in the Bibliothek der schönen Wissenschaften und freyen Künste, a journal directed against narrow dogmatism and dedicated to a discussion of contemporary literature and theory. In 1762, Der Hypochondrist, a moral weekly, patterned after Addison's and Steele's Tatler, made its first appearance. The moral weeklies are a peculiarly 18th century phenomenon. First begun in England early in the century and aimed at the middle class, they contained a colorful mixture of moral guidance, rules of decorum, literary criticism, and sometimes poetry and fiction. They could succeed only in a time which had a large middle-class population eager for reading material with which it could identify. Hettner is unduly critical of the German weeklies, the contents of which he regards as enormously inferior to the sparkling wit and entertaining variety of their English counterparts.[4] Bodmer's and Breitinger's Discourse der Mahlern, (1721), for example, contains in nuce many of the theories which the two critics develop in their later writings. In addition, their observations of individual and social behavior are portrayed in a vivid and provocative style. In a

similar fashion, Gerstenberg contributed literary criticism
along with literary satires and parodies to the Hypochondrist, (1762) which efforts afforded him an opportunity to
engage in a critical discussion before he published his
more intense literary criticism in the Briefe. Gerstenberg
continued his literary criticism after concluding the
letters and contributed 105 literary critiques to the
Hamburgische Neue Zeitung between 1767 and 1771. These
Rezensionen, along with the Briefe, constitute the primary
collection of his critical canon.[5]

The most profound impact on Gerstenberg's thought can
be traced to the writings of John Home (Henry Lord Kames)
1722-1808. The Briton reiterated ideas which had been fer-
menting on the continent and in England during the latter
part of the 17th century and most of the 18th century.
Home had declared war on the classicistic tradition and
stated unequivocally that rules inhibit the imagination.
Displaying a Klopstockian disdain for rules, he regarded
literary conventions as relative and arbitrary.[6]

Central to the continuing discussion of the nature of
literature is of course the interpretation of mimesis.
Gerstenberg correctly recognized that as the phrase "imitation of nature" had rolled through the centuries, it had
created a considerable amount of confusion. Imitation of
nature had evolved to mean both, the imitation of reality

and the adherence to classicistic and neo-classicistic
rules. In order to clarify the problem, Gerstenberg divided
imitation into "Nachahmung von Mustern" and "Nachahmung der
Natur" (Gerth, p. 36).

"Die Nachahmung von Mustern," the copying of foreign
literatures, in particular the works of the French dramatists, is roundly condemned by Gerstenberg. According to
Gerstenberg, the lack of originality in Germany had
reached alarming proportions; he calls it a "Seuche der
Nachahmung."[7] Although he has praise for Wieland's newly
published novel, Agathon, (1766) he does not fail to point
out Wieland's debt to Fielding, Rousseau, and Cervantes
(Rezensionen, p. 47). And in a later essay he insults
Wieland by stating that he, in spite of his obvious talent,
"so gar sehr an der Nachahmung klebt, dass er auch nicht
einmal seinen eignen Ton hat" (Rezensionen, p. 367).
Gerstenberg advises that the best procedure for a budding
author is to study those authors to whom he feels drawn,
and then to forget them-- "und vergessen kann man sie, wenn
man aus ihnen sich selbst schätzen gelernt hat" (Rezensionen, p. 367). Gerstenberg is urging the author to rely
upon himself. His advice to study the works of established
authors implies that the neophyte can learn from them, but
that rules should not be applied mechanically, but rather
internalized. The conservative and cautiously dependent

tone of literary criticism, which had attempted to dominate
the voices raised in opposition, is clearly changing to one
of confidence in the creative power of the individual and
the nation.

"Nachahmung von Mustern" is divided by Gerstenberg
into two models, "Nachäffung" (Rezensionen, p. 327) and
"Nacheifern" (Gerth, p. 37). "Nachäffung," the total imitation of foreign literature, is rejected emphatically.
"Nacheifern," or emulation, as Young calls it, is on a
somewhat higher scale. It is alleged to be the result of
an inner relationship between the imitative writer and the
original writer and according to Gerstenberg, results in a
more convincing work of art than is achieved by the more
mechanical "Nachäffung." Gerstenberg uses Gleim as an
example and maintains that in his lyrics in imitation of
Anacreon, Gleim is in fact expressing his own essence
through the form he is imitating. Gleim is able to
accomplish this because the two writers are spiritually
related, whereas Gleim's odes in imitation of Horace are
less successful because no spiritual relationship exists
between him and Horace (Rezensionen, p. 357). In other
words, Gleim is not a crude copyist, but rather an original imitator.

In his concession to Gleim, Gerstenberg seems to be
saying that a good imitation is commendable, whereas a

poor one is to be condemned. Certainly he is inconsistent
in the rejection of literary imitation. At best, he is
highly subjective in his judgment. Gleim's greater success
in imitating Anacreon than in imitating Horace does not
prove their spiritual relationship, nor should spiritual
relationship, if indeed it does exist, grant permission to
imitate. Perhaps Gerstenberg's praise of Gleim is best
regarded as an olive branch to a poet he admires. After
all, Gerstenberg himself had not long before passed through
his anacreontic phase; his Tändeleyen, published in 1759,
were so successful that they had experienced a third edition
by 1765.[8]

Gerstenberg's general rejection of copying existing
masterworks implies that he wants the artist to be a
creator, not an imitator. This, however, did not prevent
him from struggling with the Aristotelian dictum that art
consists of the imitation of nature. Gerstenberg did not
formulate his thoughts on the imitation theory in an analytical
and precise fashion, but rather disbursed his comments
throughout the Briefe and Rezensionen.

For Gottsched mimesis requires complete identity
between empirical and theatrical reality. Gerstenberg
is critical of Gottsched's interpretation and argues
that it rests on a misunderstanding of Aristotle's
intent: "Unter der theatralischen Nachahmung der Natur

verstanden die Alten etwas anders, als die Neuern. Ihr
Zweck war niemals, die Nachahmung in dem Grade illusorisch
zu machen, dass sie mit der Natur selbst hätte können ver-
wechselt werden" (Rezensionen, p. 281). Gerstenberg goes
on to say that the moderns see mimesis as an entirely
different process, for they attempt "der wirklichen Natur
so nahe zu kommen, als möglich ist" (Rezensionen, p. 281),
a procedure which results in a forced naturalism. Gottsched's
rule that the length of the action depicted on stage must be
identical with the length of the drama is an example.
Gerstenberg is not satisfied with either approach, the
crude "naturalism" of Gottsched or the solely artistic
rendering of reality he perceives in the ancients, but
seeks to determine a middle ground. This he ascertains in
the writing of Klopstock:

> Man muss ein Genie wie Klopstock haben, um
> hier die einzige wahre Mitte auszufinden.
> Nie hat ein Dichter sich gewissenhafter an
> die Natur gehalten, und dabey den alten Chor
> vortrefflicher zu ersetzen gewusst als er.
> (Rezensionen, p. 281)

According to Gerstenberg, Klopstock remains true to nature
because the action of his Hermanns Schlacht, 1769, for
example, is rooted in history. At the same time Klopstock
uses the artistic device of the Bardengesang as a substitute
for the Greek chorus. Thus he achieves a poetic rendition
of reality based on observation.

Inherent in Gerstenberg's analysis of mimesis is the

postulate that art is <u>not</u> nature, an idea that had been especially stressed by J. E. Schlegel. On the other hand art cannot be completely removed from nature. What Gerstenberg hopes to achieve with his middle ground is an <u>illusion</u> of reality on the stage, not reality itself. "Nachahmung" becomes "Nachbildung," an ability to observe nature and represent it artistically. According to Gerstenberg, this talent is possessed only by the genius.[9]

Gerstenberg stresses that the illusion of reality is not achieved by a photographically authentic reproduction of nature, but that an additional element is essential.

> Um diese Illusion hervorzubringen, sage ich,
> muss der Dichter die <u>beobachteten</u> Gegenstände
> <u>bildlich</u> denken, und <u>mit Wirkung</u> ausdrücken
> können, welches zusammengenommen ich unter
> Nachbilden begreife. Das Nachbilden ist also
> derjenige höchste sinnliche Ausdruck, der die
> Illusion erreicht. (<u>Briefe</u>, p. 225--emphasis
> mine)

For Gerstenberg mimesis means "Nachbildung," the combination of careful <u>observation</u> and the <u>artistic</u> <u>rendition</u> of what is observed, a feat which is accomplished with the aid of the imagination. The third element essential to achieve illusion of reality through "Nachbildung" is the writer's astuteness and enthusiasm, which will assist in maintaining the illusion and thereby leave an effect in the heart and mind of the spectator. Once the illusion of reality is achieved, the emotional impact on the spectator/reader can be profound, blurring the borders between fantasy and reality and indicating to what extent the illusion is complete.

> Wenn uns also in der Shakespearschen Beschreibung der Felsen von Dover, der Gegenstand so fürchterlich wird, dass wir schon durch die blosse Vorstellung den Schwindel bekommen; wenn uns die Wharheit seiner sittlichen Gemälde oder Nachbildung so gewaltsam hinreisst, dass wir nicht mehr Zuschauer, sondern Acteur sind... . (Briefe, p. 231)

In fact, Gerstenberg contends, the "realism" can be so intense, the illusion so great that the events portrayed move the reader so intensely, that he does not seem to hear and see them, but actually sees and hears them (Briefe, p. 223). The spectator is permitted to mistake art for nature, but the artist must not; the spectator's reaction is not the result of the precisely authentic reproduction of nature, but of the artist's ability to stimulate his imagination. In order to achieve that, the artist must be creative and not imitative, for according to Gerstenberg the nature of art does not consist of Mimesis but of Poiesis.

2. Gerstenberg's Analysis of Shakespeare and its Effect on the German Drama.

In the fourteenth through eighteenth letters of the Briefe über die Merkwürdigkeiten der Literatur, Gerstenberg writes extensively about the theater of Shakespeare. Along with his analysis of Shakespeare's dramas, he develops a

theory of drama pertinent to and influential on the German
stage. According to Gerstenberg, Shakespeare should not be
judged by classicistic rules, as had been the tendency in
18th century Shakespeare criticism. Lessing, too, tries
to justify Shakespeare in Aristotelian terms. But
Gerstenberg, who intensifies Bodmer's and Breitinger's,
Klopstock's, Schlegel's, and Gellert's dispute with convention, has less patience with the rules than they. He
largely regards them as oppressive and useless: "Wie
ist es möglich, dass man noch immer die Unbrauchbarkeit so
vieler Regeln...nicht erkannt haben sollte?" (Rezensionen,
p. 57). Gerstenberg argues that the rules are not "natural"
as most theoreticians maintained, but have been "invented"
and therefore are not permanently binding. And even if it
were possible to determine unalterable laws from existing
systems, it is too early in man's history to formulate
them (Rezensionen, p. 57).

Gerstenberg maintains that Shakespeare's dramas should
not be approached from the point of view of the Wirkungs-
theorie, the concept handed down from antiquity that the
major function of tragedy is the arousal of emotion
and of comedy the arousal of laughter. He recognizes that
Shakespeare's drama does arouse the emotions, as all great
drama does, but Shakespeare subjugates that function of the
theater to another purpose, namely the psychological

portrayal of character:

> Aber merken Sie sich, dass ich ihm die Erregung
> der Leidenschaften nicht streitig mache, sondern
> sie nur einer höheren Absicht unterordne, welche
> ich durch die Zeichnung der Sitten, durch die
> sorgfältige und treue Nachahmung wahrer und
> erdichteter Charaktere, durch das kühne und
> leicht entworfne Bild des idealischen und
> animalischen Lebens andeute. (<u>Briefe</u>, p. 112)

This definition of the nature of the drama clearly places
the character in a central position. Unlike Aristotle, who
had subjugated character to action, the increasing tendency
is to focus on character, a notion present before Gerstenberg
but formulated more strongly by him and later by Lenz. The
desire to understand the universe and explain events by
exploring and understanding the nature of man is at the
heart of this notion. It reflects a general turning inward
and interest in psychological processes evidenced by the
Enlightenment, pietism, and the cult of sentimentality.
The focus on man, rather than on events, indicates the
belief that man is in control of his world and capable of
solving his problems. Structurally, the focus on character
results in an episodic, rather than a dramatic structure,
because specific dynamics are inherent in action whereas
character can be explored in a non-sequential fashion.

Because of his emphasis on character, a great portion
of Gerstenberg's Shakespeare criticism concentrates, like
Schlegel's, on Shakespeare's portrayal of dramatic character.

Gerstenberg attributes Shakespeare's ability to create plausible characters to his knowledge of human nature. The result is a many-faceted, individualized character, not a one-sided, generalized one. Using Lord Kames' words, Gerstenberg describes Shakespeare's ability to create realistic characters as a talent

> jede Leidenschaft nach dem Eigenthümlichen
> des Charakters zu bilden, die Sentiments zu
> treffen, die aus den verschiedenen Tönen der
> Leidenschaften entspringen, und jedes Sentiment
> in den ihm eignen Ausdruck zu kleiden.
> (Briefe, p. 121)

The stress is on the individual; peculiarities of character, the import of a particular emotion, and the specificity of its expression. Although individualism has support in the German Enlightenment because of its faith in man's ability to reason, it gained greater prominence in the theory and literature of Storm and Stress.

Shakespeare's detractors had primarily been critical of the irregularities of his dramas. Even Schlegel is ill at ease with Shakespeare's dramatic structure. For Gerstenberg, however, the three unities are no longer applicable, and he can therefore examine Shakepeare's dramatic technique with a fresh eye. Because creating a dramatic illusion is a necessity for Gerstenberg, he argues that the unities of time and place could be detrimental because they can interfere with illusion (Rezensionen, p. 101). Nor does Gerstenberg agree with the need for unity of action which is the primary classicistic criterion for distinguishing

epic and dramatic poesy. Convention requires that only those
scenes which contribute to the progress of the action are
permitted in a drama, which should be, as Lessing reiterates,
a chain of causes and effects. Gerstenberg, however, isolates two consecutive actions within a tragedy, which he calls
"Handlung" and "rührende Handlung" (Rezensionen, p. 101).
Therefore, he concludes, the dramatist must write two kinds
of scenes, scenes which further the main action and others
which affect the pathos.

> Dieses thut er...durch abgesonderte kleine
> Handlungen [italics mine] die zwar keine
> eigentliche Folge auf die Entwicklung der
> Fabel haben, aber doch das Interesse
> dieser Entwicklung vorzüglich erhöhen.
> (Rezensionen, pp. 101-102)

Gerstenberg has identified a major characteristic of Non-
Aristotelian drama. The fragmentation of acts into multi-
faceted secondary scenes destroys unity of action and gives
the drama an epic quality. Fragmented dramatic composition
had been avoided in eighteenth century drama. Gerstenberg
makes a hesitant beginning with Ugolino, and the new epic
structure progresses in the dramas of J. M. R. Lenz.

In the dramatic works of Shakespeare, Gerstenberg has
isolated an outer structure and an inner structure or
pattern, which must be analyzed from two different perspectives and requires two sets of rules, "Regeln für die Handlung und Regeln für das Pathos derselben" (Rezensionen,
p. 101). Gerstenberg is the first German critic who is not

primarily looking at the effect, but at the composition and
structure of Shakespeare's dramas. He is attempting to
comprehend the essence of Shakespearian drama which Guthke
calls "Dichtung in ihrem Sein."[10] In his review of <u>Julius
Caesar</u>, for example, Gerstenberg is moved to exclaim, "Was
ist hier gigantisch? Was wild? Was unförmlich?" (<u>Briefe</u>,
p. 163) As his analysis of an outer and an inner action
indicates, he has determined that Shakespeare's dramas are
constructed according to Shaftesbury's "inner rule." The
concept of inner form isolates patterns or sequences, be
they linguistic, thematic, or structural, within the drama,
thus giving it cohesion and unity. As understood in the
terminology of the time, "inner form" is the product of
genius. Gerth cites Schwinger as follows: "Bei Shaftesbury
ist die 'inward form' des Genies...gleichzeitig dynamische
gestaltende Kraft und eine geistige Gestalt, der von jener
Kraft gewirkte, sich gleichbleibende, proportionierte
Zustand." (Gerth, p. 80)

Gerstenberg points to some of the elements of inner
form present in Shakespeare: "Ich sehe durchaus ein ge-
wisses Ganze, das Anfang, Mitte und Ende, Verhältnis,
Absichten, contrastirte Charakter, und contrastirte Groupen
[sic] hat" (<u>Briefe</u>, p. 161). The concept of the validity of
an open ended drama does not play a role here, and Gerstenberg is decidedly affected by the demands of traditional

dramatic structure when he stresses the beginning, middle, and end he purports to identify in Shakespeare's dramas. More indicative of inner form is the relationship between character and situation he identifies in The Merry Wives of Windsor: "sehet da Charakter und Situationen, die sich drehen und winden, sich vermischen, sich durchkreuzen, um ein einziges Gewebe zu machen" (Briefe, p. 155). He sees Shakespeare's dramas as a multicolored fabric in which everything is "in gleichem Grade vermischt, und in ein grosses Ganze zusammengewachsen" (Briefe, p. 125). In other words, Shakespeare's dramas possess an inner unity.

One of the most cogent sentences uttered by an 18th century critic is probably the following: "Sie erinnern sich, dass ich Ihnen bereits zugegeben habe, Shakespears Drama sey nicht das Drama der Alten, und könne folglich keine Vergleichung dieser Art dulden" (Briefe, p. 139). At last a critic has appeared on the German literary scene who unequivocally admits that there are two types of drama, Aristotelian and Non-Aristotelian, and that both are equally valid! In stressing the composition of Shakespeare's dramas, Gerstenberg has authenticated their validity. Clearly, it is a composition unlike Greek drama and is guided by rules of its own. Gerstenberg concludes one of his arguments with the following: "Mir ist es genug, den Ungrund des allgemeinen Vorurtheils aufgedeckt zu haben,

dass es Shakespearn an Kunst fehle" (<u>Briefe</u>, p. 156). With
that and similar remarks, he firmly propels the state of
German drama. On the other hand, it must be stressed that
Gerstenberg does not break with tradition as pervasively as
Lenz and the other Storm and Stress dramatists. The attempt
to identify a cohesive structure within Shakespeare's
dramas is indicative that Gerstenberg has not freed himself
from demands for conventional form. This is particularly
evident in the seventeenth of his <u>Briefe</u>, where he purports
to detect Aristotelian tendencies in Shakespeare and maintains that Shakespeare does not always disregard the
unities, but merely sees them from a different point of
view. Thus, he recognizes in Shakespeare's <u>scene undivi-
dable</u> the Aristotelian unity of place.

> allein was meint Schakespear mit dem, was
> er <u>scene undividable</u> nennt? Ich müsste mich
> sehr irren, wenn wir hier nicht das Drama
> der Alten wiederfänden, das sich auf die
> Einheit des Orts gründet, das folglich zu
> Schakespears Zeiten nicht unbekannt war,
> sondern nur von einer andern Seite be-
> trachtet wurde, als von der wir es betrachten... .
> (<u>Briefe</u>, p. 140)

And in <u>Ugolino</u>, which is rightfully considered to be the
first drama incorporating a variety of Non-Aristotelian
dramatic techniques, he nevertheless observes the
<u>Ständeklausel</u>, the evocation of terror albeit without a
cathartic resolution, and at least an outward conventional
structure.

3. In Search of a Linguistic Model

In conjunction with their belief that human affairs can
be managed rationally, Enlightenment critics and theoreticians had also developed a direct approach toward language:
they were of the conviction "dass die Sprache--vernünftig
angewendet--imstande ist, die Wirklichkeit ganz zu fassen"
and lived in a "naiven Sprachrealismus" (Gerth, p. 84).
Bodmer and Breitinger, however, had already pointed out the
affective quality of language; Friedrich Leopold Stolberg
lamented language's inability to truly express emotions;
Klopstock, and particularly Hamann, struggled with the dis-
crepancy between thought and word. It is no surprise, then,
that as the emphasis on emotion and the expression of inner
experience, together with a tendency toward an aesthetic
rather than a didactic concept of literature progressed, a
new view of language developed.

Batteux regarded words as signs and described their
function as follows:

> Die Worte drücken eine Leidenschaft nur
> vermittelst solcher Zeichen aus, bei welchen
> man sich eine Empfindung zu denken ein ge-
> worden ist, sie sind gleichsam nur der
> zurückprallende Strahl der Leidenschaft...
> Kurz die Worte sind eine Sprache des Willkürs...
> die Gebärden und die Töne sind die Sprachkunde
> der einfältigen Natur.[11]

Gerstenberg, like Herder and Hamann, considered words to be

arbitrary signs or symbols (Zeichen) of reality. Hamann
refers to words as signs in Kreuzzüge des Philologen, "Da
wörter und Gebräuche Zeichen sind...."[12] Using an image of
an eclipse which can be viewed only indirectly, he analyzes
the relation between word and thought as follows: "Reden
ist übersetzen--aus einer Engelsprache in eine Menschen-
sprache, das heisst, Gedanken in Worte,--Sachen in Namen,--
Bilder in Zeichen."[13] Herder also attempts to analyze the
relationship between a word and its meaning, the "Zeichen"
and the "Bezeichneten,"[14] or, in linguistic terminology, the
"signifier" and the "signified." Contradicting Lessing's
assertion that there is a comfortable correlation between
Zeichen and Bezeichnetem, he maintains:

> Die artikulirten Töne haben in der Poesie
> nicht eben dasselbe Verhältnis zu ihrem
> Bezeichneten, was in der Malerei Figuren und
> Farben zu dem Ihrigen haben. Die Zeichen der
> Malerei sind natürlich: die Verbindung der
> Zeichen mit der bezeichneten Sache ist in den
> Eigenschaften des Bezeichneten selbst gegründet.
> Die Zeichen der Poesie willkührlich: die artikulirten
> Töne haben mit der Sache nichts gemein, die sie aus-
> drücken sollen; sondern sind nur durch eine allgemeine
> Convention für Zeichen angenommen. (Herder, p. 135)

According to Herder, poetry affects the reader through the
connotation of the word:

> Bei keinem Zeichen muss das Zeichen selbst,
> sondern der Sinn des Zeichens empfunden werden;
> die Seele muss nicht das Vehikulum der Kraft,
> die Worte, sondern die Kraft selbst, den Sinn,
> empfinden. (Herder, p. 137)

82

The poem remains closed until the reader has experienced the "spirit" of the word. Herder describes that spirit or essence as a power, a "Kraft" which "dem Innern der Worte anklebt" (Herder, p. 139).

Gerstenberg echoes Herder when he writes, "Worte... sollen Zeichen unsrer Begriffe seyn" (Briefe, p. 339) and "Töne sind Zeichen, Worte sind auch Zeichen, nur auf eine andre Art" (Briefe, p. 334). Gerstenberg sees poetic language as a symbolic medium; words are signs which are capable of evoking a picture or image, a process induced by the imagination: "Mich dünkt also, man könne nicht behaupten, das Wort werde auch da wider seinen Zweck gebraucht, wodoch in der That der Zweck erreicht wird, nämlich, dass der Zuhörer es beides als Zeichen versteht, und als Gemälde empfindet" (Briefe, p. 340). By translating the sign into an image, the reader "experiences" the "thrust" of the word. The image produced by the word permits the reader to perceive the emotion the author wishes to express, "woran wir die Empfindungen, die in dem Herzen eines anderen vorgehen, symbolisch erkennen" (Briefe, p. 334, emphasis mine). Thus, the word becomes a symbol whose content is determined through the thrust of the imagination. Symbols can be universal, nevertheless they are arbitrary. Gerstenberg's focus on the symbolic nature of poetic language indicates that he regards the linguistic

sign as arbitrary. Although Gerstenberg did not develop
his theory of language to the extent Herder did, his view
nevertheless resemble those of Herder. According to
Gerth: "Das entspricht genau der Herderschen Auffassung und
charakterisiert Gerstenbergs Erkenntnis der Grenzen, welche
die Sprache der Ausdrucksdichtung setzt" (Gerth, p. 85).

Gerstenberg is well aware of the complex nature of
poetic language and recognizes that it has the power to reveal and to conceal, "ist es nicht gerade ein Hauptvortheil
für die Poesie, dass sie mit ihren Zeichen, besser als
irgend eine andre Kunst, das Widrige eines Bildes in
Schatten zu verhüllen weiss" (Rezensionen, p. 193). The
logical conclusion is that if literature is capable of veiling the unpleasant, it is also capable of veiling the truth.
And indeed, a philosophy of language which regards words as
arbitrary symbols of reality and is aware of the role played
by the imagination which is by nature subjective must recognize the possibility of the dubious truth value of the
written word. This did not escape Gerstenberg:

> Weder eine Beschreibung noch eine wirkliche
> Abbildung giebt ein ganz vollständiges Bild.
> Wer den Gegenstand genau kennen will, wie er
> ist, muss nicht die Copie sondern ihn selbst
> ansehen. (Rezensionen, p. 194)

Certainly the opportunity for language skepticism exists
here and it does surface in a number of the works of the
epoch, in Lenz's Hofmeister and his Soldaten, for example,

and in Gerstenberg's own drama, <u>Ugolino</u>. As a whole, however, the language theory of Storm and Stress overtly pursued another interest. No longer was language merely a
tool for communication, or even a stimulus for the imagination, but it became <u>Ausdruckssprache</u>--the means by which the
soul's innermost feelings and emotions are expressed. Although an understanding of the word as arbitrary sign or
symbol for the emotion expressed implies a recognition of
the limitations of language, Gerstenberg attempts to overcome those limitations. He continues the paragraph quoted
above as follows: "Wenn aber gleich in dieser Absicht
eine jede Nachahmung mangelhaft bleibt, ist darum das Bild,
was sie in der Seele zurücklässt, gar Nichts? (<u>Rezensionen</u>,
p. 194). Indeed it is not, because the inherent barrier
between word and emotion can be overcome by the affective
participation of the reader himself: "Empfindung kann nur
durch Empfindung begriffen werden" (<u>Rezensionen</u>, p. 349).
Increasing emphasis is placed on the writer's emotional
involvement in the creative process, but Gerstenberg also
stresses that the writer must consciously use imagery and
certain stylistic devices, such as inversion and a conscious
choice of words--"Wendungen, Inversionen, Worte, und
Bilder...durch welche sich der Ausdruck der Empfindungen
von dem Ausdruck des kalten Verstandes allemal, mehr oder
weniger, unterscheidet" (<u>Rezensionen</u>, p. 349).

For Gerstenberg, the result of poetic language is not
"gar Nichts" but rather an impression of the emotion described in the soul of the reader. A poet, "der sich auf
dem rechtn Pfade der Natur fühlt, und sein eignes Gefühl
treulich ausdrückt" (Rezensionen, p. 350), is capable of
accomplishing this.

Gerstenberg limited his theory to poetic language; he
did not include a discussion of the relationship between
"rational" language, ("der Ausdruck des kalten Verstandes")
and its symbolic character, as Herder did in his Fragmente,
(1766-7) and in his Abhandlung über den Ursprung der
Sprache, (1770). Based on the Lockian model of language as
arbitrary signs, a view which influenced Christian Wolff,
the Swiss critics, Mendelssohn, Herder, and others, (Gerth,
p. 84), rather than the Leibnizian one of language as
natural signs, Gerstenberg pursued the interrelationship
between linguistic symbol, emotion, and imagination. Contrary to modern criticism, meaning was not to be ascertained
by analyzing syntax and semantic sequences, but by emotional
participation, a highly subjective function.[15] Although
Gerstenberg attempts to overcome the barriers between
language and emotion, he recognizes the limits which
language sets for Ausdrucksdichtung; certainly the onset of
language skepticism is apparent in his theory, a factor
which plays an increasingly important role in future literature.

4. Ugolino--Conventional Structure or Inner Form?

According to A. Wagner, Ugolino, published in 1768,
"war eine historische Notwendigkeit."[16] Kistler calls it
"the first drama of any consequence which created an
atmosphere of highly charged emotional feeling and, in this
respect, corresponded to the esthetics of the Storm and
Stress."[17] Nevertheless, in spite of its alleged pivotal
position, literary history and criticism has paid it pre-
cious little attention. Martini grants it one sentence:
"Gerstenberg's Drama Ugolino wagte für das schauerliche
Ereignis des Hungertodes des Grafen Ugolino und seiner
Söhne im Gefängnis von Pisa einen pathetischen psycholo-
gischen Naturalismus."[18] Recent criticism offers psychological and sociological interpretations.[19] Other critics
note that the unities observed in the drama are no longer
the classical three unities and point to the symbolism of
the work.[20] However, the dramatic techniques utilized by
Gerstenberg and the theories out of which they evolved have
not been developed in detail. A general emphasis in Storm
and Stress criticism as a whole seems to be _that_ the movement stressed the emotions, not _how_ that emotional emphasis
was achieved. But the question of _how_ to express emotion
in literature was, as their theories reveal, pursued in
a conscious manner by the exponents of Storm and Stress.

Gerstenberg's biographer, Wagner, is correct when he states that Gerstenberg's primary concern when writing Ugolino was dramatic form.[21] Unfortunately, his conclusions concerning the dramatic structure of Ugolino are incomplete.

It has been often mentioned that Gerstenberg observes the three unities and the traditional five-act structure. The theme selected by Gerstenberg, the incarceration of a man and his sons and their reaction to impending death by starvation quite naturally assumes at least the unity of place. The scene opens on a stormy night in a tower room, which has become the prison of Gheradesca and his three sons. Yet, the tower is obviously more than the antique place in which the action occurs. The tower, long a symbol in literature of inwardness and isolation--notably in La vida es sueño and Hofmannsthal's Turm--represents inner space; it is no longer merely a room in a prison, but has become a chamber of the mind. By observing the occurrences inside the tower, the spectator is able to look into the characters' mind and participate in their emotional experiences. Eventually, the spectator is drawn into the drama and into the characters' mind; like the prisoners, he has no other "place" into which to escape.

There is no action in Ugolino; the events that lead to the unfortunate imprisonment occurred before the drama begins

88

and are not unravelled on stage. Analytical drama is not
Gerstenberg's intent. He is searching for a new kind of
drama, a drama that has come to fruition with Shakespeare,
a drama that represents "ein Bild der sittlichen Natur"
(Briefe, p. 112). Therefore action is secondary and unim-
portant. It is the characters who dominate, magnificently
and sometimes frighteningly.

.The death scenes on stage are a decidedly Non-
Aristotelian innovation. Antiquity preferred unpleasantness
to occur off-stage and have it reported by a messenger.
But J. E. Schlegel already talks of the necessity of
depicting unpleasantness in order to present a whole
picture of reality, albeit portrayed in an aesthetically
pleasing manner. In a letter to Gleim, Gerstenberg
writes that he attempted in Ugolino to avoid a fable
which could become "abscheulich und ekelhaft" (Gerth,
p. 43). Nevertheless, the deaths occurring before
the spectators' eyes are described in graphic terror.
"Francesco: Er [death] hat mich ergriffen--Gott! Gott!
Anselmo: Erbarmer! Erbarmer! Erbarmer! Noch windet der
Wurm sich? Noch? Noch? Wehe mir! Sterben ist grauenvoll."[22] He repeats the phrase "Sterben ist grauenvoll"
and adds "Geboren werden ist auch grauenvoll!" (p. 54).

The latter utterance indicates that Gerstenberg is not really interested in portraying the pain of dying, but the pain of living. His intent is to create a portrait of human nature in which the shadings and nuances of emotion are explored. The author is depicting the suffering of the characters without ennobling their experience. There is no tragic hero in Ugolino, no redeeming death. The step away from classical tragedy is enormous. Ugolino is the major manifestation of realism on the German stage before Lenz's Der Hofmeister and Die Soldaten.

The unity of time also appears to be observed: the events on stage take place during one brief, stormy night. Yet it becomes immediately apparent that it is no longer historical time which is in question. The captives in the tower have been largely cut off from contact with the outside world; the historical events leading toward their imprisonment are no longer of any consequence, and there is almost no interaction between the inhabitants of the tower and their former environment. They seem to exist in a time warp; instead of the concrete time period of classicistic drama, the characters of Ugolino operate in a state of perpetual timelessness. Their pain is not the result of harmatia, their suffering and punishment is not one with which the spectator can come to terms. Instead they experience existential pain, timeless in its scope and univer-

sal in its implications. No longer is there a moral lesson
here with which the spectator can confidently leave the
theater. Instead he sits in awe and marvels at the con-
volutions of human nature, just as Gerstenberg had intended.

Gerstenberg selected a traditional five-act structure
for Ugolino. Each act consists of one scene only. The
action, no outer action in the conventional sense, but the
inner progress of Ugolino's and his sons' increasing despair, appears to consist of an homogeneous whole, for there
are no splinter scenes or side actions. In that sense the
drama certainly manifests a classicistic structure. Yet the
scenes do not logically lead from one into the other nor do
they move the action forward to a logical conclusion. Instead each act represents a state of frenzied stasis. The
drama is no longer a cohesive whole in which the action
develops toward a climax and denouement, but each individual act is split asunder by the acute tension existing
among the characters. Part of that tension is maintained by
the four songs Gerstenberg has interpolated in Acts II,
IV, and V. Traditionally lyrical presentations within a
drama and the actions of the Greek chorus have functioned
as a commentary or explication of the action. Ugolino is
one of the first dramas in which songs interrupt the dialogue and are used to heighten the emotional effect. It is

an innovation continued by Lenz and by Büchner and adds a
certain epic quality to the drama, for the songs often contradict and thereby expand the action.

The four songs in <u>Ugolino</u>, all of which are sung by
Anselmo, stand in peculiar contrast to the dialogue. In the
first scene in which a song appears, Anselmo is convinced
that help from outside will soon arrive. Yet, in the song
requested by his father, which was taught to him by his
mother, he sings of death:

> Um und um von Nacht umflossen,
> Ach! von Schauern übergossen,
> Wall' ich bebend an mein Grab!

The second half of the stanza asks for divine interference:

> Leite mich im finstern Tale,
> Quell des Lichts! mit deinem Strahle!
> Blicke mild auf mich herab! (p. 30)

When Anselmo completes the song, Ugolino thanks him, and
then states that he wanted to ask him to repeat the song,
but that he is not up to it: "Aber ich bin diesmal zu
weich," whereupon he cries vehemently" (p. 30). The lyrics
are not in keeping with the spirit of hope Anselmo attempts
to foster, nor have they succeeded in offering the consolation intended in their content.

A similar situation exists the second time Anselmo is
asked to sing: Ugolino has just reminisced about past
happy times. "Ugolino: Zu bedauern ist's, dass dies Leben

nicht immer fortwährt. Man ist auf der Welt so glücklich.
Gaddo (seufzend): Ach ja! das Leben ist so was Süsses"
(p. 50). This in stark contrast to the grimness of their
situation. Following these remarks, Ugolino speaks of an
afterlife: "Das menschliche Leben ist zwar sehr glücklich;
aber das höhere Leben nach dem Tode ist doch viel glück-
licher" (p. 50). At this point Francesco is reminded of the
dying song of their patron saint, St. Stephen, and Ugolino
asks Anselmo to sing it:

> Ich soll den Lichtquell trinken
> Am himmlischen Gestad'!
> Ach! wo das Lied der Sterne strömt,
> Am himmlischen Gestad',
> Da strömt ihr Silberstrom
> Unsterblichkeit!
> Ihn soll ich schaun! Gedank'!
> Unauszudenkender Gedank'!
> Ach! ich verstumme dir! (p. 50)

Again, the song does not continue the mood of confidence and
joy which Ugolino attempted to establish. The first verse
suggests that the singer does not want to, but has to experience the beyond. Coming face to face with divinity is
an "unthinkable thought." The twice repeated "Ach" ac-
centuated by an exclamation point and the verse's ebbing
into silence express the singer's terror. The song contradicts the situation.

Light imagery appears in both of the songs sung by
Anselmo. The "Quell des Lichts" of the first song becomes

"Lichtquell" in the second. Light traditionally symbolizes
the divine, but it can also represent reason. In the first
stanza of the first song in particular, Anselmo is address-
ing reason:

> Stillen Geists will ich dir flehen!
> Weisheit, blick' aus deinen Höhen,
> Blicke sanft auf mich herab!
> Leite mich im finstern Tale,
> Quell des Lichts! mit deinem Strahle!
> Sende mir dein Licht herab! (p. 30)

In the first half of the stanza, there is a specific reference to reason. In the second half, the singer addresses
the source of light, or God, and light itself, symbolizing
wisdom or reason emanating from the divine. But as the
second stanza indicates, neither God nor reason are providing consolation. The mood is one of hopelessness and
despair.

In the other two songs of the drama, the same dis-
crepancy between dialogue and lyric exists. Gerstenberg
uses the lyrical interludes to further demonstrate the
paradoxes and inconsistencies of the human psyche.
Structurally, the interjection of the songs helps to
create a fragmented and episodic, rather than an homogenous act. In spite of its apparent traditional structure
and observation of the unities, Ugolino is the most innovative drama written in Germany up to that time.

As science has known for quite some time, even in

disintegration patterns exist, and each destruction of
form is accompanied by an inherent birth of a new form.
W. H. Rey calls it in his work _Die Poesie der Antipoesie_,
"Formauflösung und Reintegration."[23] Certainly, here we
must turn to Shaftesbury's "inner form" to determine what
holds _Ugolino_ together. In that respect, the instrumental
music interspersed throughout the drama has a different
function than the songs. Wagner has noted Gerstenberg's
preoccupation with music in relationship to Kleist, "aber
was sind denn die Kleistschen 'Leitmotive' anderes, als
die Abwandlungen der seelischen Situationen _Ugolinos_, was
anders als Motive, den seelischen Strom hinab- und hin-
aufzuleiten. In diesem Sinne ist jedes grosse Seelendrama
musikalisch."[24]

The references to music, together with actual music on
and off stage and fading in and out of the episodes, give
the drama an inner cohesion. In Act II, Anselmo compares
the three pebbles rolling off the tile roof--Francesco's
signal that the jump from the tower has been successful--to
the sound of music. Toward the end of the act, he accom-
panies his singing on his lute. Later, before he breaks
into the forced hilarity of a hunting ditty, he whistles.
And in Act V, the music reaches a crescendo, this time
coming from off-stage and ending, according to Gerstenberg's direction, on a sublime note.

In a similar fashion, certain words and phrases are repeated throughout the drama. The youngest child, Gaddo, is repeatedly called "der arme Gaddo" or "der kranke Gaddo." The death lament is reinforced by the constant use of the word "traurig." And as H. Schmidt points out, "in the first act alone, the word 'Vater' is spoken thirty-seven times."[25]

Thematic unity is, of course, achieved through the spectre of impending starvation. The primitive and abiding urgency for food is expressed by the increasing desperation of the youngest child. Early in the play when there is still hope, Gaddo happily looks forward to eating, "Ach lieber Gott, dann wird gegessen werden" (p. 18). Later, when Anselmo rhapsodizes of freedom and his father's house, Gaddo responds with "Was geht mich Freiheit an! Hab' ich doch zu essen!" (p. 24). And towards the end, when the horror is reaching its final stages, he cries out, "Gib mir Speise, Francesco, oder ich sterbe!" (p. 32).

An elemental principle of dramatic structure is that of character contrast. Thus, the hero of a classical tragedy must have an antagonist, who is involved in his downfall, present on stage--Creon in Sophocles Oedipus, for example. For Ugolino, there is no visible antagonist on stage. Ruggieri, who is responsible for the imprisonment, does not participate in the occurrences on stage.

Ugolino's adversary seems to be life as a whole. Yet, character contrapositions exist within the drama and contribute to its inner structure. The rational Francesco is contrasted by the hot headed Anselmo. "Du bist ein Geck," he tells his brother who questions his priority in daring the jump from the tower, "Die Sache ist zu ernsthaft, um ein Wortspiel daraus zu machen" (p. 21). By the same token, the trusting and naive child, Gaddo, functions as a counterpoint to Ugolino's rage. In the last act, Ugolino kills Anselmo, the son who is most like himself, and by killing his child commits spiritual suicide, although his own suicide does not occur. In a sense, Ugolino is his own adversary, and the paradoxes of his nature are visually represented in the contrasting figures of his children.

The problematic ending of Ugolino causes the same dissatisfactions occasioned by the endings of Die Soldaten and Der Hofmeister. It does not integrate the tone of the drama and appears contradictory and contrived. That Gerstenberg struggled with the conclusion of his tragedy is evidenced by the history of its final scene. Originally, Gerstenberg had planned to end the drama with Ugolino cursing the hour of his birth. Upon Lessing's urgings, however, he altered the conclusion to depict an Ugolino who inwardly triumphs over adversity. In his final monologue he reaffirms his faith in a divine order and accepts his

state in what he suddenly professes to perceive as a
harmonious universe. The artificially imposed classicistic
ending has the effect of a dam built against a raging sea.
It has not evolved organically out of the action and does
not negate the chaos within. It emphasizes, however, that
a classicistic ending is a paradox in Non-Aristotelian
drama. Ugolino's spiritual atonement in the final scene
can not only be seen as a legacy of a dramatic convention
to which Gerstenberg returns, but it also reflects his own
position--that of finding himself in the center between
antiquity and modernity. Because Ugolino's final monologue
has not developed out of the drama itself, it contradicts
the mood of the drama, and Ugolino remains basically open-
ended. Anselmo's questions from a Klopstockian ode immediately preceding Ugolino's monologue imply this: "Ist
am Ziel denn nicht Vollendung? / Nicht im Tale des Tods
Wonnegesang?" (p. 60).

As discussed previously, for Gerstenberg the illusion
of reality, in this case, inner reality, is created not by
an authentic reproduction of nature, but by the poetic
rendition of the writer's observation. In order to achieve
a poetic representation of reality, the writer must pay a
great deal of attention to language, and this, of course,
Gerstenberg did. Since his emphasis is on the representation of psychological realism with its accompanying focus on

the emotions, he tried to achieve a language that would most accurately express the writer's intent and affectively involve the reader. Characteristics of an emotionally charged language are inversion, exclamations, emphasis on adjectives, and emphasis on imagery. This Gerstenberg achieves in _Ugolino_. Exclamation and question marks are, of course, the preferred punctuation of Storm and Stress, and Gerstenberg is no exception. Incomplete sentences appear frequently, "Wenn wir uns wiedersehn, so--" (p. 51), and adjectives are manifold, "Seinen kranken, gelähmten, verschmachtenden Bruder schlägt Anselmo?" (p. 48). Occasionally, Gerstenberg lapses into 17th century mannerism, "und deine süssen Lippen, deine Nektarlippen, deine Wonnenlippen" (p. 41). The resulting hyperbole can perhaps be attributed to a misapplied admiration of Longinus, joined with his admiration for Gleim.

In addition, Gerstenberg uses nouns formed from adjectives, "der Ungenügsamste" (p. 23), "Unglücklicher," (p. 27), "Ärmster," (p. 43). Inversion, rearranging syntax so that the word which is to be stressed begins the sentence, is also utilized, "Bleich war das Antlitz unsers Vaters" (p. 43). Imagery also appears frequently. Anselmo gives Gaddo an imaginary gift of a lush forest filled with deer and nests, for example, after the younger brother has shamed him with his own generosity. The fantasy created by Gaddo and Anselmo becomes bitter reality when Anselmo, temporarily maddened, accuses Gaddo of stealing eggs out of his nests and tries to kill him.

At the same time Gerstenberg consciously attempts to create an expressive language--eine Ausdruckssprache--and gestures also play a major role in his drama. The stage directions imply that the actors are to express visually what they are experiencing internally. There are frequent directions like the following: "reisst sich die Haare aus" (p. 34), "in dem er sich die Hände reibt" (p. 29), "schlägt sich vor die Brust und entfernt sich schnell" (p. 54), and many others. In the first act alone, there are eleven directions for specific and involved gestures underlining emotions expressed. Similarly, the actor is directed to express his emotions not just through his words, but through the tone of his voice, and he is informed he must speak with a voice that is "keuchend," (p. 29), "traurig," (p. 30), "bestürtzt," (p. 43), and so on.

Modern drama has increasingly relied on gestures. The stylization of Expressionism or Artaud's Theater of Cruelty is an extended gesture--an attempt to convey meaning and to communicate not only through words, but also through visual effects. The danger of the elusiveness of language is thus avoided. The extremely stylized figures of the

commedia dell'arte, for example, could never be mistaken
for what they were not intended to be. The reliance on
gestures in modern drama reflects language skepticism and
is an attempt to represent that which cannot be expressed by
words alone. It could be said that that skepticism is already present in a drama whose author feels compelled to
reinforce his characters' words through gestures as frequently as Gerstenberg does in Ugolino.

It has become apparent that Gerstenberg's objective
is to create a drama which explores the intricate manifestations of human nature. His aim is to create an illusion of reality--inner reality, in Ugolino's case. He
describes a successful illusion of reality as follows:

> Sobald der Vorhang aufgezogen wird, denken
> wir nicht mehr an das Theater, sondern an
> den Ort, den das Theater vorstellen soll,
> nicht an den Schauspieler, sondern an seine
> Rolle, nicht an die Zeit, Abends von fünf bis acht
> Uhr, da wir ausserhalb Hauses sind, sondern
> an diejenige Zeit, die uns der Dichter
> andeutet, Morgen, Mittag, oder Mitternacht;
> wir sehen mit eben dem guten Glauben in die
> Bühne hinein, als ob wir, wenn ich diese
> Vergleichung brauchen darf, in einen
> Guckkasten sähen. (Rezensionen, p. 104)

In Gerstenberg's description, we have intimations of the
19th century Illusionsbühne. The movement toward realism is
gaining momentum in German drama. With Ugolino, Gerstenberg has brought psychological realism to the German stage.

CHAPTER IV

DRAMATIC THEORIES OF J. M. R. LENZ:
THE "ANMERKUNGEN ÜBERS THEATER" AND OTHER THEORETICAL ESSAYS

An astonishing phenomenon in literary history is the
emotional tone and subjective stance literary historians
and critics adopt when describing the "alleged" emotional-
ism of the Storm and Stress movement. This is particularly
true in 19th and early 20th century criticism, but it
nevertheless continues to surface even in contemporary
assessments of Storm and Stress. It seems to be practiced
by both detractors and admirers of the movement, and occurs
most intensely in the evaluation of J. M. R. Lenz. Wagner,
for example, describes him with unrestrained enthusiasm as
a "prachtvoller deutscher Jüngling,"[1] while Gundolf, on
the other hand, refers to Lenz's theoretical essay as
"seine konfusen Anmerkungen übers Theater," and concludes
that "Für die Geschichte Shakespeares in Deutschland be-
deutet Lenz nichts Neues, für die Geschichte der deutschen
Literatur bestenfalls eine Kuriosität."[2] And one of the
most influental contemporary histories of German literature, that of Martini, stresses Lenz's relationship to
Goethe, inducing the reader to conclude that the author's
biography must somehow detract from the significance of his

dramatic theory and practice.[3] Unfortunately, the emphasis
upon the problematical personalities of several Storm and
Stress writers and the proclivity for highlighting the
content rather than the style, form and structure of
Storm and Stress literature, have relegated the _experimental_
nature and _theoretical_ aspects of the movement to a
secondary rank which has created a distorted picture of
Storm and Stress. On the whole, there has been a marked
tendency to view the period primarily as a sudden revolt
against the Enlightenment and an attempt to elevate the
forces of emotion over the power of reason. But throughout the 18th century many of Germany's leading dramatists
were involved in a confrontation with the Aristotelian
tradition, and this rebellion caused an increasing distancing
from classicistic dramatic precepts. In the early 1770's
the preoccupation with a new and valid dramatic form for
the German stage crystallized in the persuasive Shakespeare
essays of Herder and Goethe, and particularly in the
dramatic theories and practice of J. M. R. Lenz.

As is well known, Lenz introduced his essay "Anmerkungen
übers Theater" with the remarks that it had been read to a
circle of his friends two years before Herder's and Goethe's

Shakespeare essays were published. Lenz's claim resulted
in an immediate controversy--Wieland declared that he also
had a hand in acquainting the Germans with Shakespeare[4]--
and the date of the essay continues to be the subject of
scholarly speculation.[5] It is irrelevant to the purposes
of this discussion whether Lenz's essay preceded, followed,
or appeared simultaneously with those of Herder and Goethe.
All three writers are obviously expressing views which were
shared by many thinkers concurrently. Germane to our
discussion is the fact that Lenz, unlike Herder and Goethe,
addresses himself to specific dramatic principles in his
essay and demonstrates in considerable detail why Greek
precepts are no longer applicable and should therefore
be rejected. Lenz's dramatic theories, and in particular,
his dramas, rather than those of other Storm and Stress
writers, have become the model for Büchner, Grabbe, Wedekind, Brecht, and other contemporary dramatists.

1. The Structure and Style of the "Anmerkungen."

Because the essay is written in the innovative style
favored by Storm and Stress writers, the "Anmerkungen" pose

difficulties for all who are accustomed to an analytical approach in theoretical essays. One could argue that Lenz's rejection of the Aristotelian tradition is visually expressed by his revolutionary syntax; that recognition, however, does not assist the reader to simplify the complex stylistic and structural patterns or clarify the development of Lenz's thought and theories.

In spite of its unconventional linguistic structure, the essay is not "confusing," as Gundolf contends. Granted, a 20th century reader, accustomed to a variety of stylistic experimentation, is more comfortable with Lenz's style than an 18th century "classicist" must have been. However, it is precisely the stylistic innovations (in addition to content) which comprise the value of Lenz's essay as a major stylistically and theoretically _modern_ document which endeavors to make an impact on the reader both by its content _and_ form. The terminus "modern" is used here to denote non-classical literature as it was later defined by August Wilhelm Schlegel.

On a superficial level, the "Anmerkungen" can be divided into sections treating specific topics. The introduction consists of a brief history of the theater followed by an investigation into the nature of poetry and the poetic genius. The next two sections, containing Lenz's major dramatic theories, concern themselves with the primacy

of character in relation to action in tragedy and with the
three unities. This is followed by an assessment of
French literature and a comparison between Shakespeare and
Voltaire. The conclusion then explores the difference between antique and modern drama, contains additional remarks
about Aristotle and ends with a comparison between comedy
and tragedy. A separate paragraph follows introducing
Lenz's attached translation of Shakespeare's <u>Love's Labour's</u>
<u>Lost</u>, which he had published with the title of <u>Amor</u> <u>vincit</u>
<u>omnia</u>. In his analysis of the "Anmerkungen," T. Friedrich
approximately follows the above schema, but contends that
the essay seems to lack an inner logic. Friedrich contributes the lack of inner logic to the fact that the essay
was written in sections, with the introduction and conclusion as later additions and portions inserted into the main
body of the essay. To demonstrate his thesis, he maintains that contradictions exist within Lenz's remarks concerning Aristotle. It is obvious that Lenz rejects
Aristotelian theories in the body of the essay; he speaks
of "die so erschröckliche, jämmerlichberühmte Bulle von
den drei Einheiten,"[6] refers to Aristotle in a mocking
tone, "Ich habe eine grosse Hochachtung für den Aristoteles,
obwohl nicht für seinen Bart,"(p.721) and declares, "aber
fort mit dem Schulmeister, der mit seinem Stäbchen einem
Gott auf die Finger schlägt,"(p.730). With this Friedrich

agrees. He argues, however, that Lenz modifies his views in the concluding remarks when he explains that the Greeks necessarily subjected character to action because of the religious nature of their drama and thereby achieved unity: "Wie konnte Aristoteles also anders..." (p.742). In Friedrich's opinion, Lenz changed his views after the publication of Blätter von deutscher Art und Kunst, in which Herder examined the religious origin of Greek drama and analyzed Shakespeare's drama from an historical perspective. According to Friedrich, portions of the "Anmerkungen" were written before Herder's essay; its publication had an impact on Lenz, caused him to alter his position, and brought about a lack of inner logic and unity.[7]

Friedrich's assertions are incorrect. Whether the essay was written in chronological order or not a unifying or guiding principle in its content as it exists emerges and provides it with an inner structure and unity. From its inception to its final paragraphs, the essay is consistent, in that it embodies a dialectical confrontation with Aristotle. Periodically, the focus on Aristotle recedes and other aspects occupy the foreground, but Aristotle is never absent. He consistently functions as the antagonist against whom all argument is directed.

Chronologically, the essay can be divided into two major parts, a direct confrontation with Aristotle and an

indirect confrontation. The following schema of Lenz's
debate with Aristotle emerges:

Direct Confrontation

		ARISTOTLE	LENZ
1.	History of drama	Antique drama French classicism	Condemnation of effect on German drama
2.	Concept of mimesis	Source of art is "Nachahmung der Natur"	Two sources of art, "Nachahmung" and "Anschauung"
			"Nachahmung" as mechanical necessity
3.	Character	Stress on action; attitude and morals of characters affects action	Stress on characters; characters instigate action
		Tragedy imitation of action	Action not ultimate purpose of tragedy
		Actions determine character	Premise no longer possible (characters determine action)
		Fable (action) final purpose of tragedy; tragedy could not exist without action, but could exist without characters	Does not agree-- modern man wants to know causes of actions, not just actions themselves

		ARISTOTLE	LENZ
3.	Character (continued)	Dramatists who do not create characters are still dramatists	Not true in modern times
		Second rate poets create fables inferior to character and diction; proves that fable is of primary importance	Not valid reasoning; modern drama requires powerful characters who create their own events
		Tragedy is the imitation of an action and thereby of character	The opposite can occur
4.	Unities	Fundamental law	Too restrictive
		Unity of action	Episodic structure
		Unity of place	Because of chorus
		Unity of time	Length of time not significant

Indirect Confrontation

		ARISTOTLE	LENZ
5.	French Theater	Determined by classicistic rules	Prefers Dante, Klopstock, Shakespeare
		French characterizations weak	Shakespeare's characters superior
		Voltaire's Caesar	Shakespeare's Caesar
6.	Concluding Remarks	Aristotle's historical determination fatum phobos	Aristotelian precepts no longer valid

The Lenzian confrontation with Aristotle proceeds as follows: The introductory paragraphs contain a brief history of the theater, but focus primarily on the drama of the ancients. The reader becomes immediately cognizant of the fact that he will not be offered fresh insights into the nature of the drama without first encountering the drama of classical antiquity. Lenz inserts a transitional paragraph after his brief history of the drama, and then the direct confrontation with Aristotle begins.

The pace is relatively languid during the discussion of the nature of art. Lenz introduces the time-honored concept that art consists of an imitation of nature and concludes the paragraph with an appropriate quotation from the Poetics. The immediately ensuing ironic reference to Aristotle as "ein grosser Kunstrichter mit einem Bart" (p. 721) prepares the reader for the following refutation of Aristotle. The lengthy section developing Lenz's premise that the nature of art consists in both "Nachahmung" and "Anschauung" ends with a paragraph on imitation, which relegates the concept of imitation to a mechanical necessity: "Dass das Schauspiel eine Nachahmung und folglich einen Dichter fordere, wird mir doch wohl nicht bestritten werden," (p. 725). This undermines the power of the concept as profound insight and binding law. In fact, Lenz maintains, imitation plays a role in most of man's pleasures:

> Ich getraue mich, zu behaupten, dass tierische
> Befriedigungen ausgenommen, es für die
> menschliche Natur kein einzig Vergnügen gibt,
> wo nicht Nachahmung mit zum Grunde läge--die
> Nachahmung der Gottheit mit eingerechnet usw. (p.725)

and concludes the segment with an incomplete sentence,
"Herr Aristotles selber sagt..." (p. 725). The allusion
here is clear although the sentence remains unfinished--
Aristotle agrees that imitation is a component in many
human activities. But imitation does not automatically
produce art because the creation of art requires an additional element which Lenz calls "Anschauung." He has
successfully questioned Aristotle's authority and under-
mined his power as the sole and final arbiter in matters
of poetic theory.

In the ensuing section, Lenz's analysis of dramatic
character, his dialogue with Aristotle, increases in fer-
vor and intensity. It consists of rapid statements about
Aristotle's position via quotations from the Poetics and
their immediate refutation by Lenz. In the fourth paragraph of the section, for example, this exchange takes
place: Aristotle: "Die Begebenheiten, die Fabel ist also
der Endzweck der Tragödie, denn ohne Handlungen würde es
keine Tragödie bleiben, wohl aber ohne Sitten." Lenz:
"Ohnmöglich können wir ihm hierin recht geben, so sehr er

zu seiner Zeit recht gehabt haben mag" (p. 727). Aristotle: "Die Trauerspiele der meisten Neuern sind ohne Sitten, es bleiben darum ihre Verfasser immer Dichter." Lenz: "In unsern Zeiten durchaus nicht mehr" (p. 728). And in the following paragraph, Aristotle: "Ein Zeichen für die Wahrheit des Satzes, dass die Fabel, die Ver- und Entwicklung der Begebenheiten in der Tragödie am meisten gefalle, ist, weil die, so sich an die Poesie wagen, weit eher in Ansehung der Diktion und Charaktere fürtrefflich sind, als in der Zusammensetzung der Begebenheiten, wie fast an all unsern ersten Dichtern zu sehen." Lenz: "Dies will nichts sagen..." (p. 728). The section consists of seven separate exchanges between Lenz and Aristotle. A similar pace continues in the brief passage in which the three unities are examined. It and the preceding segment come close to the nature of a dramatic dialogue; they represent a rapid exchange of ideas, a verbal fencing match patterned after stichomythia. The sections on imitation, characterization, and the three unities entail the substance of Lenz's dramatic theories. They are also the portions of his essay in which the presence of Aristotle is most conspicuous. They indeed represent the most intense confrontation of antiquity and modernity in German dramatic theory up to that time.

In the following paragraphs the figure of Aristotle

recedes; Lenz no longer addresses him directly, but the disputation continues on an indirect level. The majority of this portion of the essay is devoted to a critique of the French classicistic theater. It begins with two transitional paragraphs in which Lenz comments on the nature of epic and dramatic poetry and stresses the role and function of the dramatist. This is not an arbitrary deviation, but rather the discussion evolves out of the preceding reference to the Aristotelian distinction of time in epic and tragic poetry. Lenz disputes that length of time denotes the major difference between tragedy and epic and instead purports to see that distinction in the presence or absence of a narrator: "Es springt in die Augen, dass in der Epopee der Dichter selbst auftritt, im Schauspiele aber seine Helden" (p. 731). Having broached the subject, he now briefly enumerates the activities of the dramatist.

The critique of French classiscistic drama then follows. During the first two paragraphs of this segment, the name of Aristotle is mentioned five times. Lenz makes it clear that he equates French neo-classicism and classical antiquity: "Man braucht nicht lange zu beweisen, dass die französischen Schauspiele den Regeln des Aristoteles entsprechen..." (p. 734). He acknowledges that the French dramatists have exaggerated classical rules; nevertheless, they see the drama through "Aristotele's Prisma" (p. 733),

and his spirit dominates their theater. Lenz, however, no
longer considers Aristotelian precepts valid; therefore, a
dispute with French neo-classicism is at the same time a
dispute with Aristotle.

Stylistically, the passage on the French theater differs from the preceding portion of the essay because Lenz
no longer utilizes the device of direct quotation followed
by an immediate refutation. Structurally, however, the
segment adheres to the established model. Lenz is not concerned with dramatic theory in this section, but with
dramatic practice. He cites examples of French ineptness
and follows them with samples of Shakespearian expertise.
Rather than Aristotle-Lenz, we now find the dialectical
opposites of French classicistic drama-Shakespearian
drama, for Lenz's own views are now presented through
Shakespeare's dramas. Shakespeare's diversity, for example, counterpoints French monotony: "Ists nicht an dem,
dass Sie in allen französischen Schauspielen (wie in den
Romanen) eine gewisse Ähnlichkeit der Fabel gewahr werden,
welche, wenn man viel gelesen oder gesehn hat, unbeschreib-
lich ekelhaft wird" (p. 735), whereas: "Der Witz eines
Shakespeares erschöpft sich nie und hätt' er noch soviel
Schauspiele geschrieben" (p. 735). By the same token,
French dramatists are incapable of producing convincing
characterizations: "Es ist keine Kalumnie...das die

Franzosen auf der Szene keine Charaktere haben" (p. 736),
as is clearly demonstrated in Voltaire's portrayal of
Brutus. The scene in question is Brutus' monologue in
which he struggles with the resolution of Caesar's death.
Voltaire does not depict Brutus' inner conflict whereas
Shakespeare develops the scene in great detail illustrating
the enormity of Brutus' decision through dialogue and
action. Lenz is merciless in his rejection of French
classiscistic drama, and particularly Voltaire, a stance
we would probably regard as unjustified today. Nevertheless, his intent and the result he achieves in the "Anmerkungen" is a diametric opposition of antique and modern
theater, first through the binary opposites of Aristotle-
Lenz and then French classicism-Shakespeare.

As has been mentioned previously, Friedrich considers
the last segment of the "Anmerkungen," which begins with
"Noch ein paar Worte übern Aristoteles," to be a contradiction of his earlier assessment of Greek drama added
after the publication of Herder's Shakespeare essay.
Friedrich argues that the last section of the essay re-
constitutes Aristotle, in that the nature of Greek drama is
relativized and seen in its historical manifestations.
Lenz reasons that because of the religious nature of
antique drama and the fact that the ancients' belief in
fatum was the determining factor in their moral and philo-

sophical value system, they had no choice but to subject character to fable.

> Da nun fatum bei ihnen alles war, so glaubten
> sie eine Ruchlosigkeit zu begehen, wenn sie
> Begebenheiten aus den Charakteren berechneten,
> sie bebten vor dem Gedanken zurück. Es war
> Gottesdienst, die furchtbare Gewalt des Schick-
> sals anzuerkennen, vor seinem blinden Despotismus
> hinzuzittern. (p. 741)

This attempt to justify Aristotelian precepts, however, is not unexpected, for it also occurs in other portions of the essay. When discussing the relationship of character to action, Lenz refutes, of course, the Aristotelian dictum that action must dominate character, but includes the following mitigation of Aristotelian thinking: "Aristoteles konnte nichts anders lehren, nach den Mustern, die er vor sich hatte, und deren Entstehungsart ich unten aus den Religionsmeinungen klar machen will" (p. 726). Not only does the conclusion not contradict the body of the essay, but it also reiterates Lenz's position that antique drama-tic theories are no longer valid.

> Damit wir nun, unsern Religionsbegriffen und
> ganzen Art zu denken und zu handeln analog,
> die Gränzen unsers Trauerspiels richtiger
> abstecken, als bisher geschehen, so müssen
> wir von einem andern Punkt ausgehen, als
> Aristoteles. Das Trauerspiel bei uns war
> also nie wie bei den Griechen das Mittel,
> merkwürdige Begebenheiten auf die Nachwelt zu
> bringen, sondern merkwürdige Personen. (p. 743)

In the conclusion as in the body of the essay, Lenz upholds the primacy of character over action. At no time throughout the essay does he castigate antique characterizations, only those of the French neo-classicists. He is therefore not inconsistent when in the conclusion he praises the power of Sophocle's _Oedipus_ to move a modern audience. The chronology of Lenz's interest in historical relativism cannot be assessed from the structure or content of the essay. What can be determined is that Lenz remains adamant throughout the essay in his view that modernity requires a new dramatic vision.

In spite of the clearly developed "inner" structure of the "Anmerkungen," the essay poses difficulties for the reader. These are the direct result of the fact that Lenz submerges his dialogue with Aristotle in a superstructure of stylistic innovations. A conventional mode of expression or automatization of language reflects social and artistic stasis. Lenz's struggle with a new mode of expression can be directly related to the new vision of reality he attempts to formulate in the essay. Unquestionably, his style is influenced by Lawrence Sterne, whose impact on 18th century German writers has been well documented.[8] Whereas many authors adopted Sterne's themes directly and imitated his _Tristram Shandy_ and _Sentimental Journey_, his impact on Lenz seems to be of a philosophical and stylistic nature.[9]

Like Sterne's novel, the syntactical structure of
Lenz's essay is carefully designed to involve the reader
directly and engage him/her in a dialogue with the text.
Lenz consistently uses apostrophe--"Mit Ihrer Erlaubnis
werde ich also ein wenig weit ausholen..." (p. 719). "Denn
--und auf dieses Denn sind Sie vielleicht schon ungeduldig"
(p. 723) and numerous other instances. Reader and author
are united in a common effort--an attempt to discover the
nature of modern drama, "Wir [emphasis mine] sind alle
Freunde der Dichtkunst..." (p. 720), "Unsere [emphasis mine]
Seele ist ein Ding..." (p. 721), "Was haben uns [emphasis
mine] die Primaner aus den Jesuitenkollegien geliefert?"
(p. 733).

The tone and syntax of the essay is loose, informal,
and conversational. The several digressions which develop
out of preceding statements, notably on the nature of the
dramatist, and on comedy in the next to last paragraph, are
representations of spontaneous thought in process.[10] The
frequent occurrence of asyndeton, and the use of dashes,
exclamation, and question marks, underlines the conversational nature of the essay: "Das Fenster--wie gemein!
aber Pompejus Statue--warum sie ihm nicht lieber in den

Mund gesteckt wie die alten Maler ihre Zettel," (p. 740).
Through his style, Lenz is expressing his struggle with
the Aristotelian tradition and his own attempt to formulate
a modern vision of dramatic art. He is not submitting an
established, rigid "system," but positing a viable new
theory of poetics. Formal rhetorical techniques would be
inappropriate to a still evolving dramatic vision, for they
tend to systematize. Instead, Lenz is engaging the reader
in a dialogue, enabling the reader to observe his debate
with the classical tradition, and inviting him to participate in the genesis of a new theory of the drama.

The frequent rhetorical questions imply that the old
rules are no longer valid: "Die Schauspiele der Alten
waren alle sehr religiös, und war dies wohl ein Wunder, da
ihr Ursprung Gottesdienst war?" (p. 741). No answer is
necessary here; instead, the author is attempting to modify
the constraining reverence for convention and provoke the
dramatist toward a new vision.

Probably most annoying to the reader is the abundance
of aposiopesis occurring throughout the essay. In fiction,
recurring incomplete sentences and the resulting innuendo
demonstrate a character's inability to develop and follow
a line of thought to its logical conclusion and leave the
reader uncertain and insecure. Aposiopesis is also a
rhetorical figure which illustrates the powerlessness of

language to express innermost thoughts, a "Verschweigen des
Wichtigen."[11] A careful analysis of the frequent instances
of aposiopesis in the "Anmerkungen" reveals that this
stylistic device is not used as an indication of erratic
and incomplete thought, nor is it employed here by Lenz to
imply the insufficiency of language as a vehicle for expression, although the latter is frequently the case in his
dramas. Lenz primarily seems to be experimenting with an
innovative stylistic manifestation. Lenz uses aposiopesis
either in sentences which are irrelevant to the material
presented: "Ich habe in dem ersten Abschnitt meines
Versuchs Ihnen, meine Herren, meine unmassgebliche Meinung--
mir eine fertige Zunge geben--meine Gedanken geschwind und
dennoch mit gehöriger Präzision--" (p. 724), or in interrupted sentences. These latter either follow an unequivocal
statement, or the caesura occurs after a point has been
made, leaving no doubt in both instances as to the intent
of the incomplete sentence. Thus, a discussion of Aristotle's position on character and action ends with a quote
from the Poetics: "Es ist aber das Trauerspiel die Nachahmung einer Handlung, und durch diese Handlung auch der
handelnden Personen," (p. 729), to which Lenz adds the
following sentence fragment: "Umgekehrt wird--" (p. 729).
The implication is clear that the opposite of Aristotle's
dictum would read that tragedy is the imitation of acting

characters and thereby the imitation of an action. The
interrupted sentence serves as an invitation to the reader
to think for himself and consciously participate in the
evolution of a new dramatic theory.

An example of a sentence which terminates after the
meaning is quite clear is the following: "Die Sinne, ja
die Sinne--es kommt freilich auf die spezifische Schleifung
der Gläser und die spezifische Grösse der Projektionstafel
an, aber mit alledem, wenn die Camera obscura Ritzen hat--"
(p. 723). It cannot escape the reader that Lenz means that
the senses can be mistaken and perception can be flawed.

Aposiopesis, as used by Lenz, is a stylistic device
which challenges the reader to become more closely involved
in the essay and join in the development of the author's
thought. Like asyndeton, it also reflects thought in process more authentically than a more formal and rigid style.
The stylistic innovations introduced by Sterne and by the
exponents of Storm and Stress in Germany anticipate the
stream-of-consciousness technique of Joyce, Proust, and
Döblin. The loose, non-conventional style of stream-of-
consciousness and its concentration on inner consciousness
also demands that the reader participate in ongoing thought
processes and requires a much more intense participation by
the reader than the traditional novel demands. The stylistic devices utilized by Lenz in the "Anmerkungen" do not

detract from the inner structure and logic of the essay, but they do give it an air of mutability and flexibility. Significantly, the rhetorical fluidity and syntactical ambiguity of the essay allude to the multiplicity of modern dramatic theories and experimentation to follow.

In that sense, the Lenzian dialogue with the reader prefigures the focus on the reader of Dilthey's and Gadamer's hermeneutics and of reception theory. For Dilthey, the reader becomes involved in an active dialogue with the text and thereby experiences and understands it. Understanding is not <u>caused</u> by the text, but occurs through a circular movement of mind (the hermeneutical circle) in which parts and whole become interrelated. According to Gadamer: "Der Text bringt eine Sache zur Sprache, aber dass er das tut, ist am Ende die Leistung des Interpreten. Beide sind daran beteiligt."[12] A new awareness of the role of the reader in the interpretative process is the cornerstone of reception aesthetics. Emphasis is placed on the historicity of the work of art and the reader and, like hermeneutics, reception theory stresses the dynamics of the reader-text interaction. For Jauss: "The historical life of a literary work is unthinkable without the active participation of its audience."[13] Lenz's direct confrontation with the reader seems to indicate an awareness of the major role played by the reader in the interpretation of

the text. Not only the content, but also the stylistic
innovations are calculated to make a visual and intellectual
impact upon the reader who then becomes an active participant in the formulation of a new dramatic theory.

2.   Lenz's Interpretation of Mimesis and its
     Implication--From Authenticity to Abstractness.

As can be expected, Lenz uses the Poetics as his point
of departure in his confrontation with the concept of
mimesis. In the "Anmerkungen übers Theater" Lenz agrees
as a matter of course that the essence of art consists in
the imitation of nature; "Dass das Schauspiel eine Nachahmung und folglich einen Dichter fordere wird mir doch
wohl nicht bestritten werden" (p. 725). In fact, Lenz
reiterates Aristotle's premise that it is natural for man
to imitate and suggests that imitation plays a major role
and provides a primary source of pleasure in most human
activities.

> Ich getraue mich zu behaupten, dass tierische
> Befriedigungen ausgenommen, es für die
> menschliche Natur kein einziges Vergnügen
> gibt, wo nicht Nachahmung mit zum Grunde
> läge--die Nachahmung der Gottheit mit
> eingerechnet usw. (p. 725)

But the love of imitation does not exhaust the question of
the nature of dramatic art for Lenz. Clearly, factors
other than imitation, which he regards as such an obvious
agent in many human endeavors, are involved in the genesis

of dramatic art. Lenz reminds the reader that the writing
of a drama requires a "poet," "einen Dichter" (p. 725).
A poet possesses talents and capabilities not shared by
non-poets--he is able to represent nature in an aesthetic
fashion, as opposed to the factual rendition of the historian.
The implication here is that the result of the poet's attempt
to imitate nature is no longer a copy, but a re-creation of
reality.

Lenz speaks of imitation numerous times throughout
his essay and insists that the nature of poetry is imitation,
"das Wesen der Poesie sei Nachahmung." It is, however,
imitation with a difference, "nicht Mechanik--nicht Echo"
(Titel, I p. 336) and is the most radical break with Gottsched's concept of art as "authentic copy of nature" to
occur in the 18th century.

Lenz's view of mimesis differes from the conventional
interpretation of the term in several important particulars.
Certainly Lenz, unlike a number of earlier theoreticians,
rejects the imitation of traditional literature: a poet
must create, not copy, before he is worthy of the name "poet,"
"...eh sie selbst welche machen, versteh mich wohl, nicht nach-
machen" (emphasis mine, p. 723). This trend has already been
identified in the Non-Aristotelian undercurrents preceding
Storm and Stress, notably Klopstock's, Gellert's, and
Gerstenberg's disdain for epigones. Lenz, however, does
not only abhor imitation of exhisting authors and adherence

to conventional rules, he goes one step further; he is
concerned not only with the concept of mimesis, but with
the concept of nature itself, the <u>reality</u> which the work
of art claims to represent. Here he is no longer satisfied
with the old formula of the imitation of <u>external</u> nature, a
principle which resulted in the one-dimensional character
and moral philistinism of much Enlightenment drama. In
this respect, he purports that there are <u>two</u> origins or
founts of dramatic art, of which "Nachahmung" is only one.
The second source, which Lenz regards as a function of the
intellect and which he places on a less rudimentary level
than the more impulsive "Nachahmen," he terms "Anschauen"
(p. 721). Lenz's authority for this assertion is
Laurence Sterne, "der berühmte, weltberühmte Herr Sterne,"
whom, as the epithet implies, he admires deeply and whose
aesthetic and philosophical tenets he shares. Lenz quotes
Sterne as follows: "Die Gabe zu vernünfteln und Syllogismen
zu machen, im Menschen--denn die höhern Klassen der Wesen,
als die Engel und Geister, wie man mir gesagt hat, tun das
durch <u>Anschauen</u>" (emphasis mine, p. 721).

According to Sterne and Lenz, man is no longer satisfied with a mere outward representation of life as had
been the ancients, but he is asking <u>why</u> events occur and
expects his questions to be answered on the stage. The
result is a far more complex, multi-faceted drama than ad-

herence to tradition and to conventional rules would permit.
"Anschauen" means psychological explanation, and it requires that the dramatist delve into the internal processes
of nature, and in particular, <u>human</u> nature.

> Wir möchten mit einem Blick in die innerste
> Natur aller Wesen dringen, mit einer Empfindung
> alle Wonne, die in der Natur ist, aufnehmen und
> mit uns vereinigen. Fragen Sie sich, meine
> Herren, wenn Sie mir nicht glauben wollen.
> Woher die Unruhe, wenn Sie hie und da eine Seite
> der Erkenntnis beklapst haben, das zitternde
> Verlangen, das ganze mit Ihrem Verstande zu um-
> fassen, die lähmende Furcht, wenn Sie zur anderen
> Seite übergehn, werden Sie die erste wieder aus
> dem Gedächtnis verlieren. Eben so bei jedem
> Genuss, woher dieser Sturm das All zu erfassen
> ....(p. 722)

Because of man's desire to form order out of chaos and
understand the nature of his universe, Lenz identifies a
human tendency to simplify the complexities of reality, to
reduce concepts to their single common denominators: "Wir
suchen alle gern unsere zusammengesetzten Begriffe in einfache zu reduzieren und warum das? weil er [the intellect]
sie dann schneller und mehr zugleich umfassen kann"
(p. 722). Lenz seems to be alluding to classicistic drama
and the imitation of an action which does not portray inner
experience and explore the characters' motivations in order
to understand the internal reasons for their actions. The
result is a neatly wrapped, non-threatening but deceiving
package, the idealized, external representation of nature
revealing only the tip of the iceberg and concealing the

126

imbalance within. According to Lenz, the need "unsere zusammengesetzte Begriffe in einfache zu reduzieren," (p. 722) is an understandable human trait, because such a process seems to enhance understanding. But Lenz warns of possible stagnation and stresses the dynamics and viability of continuous questioning in opposition to harmonious conclusions represented in dramatic art

> ...trostlos wären wir, wenn wir darüber das
> Anschauen und die Gegenwart dieser Erkenntnisse
> verlieren sollten, und das immerwährende
> Bestreben, all unsere gesammleten Begriffe
> wieder auseinander zu wickeln und durchzuschauen,
> sie anschaulich und gegenwärtig zu machen, nehm'
> ich als die zweite Quelle der Poesie an. (p. 722)

In other words, the drama must not focus on plot and portray smoothly structured and predictable action, but must examine the intricate and complex processes involved in human activity; it must imitate not only _external_, but particularly _internal_ nature. It must not just represent, but examine, probe, and explain.

Lenz is quick to point out, however, that the mere ability to explain does not produce literature: "Aber eine Erkenntnis kann vollkommen gegenwärtig und anschaulich sein--und ist deswegen doch noch nicht poetisch" (p. 723). The nature of dramatic art is such that it fuses imitation and critical analysis.

> Die Poesie scheint sich dadurch von allen
> Künsten und Wissenschaften zu unterscheiden,

> dass sie diese beiden Quellen vereinigt, alles
> scharf durchdacht, durchforscht, durchschaut--
> und dann in getreuer Nachahmung zum andermal
> wieder hervorgebracht. (p. 724)

The result is not a crude naturalism, for the intellectual process in operation implies not only selection, but also a poetic transformation of reality. A mere scientific rendition of what occurs is not literature. The dramatic artist is neither imitator of nature, nor sociologist nor psychologist, but in accordance with Shaftesbury's view of the artist, creates as a second maker. He is imbued with a desire not only to create, but to "imitate divinity," in that he creates on a smaller scale what God has created on a cosmic scale.

> Wir sind, meine Herren, oder wollen wenigstens
> sein, die erste Sprosse auf der Leiter der
> freihandelnden, selbständigen Geschöpfe, und
> da wir eine Welt hie da um uns sehen, die der
> Beweis eines unendlich freihandelnden Wesens
> ist, so ist der erste Trieb, den wir in unserer
> Seele fühlen, die Begierde's ihm nachzutun; da
> aber die Welt keine Brücken hat, und wir uns
> schon mit den Dingen, die da sind, begnügen
> müssen, fühlen wir wenigstens Zuwachs unsrer
> Existenz, Glückseligkeit, um nachzuäffen,
> seine Schöpfung ins Kleine zu schaffen. (p. 720)

In a society which found the artist to be more and more dispensible, the Storm and Stress movement attempted to elevate his status by comparing him to the divine creator. The analogy between artistic and divine creativity and the exhortation that the artist look inward for guidance rather

128

than outward toward existing models must not be associated
with the platonic perception of art as inspiration, however.
Plato held that the artist listens to an inner voice and
gives expression to that which divinity has instilled in
him. The platonic view regards the artist as a tool of
divinity, whereas the Storm and Stress movement sees the
artist as an equal partner, an autonomous creator in his
own right.

In addition to extending the traditional implications
of mimesis, Lenz also attempted to broaden the conventional
understanding of the concept of nature. In classicistic
poetics, imitation of "nature" does not apply to all of
creation, but is limited to the beautiful, or in Aristotle's
words:

> And since tragedy is imitation of those who are
> better, we ought to imitate good portrait painters,
> for even in giving men their proper shape and in
> making the imitation similar to them they paint
> them more beautiful than they are .14

Gottsched and his followers upheld the concept of the
beautiful as the only proper subject for art. Bodmer and
Breitinger, however, had already doubted the validity of an
aesthetic credo which excluded all but the beautiful. In
Von dem Einfluss und Gebrauche der Einbildungskrafft,
Bodmer maintains "dass auch das natürliche Bild eines
Dinges, das in sich selbst traurig, erbärmlich, hässlich,

eckelhaft, erschröcklich, ja scheusslich ist, belustiget,"[15]
a judgment which Breitinger reiterates in the Critische
Dichtkunst. Servaes believes that this assertion is motivated by the Swiss' preference for the unusual as a literary
subject, a stance which would consider the portrayal of
exceptional ugliness as valid as that of exceptional beauty.
Less extreme is J. E. Schlegel, who specifically states that
the realistic portrayal of unpleasantness on stage cannot be
avoided. In their dramatic practice, however, these writers
remained subject to the impact of the classical tradition
and did not depict excessiveness on stage. The first major
dramatic statement which decisively rejected the aesthetics
of the beautiful is, of course, Gerstenberg's Ugolino.

In a similar fashion, Lenz predictably launches a
frontal attack against the concept of "schöne Natur." In
his essay "Versuch über das erste Prinzipium der Moral," in
which he lauds the virtues of pluralism, he criticizes
Batteux and raises the following issue: "Herr Batteux
schwur hoch und teuer, das erste Prinzipium aller schönen
Künste gefunden zu haben. Ahmet der schönen Natur nach!
Was ist schöne Natur? Die Natur nicht wie sie ist, sondern
wie sie sein soll. Und wie soll sie denn sein? Schön.--"[16]

Lenz's iconoclasm against the platonic ideal of
beauty and the classicistic doctrine that art must represent "la belle nature" only is an indication of a major

transformation in the attitude toward nature which occurred
toward the middle of the 18th century. Leibniz's teleolo-
gical concept of nature had opposed the purely mechanical
determinism of Bacon, Locke and Hume. Leibniz conceived
of natural processes as an organic whole determined by
final causes or divine Providence. As a result, nature
was glorified and considered as having been designed to
serve the needs of man and thus reveal the goodness of the
creator; natural phenomena came to be regarded as the manifestation of divine grandeur. The ensuing cult of sentimentality, which manifested itself in the poetry of the ana-
creontics and the Göttinger Hainbund, fostered a euphoristic
attitude toward nature, which ignored the destructive and
hostile forces inherent in natural phenomena.[17]

While the literature of Storm and Stress retained
traces of the earlier sentimentality, it expanded its
viewpoint to include all of nature, not only its beauty
and capacity for solace, but also its terror and potential
for chaos. For Goethe nature is organic, vital, viable--
at the same time beautiful and ugly, good and evil.

> Was wir von Natur sehen, ist Kraft, die Kraft
> verschlingt; nichts gegenwärtig, alles
> vorübergehend; tausend Keime zertreten, jeden
> Augenblick tausend gebohren; gross und
> bedeutend, mannigfaltig ins Unendliche; schön
> und hässlich, gut und bös, alles mit gleichem
> Rechte neben einander existierend.[18]

This is a view shared by Lenz when he writes in the "Anmerkungen":

> Was sie [poetry] nun so reizend mache, dass
> zu allen Zeiten--scheint meinem Bedünken nach
> nichts anders als die Nachahmung der Natur,
> das heisst aller der Dinge [emphasis mine] die
> wir um uns herum sehen, hören etcetera... ". (p. 720)

Lenz considers it a grave error and denial of truth to concentrate only on the beautiful in nature, to idealize both character and situation: "Der wahre Dichter verbindet nicht in seiner Einbildungskraft, wie es ihm gefällt, was die Herren die schöne Natur zu nennen belieben, was aber mit ihrer Erlaubnis nichts als die verfehlte [emphasis mine] Natur ist" (p. 723). Lenz emphatically rejects the classicistic dogma that beauty is the highest law of art to which all else must succumb and that art must therefore idealize nature.

Although the validity of the classicistic doctrine had been questioned before Lenz, no one had dared to assault the edifice of traditional dogma with the alacrity displayed by him. The rupture with convention expressed in the dramatic theories of Lenz is acute and their effect on the development of German drama profound. According to Lenz, the idealism propounded by the classicists is no longer adequate for the stage. Instead the dramatic artist must attempt a new "realism." [19] Lenz consents that man experiences an irresistible pull toward the divine and strives to resemble it,

but is, in fact, destined to be of this world: "da aber
die Welt keine Brücken hat, müssen wir uns schon mit den
Dingen, die da sind, begnügen" (p. 720). The source of
truth no longer resides in the ideal, but in experience,
both external and internal, sensual and psychological.
The true writer must attempt to be objective and observant
and should represent nature not as he would like it to be,
but as it is: "Der wahre Dichter verbindet nicht in seiner
Einbildungskraft, wie es ihm gefällt...er nimmt Standpunkt"
(p. 723). To adopt a point of view does not imply that the
dramatist must be politically opinionated, however, as has
been asserted by Ottomar Rudolf, but requires him to be
an astute observer of human activities.[20] Unquestionably,
the emphasis on observation as the only reliable source of
truth reflects empiricist philosophy. The senses quite
naturally and indiscriminately absorb all experience; ex-
cluding umpleasant experience and stressing only the
beautiful and pleasurable would constitute a denial of
truth. According to Lenz, the dramatic artist from his
vantage point of creator and observer, cannot afford to
be capricious, but must represent a true and accurate
picture of reality. It cannot, however, escape an astute
observer of nature that at times nature is not only cruel,
but also indifferent to human suffering: "Die Natur geht
und wirkt ihren Gang fort, ohne sich um uns und unsere

Moralität zu bekümmern... ."[21] A recognition of man's
relative helplessness is an unavoidable result of such a
discovery. Lenz's observations, and indeed, the existential
questions confronting his dramatic characters anticipate the
epistemological and ontological questions of contemporary
literature.

    Lenz's insistence that the "true poet" must be objective
and observant is complicated by his awareness of the limitations of the senses and the relative nature of truth. In
order to conceptualize the creative process, Lenz refers
numerous times to glasses and prisms, objects which assist
in producing a clearer vision, but which can also distort
vision. The writer does not observe with the naked eye;
his vision is clearly determined by the historical epoch
during which he lives. Thus Lenz writes: "Die Italiener
hatten einen Dante, die Engländer einen Shakespearen, die
Deutschen Klopstock, welche das Theater schon aus ihrem
eigenen Gesichtspunkt ansahen, nicht durch Aristoteles'
Prisma" (p. 733), and referring to the Aristotelian definition of tragedy, "ein grosses Unternehmen, aber wer kann
uns zwingen, Brillen zu brauchen, die nicht nach unserm
Auge geschliffen sind?" (p. 725).

    Lenz's concept of historical relativism is in accor-
dance with the views postulated by Herder and other exponents of Storm and Stress. However, Lenz goes a step

further and not only suggests that there are no absolute
values, but seems to question the validity of perception
itself. Using the image of the double mirror, "den Gegenstand
zurückzuspiegeln, das ist der Knoten, die nota diacritica
des poetischen Genies" (p. 723), he stresses that accurate
observation is a primary component of the creative process.
Experience is gained and absorbed through the senses and
expressed in the work of art. This aspect of Lenz's
interpretation of mimesis demands that drama consist of a
"realistic" representation of reality. For Lenz, "realistic"
means primarily the serious, non-idealized treatment of ordinary individuals and events and the portrayal of psychological processes and existential situations in relationship
to the events in which his dramatic characters become involved. But the senses, which are the poet's instruments
of observation, cannot always be trusted, for they do not
operate in isolation but are determined by circumstances.
"Die Sinne, ja die Sinne--es kommt freilich auf die spezifische Schleifung der Gläser und die Grösse der Projektionstafel an, aber mit alledem, wenn die Camera obscura Ritzen
hat"--(p. 723). The Camera obscura or darkened chamber is
the mind which receives the image through the senses and
then reflects it in the work of art. If the darkened
chamber has a fissure or crack, the image which is reflected
is no longer clear, but becomes diffused and distorted.

Although accurate observation is a major component of
Lenz's concept of mimesis and is the cornerstone of the
realistic drama he envisions, his recognition of historical
relativism and allusions to the relative value of perception give the artist considerably more freedom than he has
ever had before. Lenz questions the possibility of being
totally objective in the representation of reality and
suggests that the definition of reality is a highly personal
and subjective matter. This view is an enormous step from
Gottsched's demand for an authentic reproduction of reality.
It frees the artist from the norms which have bound him
and allows him to create according to the reality he perceives
as an individual and as a product of his own time and age.

It is important to note that Lenz does not accord the
artist special privileges and powers because he regards him
as a "genius" who is not bound by rules or norms. Although
the term "Genie" appears several times in the "Anmerkungen,"
he stresses often enough that the writer must not be capricious, but that his work must be "scharf durchdacht,
durchforscht, durchschaut" (p. 724). Absolute norms are no
longer valid, however, because of the limitations of perception and the historical determinism of the individual.
The artist must therefore represent a figure with the
exactness and truth with which he recognizes it. Of vital
importance to Lenz is that the artist does not idealize

nature, but he makes it clear that the artist has the freedom to portray a figure as he sees it--as an individual or
as a caricature.

> ...nach meiner Empfindung schätz ich den
> charakteristischen, selbst den Karikaturmaler
> zehnmal höher als den idealischen, hyperbolisch
> gesprochen, denn es gehört zehnmal mehr dazu,
> eine Figur mit eben der Genauigkeit und
> Wahrheit darzustellen, mit der das Genie sie
> erkennt, als zehn Jahre an einem Ideal der
> Schönheit zu zirkeln, das endlich doch nur in
> dem Hirn des Künstlers, der es hervor gebracht,
> ein solches ist. (p. 728)

A similar reference to caricature or distortion can be
found in Pandämonium Germanicum where the image of the
mirror Lenz uses repeatedly in the "Anmerkungen" becomes a
cylindrical mirror (Titel, II, 263). In addition Lenz,
who appears as one of the characters in the play, remarks
that society reveals itself to him as consisting of "lauter
solche Fratzengesichter" (Titel, II, 260). Although Lenz
stresses realism and accurate observation on the one hand,
his acceptance of caricature suggests that art does not
have to strictly resemble nature. The next logical step
is the notion that the artist is free to create his own
forms, to become abstract.

It has become apparent that there is an inherent contradiction between Lenz's dictum that the artist accurately
portray reality and his recognition of the subjective
aspects of the creative process as he delineates it. This

contradiction is only one of the numerous paradoxes which
permeate Lenz's oeuvre and demonstrate that Lenz is the
product of a collision between two opposing aesthetic and
philosophical views--those of classicism and those of
modernism. Lenz was never able to reconcile the disparate
elements in his oeuvre, and it is the paradoxical nature of
the Hofmeister and Soldaten which account for their appeal
to the contemporary reader. Like Kleist, who was never quite
certain whether he was a classicist or a romanticist, Lenz
could not resolve his conflicting tendencies toward both
realism and the philosophical notions of idealism.

3. Character--The Representation of Man

Dramatic art during the first half of the 18th century
is singularly barren of memorable dramatic figures. Because
of a preference for typical characters and the accompanying
exaggeration of specific traits, no opportunity existed
for the creation of a powerful dramatic figure. There
is no Hamlet here, whose indecisiveness permeates the
stage, no tormented Schach Abbas or indefatigable Mother
Courage. Instead the register of dramatis persona consists primarily of predictable and one-dimensional "types"
whose major dramatic function consists in the personification of a particular virtue or vice or the representation of a specific attitude. While Bodmer and Breitinger,

Schlegel, Klopstock, and Gerstenberg had advocated the efficacy of mixed characters and had to some degree succeeded in creating such characters, it was not until the brilliant _Minna von Barnhelm_ appeared on the stage that the 18th century German theater experienced the impact of a notable dramatic character.

Lenz, like Lessing, regarded character rather than plot as the primary focus of tragedy. In this respect he contradicts Aristotle and emulates Shakespeare. That the theater of Shakespeare fired the imagination of Lenz and his contemporaries is of course, a well known fact. Lenz discusses Shakespearian drama in several essays, most notably in "Von Shakespeare's Hamlet," presumably 1773, and in the revised version thereof, "Ueber die Veränderung des Theaters in Shakespeare," 1776, in "Das Hochburger Schloss," 1777, and in the "Anmerkungen" themselves. For Lenz, Shakespeare is the dramatist _par excellence_ whose _Love's Labour's Lost_ he translated and appendixed to the "Anmerkungen."[22] No tribute could be clearer, no declaration more overt than this gesture, which unequivocally defined the direction which Lenz pursued in formulating his theory of the drama: it was not French neo-classicism from which he took his cue, nor could he agree with Lessing's modified yet substantial reaffirmation of Aristotelian dramatic principles. It was Shakespeare who provided the inspiration, the model, and the impetus.

Lenz perceives Shakespeare as a universal genius, a "Mensch, in jedem Verhältnis gleich bewandert, gleich stark..." (p. 745), who created a theater "fürs ganze menschliche Geschlecht...wo jeder stehn, staunen, sich freuen, sich wiederfinden konnte, vom obersten bis zum untersten" (p. 745). The unique feature of Shakespearian theater is, according to Lenz, its democratic appeal, its universality and tendency to evoke a response among the entire social spectrum, a theater which does not have aristocratic pretensions but speaks directly to each individual member of society.

It has often been pointed out that Shakespeare is the first dramatist to stress the tragedy of character, the "Charaktertragödie" in opposition to the tragedy of fate, the "Schicksalstragödie" preferred by the ancients. The division into "Charaktertragödie" and "Schicksalstragödie" is perhaps too simplistic a dichotomy, for certainly classical tragedy does not preclude eloquent character portraits, nor does Shakespearian tragedy exclude the role played by fate as manifested in events and situations.

Nevertheless, the focus in post-Gottschedian 18th century
dramatic theory is clearly on the portrayal of inner experience and psychological processes which demands a concentration on character. This is also Shakespeare's
orientation, as his portrayals of Lear, Hamlet and Richard
III amply demonstrate.

Lenz therefore compares Shakespeare's and Voltaire's
treatment of character in considerable detail, extolling
Shakespeare's success and deriding Voltaire's "failure."
The scene in question is the death of Caesar, and it is
Lenz's observation that while the spectator can feel the
human quality of Shakespeare's characters, those of Voltaire
are flat and lifeless. While Lenz recognizes the role
subjectivism plays in the creative process, he nevertheless
stresses "realistic" character portrayals in his criticism of
French neo-classical dramatists. In Lenz's opinion, the French
dramatists failed because they did not imitate nature, but
rather mirrored themselves in their heroes. "Sein ganzes
Schauspiel [that of Voltaire] (ich rede hier von Meister-
stücken) wird also nicht ein Gemälde der Natur, sondern
seiner eigenen Seele" (p. 736). This results in monotonous
characterizations--"...der Dichter malt das ganze Stück auf
seinen eigenen Charakter...So sind Voltairens Helden fast

lauter tolerante Freigeister, Corne illens lauter Senecas"
(p. 737). Shakespeare's characters, on the other hand, are
colorful and vibrant.

> Seine Könige und Königinnen schämen sich so
> wenig als der niedrigste Pöbel, warmes Blut
> im schlagenden Herzen zu fühlen, oder kützelnder
> Galle im schalkhaften Scherzen Lust zu machen,
> denn sie sind Menschen, auch unterm Reifrock,
> kennen keine Vapeurs, sterben nicht vor unsern
> Augen in müssiggehenden Formularen dahin, kennen
> den tötenden Wohlstand nicht. (p. 745)
> Der Witz eines Shakespeares erschöpft sich nie
> und hätt er noch soviel Schauspiele geschrieben.
> (p. 735)

The reason for Shakespeare's success is, as Herder
had also noted, that he is truly imitating nature, the
nature of his historical period, and not attempting to
follow the rules of ancient Greece, which are no longer
valid. [23]

Lenz has correctly identified the three-dimensionality
and diversity of Shakespearian character portrayals, "the
human quality" which he stresses throughout his theoretical
writings as a prerequisite for credible character portrayal.
Thus he ridicules the dramatis personae of a relatively
unknown French dramatist named Ducis whose Dante-inspired
tragedy he discusses in "Anmerkungen über die Rezension
eines neu herausgekommenen französischen Trauerspiels den
2. Dezember 1772": "Dante hätte gewiss nicht das Herz
gehabt, eine solche Figur in der Hölle erscheinen zu lassen,

142

viel weniger auf einem Theater, das uns Menschen liefern
soll" (Blei, IV, 197, emphasis mine) and condemns his
characterizations as "unnatürlich" (Blei, IV, 198).
Lenz disdains the typical character, the representation of
a trait or passion.

> Daher sehen sich die heutigen Aristoteliker,
> die bloss Leidenschaften ohne Charaktere malen,
> genötigt, eine gewisse Psychologie für alle ihre
> handelnden Personen anzunehmen, aus der sie
> danach alle Phänomene ihrer Handlungen so
> geschickt und ungezwungen ableiten können und
> die im Grunde mit Erlaubnis dieser Herren nichts
> als ihre eigene Psychologie ist. Wo bleibt aber
> da der Dichter, Christlicher Leser! wo bleibt
> die Folie? (p. 727)

A dramatic character who represents a specific trait or
passion must act according to the requirements of his
particular orientation or cathexis. No character development occurs, and the character's actions are predictable.
A multi-dimensional or mixed character, on the other hand,
acts according to the sum of his virtues and vices. The
spectator is able to participate in the processes which
ignite the action and observe the development of character.
Gustav Freytag (1890) describes as distinctly Germanic the
tendency to take a keen interest in multi-dimensional and
highly individualistic characters:

> Dies Germanische aber ist die Fülle und
> liebevolle Wärme, welche jede einzelne Gestalt
> zwar genau nach den Bedürfnissen des einzelnen
> Kunstwerk formt, aber auch das ganze ausserhalb
> des Stückes liegende Leben überdenkt und in seiner

Besonderheit zu erfassen sucht."[24]

Freytag ascribes an active role to the spectator which
suggests that the spectator wishes to participate in the
character's development: "Wir wollen auf der Bühne lieber
erkennen, wie einer geizig wird, als wie er es ist."[25]
Lenz expresses similar notions when he accuses his contemporaries of an inability to fashion distinctive characterizations in spite of their general knowledge of human
nature:

> Grosse Philosophen mögen diese Herren immer
> sein, grosse allgemeine Menschenkenntnis,
> Gesetze der menschlichen Seelenkenntnis,
> aber wo bleibt die individuelle? Wo die
> unekle, immer gleich glänzende, rückspiegelnde,
> sie mag im Totengräberbusen forschen, oder
> unterm Reifrock der Königin? (p. 727)

In Lenz's view, the diversity and complexity of nature
should be reflected in the dramatic character--that is to
say, "die Mannigfaltigkeit der Charaktere und Psychologien
ist die Fundgrube der Natur," (p. 735) a notion already expressed by Bodmer and Breitinger. Shakespeare's characters
are individualistic, complex, and original and therefore
avoid the monotony and repetition of the French characterizations, to which Lenz ascribes the vacuity of "Charakter-
masken auf einem Ball" (p. 736).

Lenz's concentration on the depiction of both outer and
inner experience, on the psychological portrayal of

144

character, "Die Darstellung des Menschen," which the
Teutsche Merkur correctly identified as the nucleus of his
"Anmerkungen," crystallizes a new direction in German
aesthetics. Man himself, the diversity and complexity of
his nature and the role it plays in the creative process,
becomes a major concern of theoreticians. The middle of
the 18th century is the time when psychological treatises
begin to appear, Kasimir von Kreuz's Versuch über die
Seele, 1754, for example. Lenz is keenly aware of the
rapidly emerging emphasis on psychological considerations,
an orientation that would have been applauded by Paracelsus.
In the "Anmerkungen" he writes of wanting to determine the
reason for man's actions in his soul, "den Grund in der
menschlichen Seele aufzusuchen und sichtbar zu machen"
(p. 727). He perceives the soul as the vessel containing
all of the individual's secrets and acknowledges the deli-
cate balance of the individual psyche, "...denn was für ein
Wetterhahn ist unsere Seele?" (p. 722). The dramatic
characterization Lenz envisions is not a psychological case
study--that has no place in the drama as his rejection of
dramatists who merely represent their own psychological
experience indicates. The realistic, psychological representation Lenz has in mind is a multi-dimensional, mixed
character, whose actions are elucidated by including his
inner experience in the dramatic representation. Lenz ex-

presses more emphatically than Gerstenberg his notion of psychologically penetrating characterizations. In that sense in particular, his dramatic theories are the perspicacious formulation of a trend which began with Bodmer and Breitinger. Lenz's insistence on the realistic, psychological portrayal of character distinguishes his "Anmerkungen" from Goethe's and Herder's Shakespeare essays which appeared about the same time and contributes to the essay's designation as a major document of dramatic theory.

It is not surprising that a dramatic theory which places the character in the foreground would oppose the Aristotelian dictum that plot is the soul of tragedy. Lenz categorically denies that Aristotle's primary dramatic principle is still valid:

> Da ein eisernes Schicksal die Handlungen der Alten bestimmte und regierte, so konnten sie als solche interessieren, ohne davon den Grund in der menschlichen Seele aufzusuchen und sichtbar zu machen. Wir aber hassen solche Handlungen, von denen wir die Ursache nicht einsehen, und nehmen keinen Teil dran. (p. 727)

Lenz's argument reflects the tenor of the era. Because man has come of age, because he has faith in reason and no longer believes in blind fate, he must attempt to find the causes for the seemingly irrational and often unfathomable events which bedevil him. Such a drama requires that the dramatic characters become the focal point, for the explanations of man's actions are to be found in his soul.

Lenz makes it eminently clear what <u>kind</u> of character he
envisions; he is not speaking of "hingekleckte Charactere "
(p. 728), but

> Es ist die Rede von Charakteren, die sich ihre
> Begebenheiten erschaffen, die selbständig und
> unveränderlich die ganze grosse Maschine selbst
> drehen, ohne die Gottheiten in den Wolken anders
> nötig zu haben, als wenn sie wollen zu Zuschauern,
> nicht von Bildern, von Marionettenpuppen--von
> Menschen. (p. 729)

An immense order! Lenz is speaking of drama which portrays
an "autonomous" hero, a free and self-sufficient individual
who has mastered his environment and operates independently
of authority. Such a drama would imbue the spectator with
a sense of admiration for the hero, "das ist ein Kerl!
das sind Kerls!" (p. 743) and inspire him.

The desire for an autonomous existence is a constant
theme in Lenz's work; he attempts to come to terms with the
invariable conflict resulting from a philosophical stance
which holds that man is an autonomous being and his simultaneous recognition of man's dependency on nature in
several essays, notably in "Entwurf eines Briefes an einen
Freund, der auf Akademien Theologie studiert," as well as
in "Über die Natur unsers Geistes" and "Über Götz von
Berlichingen."

Lenz sees man as a being who is continuously in flux

and involved in a constant process of becoming:

> Nichts in der Welt ist zu einer absoluten
> Ruhe erschaffen und unsere Bestimmung scheint
> gleichfalls ein immerwährendes Wachsen, Zunehmen,
> Forschen und Bemühen zu sein. Wir sollen immer
> weiter gehen und nie stille stehen. (Titel, I,
> 489)

To be human means to be part of a viable, dynamic process;
man's state is imperfect and incomplete, but he is capable
of growth and improvement, a view which reveals Lenz to be
in agreement with Enlightenment philosophy. The dynamic
process described by Lenz requires constant action, and
through action rather than through the power of thought man
is able to alter events.

> Unsere Unabhängigkeit zeigt sich aber noch mehr
> im Handeln als im Denken, denn beim Denken nehm'
> ich meine Lage, mein Verhältnis und Gefühle wie
> sie sind, beim Handeln aber verändere ich sie
> wie es mir gefällt. Um vollkommen selbständig
> zu sein, muss ich also viel gehandelt, das heisst
> meine Empfindungen und Erfahrungen oft verändert
> haben. (Titel, I, 575)

This, however, is only one side of the coin, for man's
drive toward freedom is continuously thwarted and restrained
by necessary and all-encompassing eternal laws: "aber
überall bleiben die ewigen notwendigen göttlichen Gesetze,
die all unsere Wirksamkeit einfassen..." (Blei, IV, 23).
Eckart Oehlenschläger argues that Lenz regards this as a
relatively fruitful state: because nature provides an
antithesis to free will a conflict results, creating a

dialectical movement toward perfection.[26] Oehlenschläger
overlooks the fact that although Lenz does not define the
nature of perfection, which he considers to be one of the
two states most desired by man the other being happiness,
he does make it clear that "autonomy" itself is one of its
major components.

> Sollte er nicht ein Wink von der Natur der
> menschlichen Seele sein, dass sie eine Substanz,
> die nicht selbständig geboren, aber ein
> Bestreben, ein Trieb in ihr sei, sich zur
> Selbständigkeit hinaufzuarbeiten, sich gleichsam
> von dieser grossen Masse der ineinander hängenden
> Schöpfung zusondern und ein für sich bestehendes
> Wesen auszumachen, das sich mit derselben wieder
> nur so weit vereinigt, als es mit ihrer Selbständig-
> keit sich vertragen kann. (Blei, IV, 26)

Lenz envisions autonomy as man's final goal, a state into
which he cannot be born, but one to which he aspires.
Lenz is speaking of a being who has separated himself
from the remainder of humanity and exists in a higher
realm.

> Wäre also nicht die Grösse dieses Triebes das
> Mass der Grösse des Geistes--wäre dieses Gefühl,
> über das die Leute so deklamieren, dieser Stolz
> nicht der einzige Keim unsrer immer im Werden
> begriffenen Seele, die sich über die Welt die
> sie umgibt zu erhöhen und einen drüber
> waltenden Gott aus sich zu machen bestrebt ist.
> (Blei, IV, 26)

Ultimate independence, however, as Lenz argues in the same
essay and as has been referred to previously, is only
attained through action, not through the power of the

intellect. This realization forces the individual who
aspires to autonomy to participate fully in the sphere of
active life and not withdraw into the spiritual and intellectual realm. Lenz, however, was fully cognizant of the
natural forces which oppose man on that level. The interaction between the desire for freedom and the demands of
nature and society may therefore be dynamic and possibly
fruitful, but it can also be ultimately debilitating,
since man is involved in a continuous conflict and cannot
hope to attain his goal of autonomy in the social and
physical realm. While the unsatisfiable longing for autonomy resembles the unfulfilled yearning of the Romantic, it
is ultimately more disturbing. F. Schlegel's notion of
infinite perfectability and the process of continuous self-
creation and self-destruction together with Novalis'
attempt to balance reality and ideality is primarily concerned with the aesthetic and philosophical realm. Although
the "progressive Universalpoesie" would ultimately encompass all areas of life, the Romantic notions did not include Lenz's emphasis on action. Lenz's faith in autonomy
through action squarely places man into the social and
political sphere and implies the rational tenet that man
can overcome his environment. As Lenz demonstrates in his
dramas and suggests in his theoretical writings, contradicting his vision of individual autonomy, the individual is

continuously frustrated by forces beyond his control.

The desire for independence which Lenz identifies as
a primary human characteristic on the one hand, and his
recognition of man's limitations and dependence on nature,
on the other, cause a dilemna which he is unable to resolve.
The paradox and resulting tension become a major focus in
both his dramas and theoretical writings. In the essay
"Über Götz von Berlichingen," for example, Lenz extolls the
expediency of action and speaks of a "selbständige
Existenz" (Titel, I, 378) but at the same time expresses
a deterministic view using the metaphor of the <u>teatrum</u>
<u>mundi</u>:

> Wir sind alle, meine Herren! in gewissem Verstand
> noch stumme Personen auf dem grossen Theater der
> Welt, bis es den Direkteurs gefallen wird, uns eine
> Rolle zu geben. (Titel, I, 381)

> Wenn jeder in seine <u>Rolle</u> ganz eindringt und alles
> draus macht, was draus zu machen ist--denken Sie
> meine Herren! welch eine Idee! welch ein
> Götterspiel! (Titel, I, 382--emphasis mine)

In the same essay he refers to "das Schauspiel des Lebens"
(Titel, I, 381), reflecting a view of life which holds
that man is destined to play a predetermined role over
which he has little or no control. The possibility of
attaining a degree of autonomy exists--"wir sind..<u>noch</u>
stumme Personen"--but has not been realized. The contradiction between man's desire for freedom and the reality
of his existence is more intensely illustrated in the essay

"Über die Natur unseres Geistes." Lenz expresses the acute

discomfort arising from his speculations:

> Jemehr ich in mir selbst forsche und über
> mich nachdenke, destomehr finde ich Gründe
> zu zweifeln, ob ich auch wirklich ein
> selbständiges   von niemand abhängendes Wesen
> sei, wie ich doch den brennenden Wunsch in
> mir fühle. Ich weiss nicht der Gedanke ein
> Produkt der Natur zu sein, das alles nur ihr
> und dem Zusammenlauf zufälliger Ursachen zu
> danken habe, das von ihren Einflüssen lediglich
> abhänge und seiner Zerstörung mit völliger
> Ergebung in ihre höheren Ratschlüsse entgegen-
> sehen müsse, hat etwas Schröckendes--Ver-
> nichtendes in sich--ich weiss nicht wie die
> Philosophen so ruhig dabei bleiben können.
> (Titel, I, 572)

The profoundly disturbing paradox with which mankind is

forced to contend is reflected in the two outcries which

follow immediately: "Und doch ist er wahr!--Aber mein

trauerndes, angsthaftes Gefühl darüber ist ebenso wahr"

(Titel, I, 572). Even though Lenz proclaims the

attainability of freedom through action, he cannot deny

man's dependency on nature, indeed, on chance and nature's

capriciousness, "Wie denn, ich nur ein Ball der Umstände?

ich--? Ich gehe mein Leben durch und finde diese traurige

Wahrheit hundertmal bestätigt" (Titel, I, 572). Only in

the ethical realm is he able to find a definite answer to

his own question, "Ist der Mensch frei?" (Blei, IV, 22).

"Die moralische Freiheit gestehen wir ihm herzlich gern zu,

aber die metaphysische gewiss nicht" (Blei, IV, 22).

Lenz contends that moral freedom consists in the exercise
of resistance to natural drives: "Was ist denn nun die
moralische Freiheit? Die Stärke, die wir anwenden können,
den Trieben der Natur nach den jedesmaligen Erfordernissen
unsrer bessern Erkenntnis und unserer Situation zu wider-
stehen" (Blei, IV, 23). A state of denial, however,
precludes action and is inconsistent with Lenz's conception of the active and autonomous tragic hero.

No, Lenz is not able to resolve the dilemma posed by
the contradiction between man's aspirations to autonomy
and dependency on nature. After he has devoted the major
portion of the "Anmerkungen" to the portrayal of the new
tragic hero, for instance, he concludes the final section
of his discussion with a brief treatise on comedy. A
curious and ominous deviation! Lenz maintains, again contradicting Aristotle, that the major focus of comedy is
the plot: "Die Hauptempfindung in der Komödie ist immer
die Begebenheit, die Hauptempfindung in der Tragödie ist
die Person, die Schöpfer ihrer Begebenheiten" (p. 743).

Surprisingly, comedy and tragedy are reversing emphases, or perhaps it is not surprising, for the "grosse
Kerl" who believes he can control events and his own
destiny but continues to fail, in other words, the "modern"
hero, is not a proper subject for tragedy or comedy, but
"dark" comedy. The "grosse Kerl" is not a tragic character,

for the source of his actions does not lie deep within his nature. Götz von Berlichingen, for instance, merely reacts to the constraints placed upon him by historical change. Lenz's tenet that the dramatist must probe the human soul and therein find the explanations for man's actions theoretically renders tragedy impossible, for once events are analyzed and their causes understood, the tragic hero's "flaw" or harmatia no longer has the significance which classical tragedy requires.

4. Language and Structure

When Lenz writes in the "Anmerkungen," "Cäsar ist in Rom nie so bedauert worden, als unter den Händen Shakespeares" (p. 733), he not only is referring to Shakespeare's ability to create powerful characters, but he is also expressing his admiration for the English playwright's innate sense of language.

As is well known, the interest in the nature and origin of language intensified as the century progressed and culminated in a series of extensive studies during Storm and Stress, notably those by Hamann and Herder. The exponents of Storm and Stress were particularly conscious of language and style, because their emphasis on the portrayal of internal and not just external nature required the use of a

style which differed from the more rational language
sufficient for the representation of external experience
only.

Lenz's theoretical writings which concern themselves
exclusively with language are limited and consist primarily of two short essays, "Über die Bearbeitung der
deutschen Sprache im Elsass, Breisgau und den benachbarten
Gegenden," and "Über die Vorzüge der deutschen Sprache,"
as well as brief remarks concerning Shakespeare's style in
the "Anmerkungen."

Lenz introduces his translation of Love's Labour's
Lost annexed to the "Anmerkungen" with the following en-
comium:

> Seine Sprache ist die Sprache des kühnsten Genius,
> der Erd und Himmel aufwühlt, Ausdruck zu den ihm
> zuströmenden Gedanken zu finden. ...Seine Könige
> und Königinnen schämen sich so wenig als der
> niedrigste Pöbel, warmes Blut im schlagenden
> Herzen zu fühlen, oder kützelnder Galle im
> schalkhaften Scherzen Luft zu machen, denn sie
> sind Menschen. (p. 745)

Lenz's emphases here are two-fold: first, he notes
language as Ausdruckssprache--Shakespeare's effort to find
means whereby his inner experience, his thoughts and emotions, can be adequately expressed and conveyed to the
spectator, and second, he observes the naturalness of
Shakespearian dialogue, a trait which gives his characters
the human quality that was lacking in the one-dimensional

characterizations dominating the German stage. This aspect
of dramatic dialogue, a preference for a more natural,
more expressive and more easily understood Umgangssprache
had already been advocated by Gellert.

Paul Böckmann identifies three major styles in Storm
and Stress language: a "erlebnisnahes und naturhaftes
Sprechen," a style which he calls "pathetisch -bewegt" and
one which he sees as "naturalistisch-satirisch." The
latter of the three Böckmann attributes primarily to
Lenz.[27] Lenz does stress naturalness of expression, but
his language also incorporates other stylistic innovations
of Storm and Stress. Nevertheless, his focus on "natural"
language distinguishes his dramas from those of his contemporaries and gives them their modern, much less
dated flavor.

Lenz enthusiastically responds to Shakespeare's
characters because he regards them as "real" people, expressing love, hate, anger in powerful language--even in dialect
if that befits the part of a character. The naturalness of
Shakespeare's style, together with its richness, its
abundance of metaphor and imagery, was experienced by Lenz
and his contemporaries as a liberation from the stilted,
sober German which had prevailed on the German stage. Eric
Blackall describes this "middle style"--(the result of a

compromise between the "artificial rhetoric of Lohenstein
and the conversational bluntness of Christian Weise")--
which had become a stage practice and against which the Storm
and Stress dramatists rebelled, as having become "stale,
flat and unprofitable."[28] Literary style, therefore, and
language as a whole, was a topic which occupied and absorbed
writers, theoreticians, and philosophers. As indicated, it
did not escape Lenz's attention.

In the essay "Uber die Bearbeitung der deutschen
Sprache im Elsass, Breisgau und den benachbarten Gegenden,"
which does not concern itself with dramatic language as
such, but with the general topic of language and is
directed toward the inhabitants of the area mentioned in
its title, Lenz calls for a rejuvenation of the German
language. The revitalization of the German language was a
foremost concern of Lenz's generation. Hamann, and in
particular Herder, extoll their countrymen to return to
folksongs, colloquial speech, 16th century German and the
Bible. Like his contemporaries, Lenz purports to recognize a greater richness and more intense affective quality
in folk language and archaic languages: "Alle rauhen
Sprachen sind reicher als die gebildeten, weil sie mehr
aus dem Herzen als aus dem Verstande kommen" (Titel, I,
453). Germans should therefore not ignore their
linguistic past: "Gotisch sollte uns kein so verhasstes

Wort sein" (Titel, I, p. 454). The Swabian dialect is seen
as a rich source of idiomatic expressions and ancient word
combinations:

> Sehn Sie den unleidlich gedehnten schwäbischen
> Dialekt, der noch in diesen Gegenden herrschet,
> mit all seinen Provinzialwörtern und oft hier
> noch erhaltenen uralten Wortfügungen und
> Redegebräuchen als die Fundgrube an... .
> (Titel, I, 450)

Although Lenz looks toward the past, and more specifically
the Teutonic past, the paragraph just cited continues with
a decidedly contemporary and cosmopolitan view suggesting
that the inhabitants of the Alsace are particularly blessed
because they can benefit from the linguistic proximity
of France: ...aus der Sie mit Hülfe der geschliffenern
Ausdrücke und Redearten der Franzosen als mit Werkzeugen
unbezahlbare Schätze für unsere gesamte hochdeutsche
Sprache herausarbeiten können" (Titel, I, 450). In the
spirit of the 17th century language societies and inspired
by the Gelehrtenrepublik, Lenz calls for a "Klopstockischen
Landtag" (Titel, I, 454), a national forum which would
provide linguistic guidance taking into consideration
"griechische Ründe, römische Stärke, englischen Tiefsinn,
französische Leichtigkeit...ohne das Eigentümliche unserer
Sprache zu verlieren, welches Kürze und Bestimmtheit ist"
(Titel, I, 452).

Lenz displays considerable sensitivity by not advocat-

ing adoption of a purely Germanic and colloquial language.
Instead, he seems to be aware of the dynamic nature of
language and its ability to benefit from foreign influences,
although he warns against an unrestrained use of non-
German vocabulary which he sees as harmful to both German
and French: "Hüten Sie sich aber, die Werkzeuge zu dem
Sprachschatz schlagen zu wollen; hieraus würde ein Deutsch-
französisch entstehen, das der Reinigkeit beider Sprachen
gleich gefährlich werden könnte (Titel, I, 450). Lenz
also displays a keen awareness of the power of language,
of its propensity to control, manipulate, and dominate.
He observes, for example, that many actions and emotions
exist which do not have a corresponding name in German, a
fact he attributes to the patient and admiring use of
foreign words by Germans. He detects a degree of domination
by another culture in this practice because in his view,
he who controls the language, particularly in reference
to actions and emotions, has the ability to dominate and
exploit the individual.

> Ich bin auf diese Ausdrücke [foreign words for
> actions and emotions] eifersüchtiger als auf
> Worte, die Sachen oder Werkzeuge bezeichnen,
> weil sie auf Sinnesart und Handlungen wirken.
> Dass eine andere Nation es in dieser und jener

> Kunst weiter gebracht habe, können wir ihr
> leicht zugestehen, willig zu ihr in die
> Schule gehen; aber dass sie Herrscher
> unserer Seele und deren Bewegungen sein soll,
> wo der Vorzug ihrer Art zu empfinden nicht
> ausgemacht ist, muss jeden wahren Patrioten
> schmerzen. (Titel, I, 453)

In addition, Lenz suggests that not only the words themselves, but the structure of language has an effect on
thought. In "Über die Vorzüge der deutschen Sprache" Lenz
argues that German is more suited to independent thought
than French: "Unsere Sprache ist den Wissenschaften und
denen die in denselben auf Erfindungen ausgehen, weit
vorteilhafter als die französiche, weil sie dem Geist mehr
Freiheit lässt" (Titel, I, 459) because of the flexibility of the verb. As of yet, there is no proof that a
culture whose language contains peripatetic verbs is more
innovative and creative than one in whose language the
verb is assigned a more stationary position, and speculations evoked by Lenz's contention are immaterial to our
discussion. Pertinent is that his argument reveals his
recognition of the power language exerts over life and
that language is in effect an extension of an individual
and of a culture whereby a powerful entity is able to
manipulate others. It is therefore of utmost importance to
Lenz that if any linguistic standards are to be formulated
for Germany they be of a democratic nature: "einen nicht

einseitigen, despotischen, sondern republikanischen
Sprachgebrauch" (Titel, I, 454). His utopian plan is
for a revitalized language of equality implemented by
representatives of all segments of society: "Zu diesem
gehört Zusammentreten mehrerer Gesellschaften, deren
Mitglieder aus den verschiedensten Ständen ausgewählt sein
müssen, um eine verständliche Sprache für alle hervorzubringen" (Titel, I, 451).

The essay ends with the statement that many difficulties could be resolved and the people could be drawn
closer together, if only they could completely understand
each other. Lenz's call for a national language forum which
would bring about such understanding indicates that he believes in the possibility that linguistic difficulties can
be resolved by a reasonable and rational approach to the
problem. On the other hand, there are a number of comments
dispersed throughout the essay which suggest a definite
awareness of the capriciousness and limitations of
language, observations which place Lenz's entreaty for a
"Klopstockian Landestag" in the same category as the reso-
lutions he appends to the Hofmeister and Soldaten. The
rather preposterous solutions Lenz proposes reveal him to
be a desperate disciple of the ideals of the Enlightenment
which are in continuous conflict with Lenz the realist. As
far as his dramatic theories are concerned, Lenz remains

firm in his opposition to the validity of the classicistic
doctrine for contemporary drama. Philosophically, however,
his faith in the infinite perfectibility of man, a notion
which resembles the views of Goethe and of the Romantics,
reveals him to be an idealist and not a realist. His desire to maintain faith in the power of reason is demonstrated by what he apparently regards as practical solutions to the theoretically surmountable problems in his
dramas. The intricacy of the events in which his characters become enmeshed however, are indicative of a disillusioned idealist who no longer believes that man can
rationally resolve the difficulties which life poses.

Lenz maintains that the individual has to act in
order to be able to speak, "überhaupt...muss man handeln um
reden zu können" (Titel, I, 456). He elaborates by ex-
plaining that there is a difference between a language
which is learned and one which we have taught ourselves,
"Das erste macht Papageien, das andere Menschen" (Titel,
I, 456). The art of teaching oneself a language involves conscious intellectual effort and applies to the
learning of a foreign language only. We have already mentioned Lenz's awareness of the limitations circumstances
place on the ability to act. Speaking one's own tongue
involves little active exertion by the learner. It is an
ability that is "erlernt" and consists primarily of repeti-

tion--it "macht Papageien." The clichés to which Marie
resorts frequently are an example of an inability to express inner experience. True communication is of course
impossible under such circumstances, and any ensuing
dialogue becomes a sham.

Furthermore, Lenz's analysis of the origin of words
and syntax indicates that he recognizes a certain arbi-
trariness and capriciousness present in the formation of
both words and syntax, at least as far as modern languages
are concerned.

> Bei den Rauhen [languages] ist es Bedürfnis,
> die die Wörter macht, bei den Gebildeten
> [languages] Übermut. Bei den ersten hat
> jedes Wort seine Stelle von der Natur
> angewiesen, seine geflissenste Bestimmtheit
> und bleibenden Wert, bei den andern verjährt
> dieses, erhält sich jenes mehr aus Eigensinn
> der Mode als aus Verdienst. Sehen sie die
> gefährliche Klippe, an der unsere Sprache
> gegenwärtig schifft. (Titel, I, 453)

Certainly, a considerable degree of language scepticism is
present in these observations. As indicated previously,
Lenz's scepticism is counterpointed by his faith in a
logical resolution of the language problem he perceives in
Germany, and the same dynamics as those apparent in the
freedom-determinism conflict seem to be at play here. The
contradictions and paradoxes within Lenz's writings underline the complexity of the aesthetic and philosophical
orientation of Storm and Stress and indicate that it involves

a great deal more than a mere rejection of rationalism and
emphasis on the emotions.

Finally, Lenz recognizes how dependent man is on
language:

> Soll ich Ihnen zu bedenken geben, wie viel nicht
> allein in den Wissenschaften, wie viel selbst im
> Handel und Wandel, und allen andern Begegnissen
> des menschlichen Lebens, die Liebe und Freund-
> schaft selbst nicht ausgenommen, auf die Sprache
> ankomme, auf die Art andern seine Gedanken und
> Wünsche auszudrücken. (Titel, I, 456)

Lenz paints an ominous picture of what will happen if agreement concerning linguistic usage and enhanced understanding
are not achieved:

> Treffen wir mit andern in Ansehung unserer
> gemeinschaftlichen Sprache keine Verabredung,
> so vereinzeln wir uns selbst auf die
> allergrausamste Weise. Sind es gar Leute, mit
> denen wir zu teilen haben, und verstehen nicht
> alle Schattierungen in ihrer Sprache, so
> entstehen daraus unzählige Verwirrungen und
> Missverständnisse, die oft mit der Zeit zu
> Hass, Feindseligkeiten, und Untergang ganzer
> Familien, Gesellschaften und Nationen
> ausschlagen können. (Titel, I, 457)

Language, then, has the power to unite and to disrupt, to
build and to destroy. It is at the same time man's primary
resource for achieving communication and contact with other
men _and_ a commanding mechanism capable of creating confusion and misunderstandings. Lenz is aware of the complex
nature of language, and although he expresses some doubts
in his theoretical writings, he suggests that misunderstand-

164

ings can be avoided through a rational approach. In his dramatic works, however, the limitations of language and a resulting language skepticism play a major role.

The section of the "Anmerkungen" devoted to a discussion of the three unities is one of the briefest of the essay. It begins with Lenz's following irreverent assessment of Aristotle's influential dramatic principle: "Auf eins seiner Fundamentalgesetze muss ich noch zurückschliessen, das so viel Lärm gemacht, bloss weil es so klein ist, und das ist die so erschröckliche, jämmerlichberühmte Bulle von den drei Einheiten" (p. 729). Lenz systematically rejects the validity of the unities of action, space, and time. He explains the difference between the structure of antique and modern drama as follows:

> Bei den alten Griechen wars die Handlung, die
> sich das Volk zu sehen versammlete. Bei uns
> ists die Reihe von Handlungen, die wie
> Donnerschläge aufeinander folgen, eine die
> andere stützen und heben, in ein grosses
> Ganzes zusammenfliessen müssen, das hernach
> nichts mehr und nichts minder ausmacht, als
> die Hauptperson, wie sie in der ganzen Gruppe
> ihrer Mithändler hervorsticht. (p. 731-32)

In accordance with his contention that the character and not the plot is the primary end of tragedy, he again places the emphasis on the tragic hero around whom the action aggregates. The plot no longer should consist of one major strand of action, but rather of a series of inci-

dents occurring in rapid succession. In that manner,
Lenz argues that it is not just a small segment of the
hero's life, the particular plot in question, which is
portrayed, but his life and activity, which are depicted
in their totality. By enabling the spectator to participate in numerous aspects of the hero's life, he is able
to gain a greater understanding of his character and motivations, he sees the hero in not just a portion of his
life, but in his "whole" life: "Was können wir dafür, dass
wir an abgerissenen Handlungen kein Vergnügen mehr finden,
sondern alt genug geworden sind, ein Ganzes zu wünschen?
(p. 731).

    Lenz's refutation of unity of action, a dramatic
principle regarded as essential by Lessing, is the result of
his assertion that the dramatic character, the realistic
psychological portrayal of man, and not the plot is the
primary end of tragedy. Modern drama must depict not only
that an event occurred, but attempt to explain why it
occurred. Aristotle, Lenz argues, insists on separating the
action from the main character, who is forced to fit into
the plot like a "Schiffstau in ein Nadelöhr" (p. 730).
According to Aristotle, the plot and each scene must be
constructed in such a manner that "when the parts are replaced or removed, the whole is dislocated and moved."[30]
Lenz, however, changes Aristotle's "Fabula autem est una,

non ut aliqui putant, si circa unum sit" (p. 730) to "Bei
uns also fabula est una si circa unum sit" (p. 731). In
direct opposition to Aristotle's notion that unity of
action does not result from concentration on the activities
of a character, because "many and indefinite things happen
to one agent, some of which do not make a unity,"[31] Lenz
wishes to depict a broader spectrum of human experience
centered on the main character. He does not consider the
structure of such a drama chaotic, because he specifically
states that the episodic plot he prefers is dominated by a
main character through whom all is brought to a harmonious
conclusion. Whether or not this actually occurs in his
dramas is, of course, another question.

Because modern drama should represent the world--"behalten Sie ihre Familienstücke, Miniaturgemälde und lassen
uns unsere Welt" (p. 730)--Lenz also finds the unities of
place and time too restrictive. Unity of place he dis-
misses as a dramatic convention arising out of the use of
the chorus: "Einheit des Orts--oder möchte lieber sagen,
Einheit des Chors, denn was war es anders?" (p. 731).
Unity of place Lenz considers much too artificial for the
realistic drama he envisions. The characters appear without logical reasons for their presence, without an organic

development arising out of the action: "Kommen doch auf
dem griechischen Theater die Leute wie gerufen und gebeten
herbei und kein Mensch stösst sich daran" (p. 731). By the
same token, Lenz does not consider unity of time an
essential dramatic principle and, in fact, regards Aristotle's dictum that a tragedy must last only twenty-four hours
as arbitrary: "Sind denn aber zehn Jahre, die der Trojan-
ische Krieg währte nicht ebensogut bestimmte Zeit als unus
solis ambitus?" (p. 731). For Lenz, as for Lessing, the
unities of time and place have relative value only and are
not binding.

After dispensing with the three unities in five brief
paragraphs, the topic does not concern Lenz again in the
"Anmerkungen." In the essay "Über die Veränderung des
Theaters im Shakespear" which Lenz read to the Deutschen
Gesellschaft in Strassburg in 1776, and which constitues a revised version of an earlier essay dated by Blei as approximately 1773, Lenz again comments upon the unities of time
and place. If the earliest mentioned date for the "Anmerkungen," namely 1772, and Blei's dating of the first version of the Shakespeare essay are correct, there seems to
be a change in Lenz's tone, which is more conciliatory in
the Shakespeare essay than it was in the "Anmerkungen."
As we have noted, Friedrich attributes apparent changes
in Lenz's attitude to the publication of Herder's

Shakespeare essay. Rather than adamantly maintaining that
Aristotelian dramatic principles are no longer valid, Lenz
here tries to justify Shakespeare by arguing that even
ancient playwrights, Aristophanes for example, did not
always observe the unity of place. In addition, he points
out that Shakespeare does not arbitrarily change the scene,
but changes it only if it is necessitated by the demands
of the action: "Man vergisst, das auch Shakespear die
Veränderung der Szene immer nur als Ausnahme von der Regel
angebracht, immer nur höheren Vorteilen aufgeopfert" (Titel,
I, 363). Lenz suggests that the dramatist's primary
concern and major purpose must be the arousal of the spectator's interest, an endeavor to which all other purposes
must be subjugated.

> Das Interesse ist der grosse Hauptzweck des
> Dichters, dem alle übrigen untergeordnet sein
> müssen--fordert dieses--fordert die Ausmalung
> gewisser Charaktere, ohne welche das Interesse
> nicht erhalten werden kann, unausbleiblich und
> unumgänglich Veränderung der Zeit und des Orts,
> so kann und muss ihm Zeit und Ort aufgeopfert
> werden. (Titel, I, 354)

In an addendum to the essay, Lenz reviews a French drama
and makes the following observation:

> Ganz überzeugt von dem Vorzug derjenigen Stücke,
> in welchen die Einheit des Orts beibehalten
> worden, wenn sie sonst an Güte den unregel-
> mässigen gleich kämen, ging ich hin, ich muss
> aber gestehen, dass ich mit ungemein veränderter
> Überzeugung zurück gekommen bin. (Titel, I, 365)

Like J. E. Schlegel, Lenz maintains that a regular drama
is not superior to an irregular one by virtue of its
adherence to the rules.

Although Lenz's tone is apparently less acerbic in
the Shakespeare essay than in the "Anmerkungen," he never
waivers in his contention that unity of action is inappropriate in modern drama because it must focus on the hero, a
circumstance which demands a multi-faceted plot. He urges
young poets not to applaud the irregularity of Shakespeare's dramas for the sake of his disregard of the unities of time and place, but rather to be aware of the fact
that Shakespeare's frequent change of scene and extended
time is not the result of capriciousness. It is an organic
development based upon the requirements of the action. Because Lenz stresses a realistic theater, change of scene
and time must not be artificial and arbitrary, but natural.

The dominant impression conveyed by Lenz's oeuvre--not
just his dramatic works, but also his theoretical writings--
is its paradoxical nature, thematically, structurally, and
to some degree stylistically. Underlying the outwardly
confusing Non-Aristotelian structure of the "Anmerkungen"
for example, is the technical device of a debate contra-
posing Lenz and Aristotle. Syntactically, the essay seems
to be an aggregate of Storm and Stress stylistic innovations. The loose, conversational style abounds with

aposiopesis, rhetorical questions, apostrophe, and the frequent dashes and exclamation marks symptomatic of Storm
and Stress punctuation, showing Lenz to be a non-traditional essayist who consciously avoids conventional rhetorical
devices. The result, however, is not an incoherent dia-
tribe, but rather a conscious invitation to the reader to
avoid submitting to an existing system, and to participate
in a dialogue and the genesis of a new dramatic theory.

Lenz's vision of an autonomous dramatic hero is
raised in the "Anmerkungen" and in "Über Götz von Berlichingen," and man's autonomy is questioned in the latter
essay itself as well as in "Über die Natur unsers Geistes."
By the same token, his call for the realistic psychological
portrayal of character is contradicted by his advocacy of
caricature. Unity of action is disavowed, a splintered,
episodic structure advocated, the goal of which, however,
seeks "wholeness" realized through the dramatic hero.
Language itself is recognized as man's sole means through
which understanding can be achieved; yet at the same time
the fluidity and capriciousness of language are not ignored.

It is important to note that the contradictions
within Lenz's oeuvre are primarily of a philosophical
nature. As far as his dramatic theories are concerned, he
is consistent in his advocacy of the following non-
Aristotelian dramatic tenets: 1) the emphasis on charac-

ter; 2) the mixture of tragic and comic elements; 3) the
utilization of natural language; 4) a multi-faceted plot;
and 5) although he somewhat softens his stance toward the
unities of time and place, he never maintains that a regular drama is superior to an irregular one.

The paradoxes occurring in Lenz's oeuvre seem to be
largely the result of a clash between the philosophical
ideals of the Enlightenment to which Lenz was heir, and the
later disillusionment and subsequent socio-political
awareness of Storm and Stress of which he was one of the
foremost advocates. Thus Lenz's intrinsic faith in personal freedom is counterpointed by his recognition of the
constraints of nature and the realities of 18th century
socio-political conditions. Instead of the autonomous individual who is capable of influencing his environment and
controlling events, Lenz has created an early version of
the contemporary anti-hero. The typical Lenzian character is
portrayed as a victim of both circumstances and his own
passions. He no longer operates in an organically whole,
harmonious world, where moral transgressions are punished
but forgiven thus restoring the old order, but finds him-
self--still dependent on fate as had been the ancients but
with no hope of forgiveness or consolation--in a world
that is rapidly losing faith in God. The wholeness or
unity of the multi-faceted plot to be affected by the

autonomous hero does therefore not occur. And finally, Lenz's advocacy of a rational approach to the solution of linguistic problems is counteracted by his recognition of the enormity of language barriers and the complexity of the communicative act itself.

Although Lenz's philosophical aims do not bear fruition, his dramatic innovations are responsible for the realization of a new realism on the German stage. The notions which he develops and surpasses have their origin in Bodmer and Breitinger and the succeeding generations of theoreticians and dramatists who challenged the classicistic doctrine and endeavored to develop a dramatic theory and practice representative of their age.

CHAPTER V

PARADOX IN THE DRAMATIC PRACTICE OF J. M. R. LENZ:

DIE SOLDATEN AND DER HOFMEISTER

1. Character: Reality and the Autonomous Hero

The dramatic works of J. M. R. Lenz reflect the incon-
gruities of life. This experience is already evident in his
theoretical writings, where it is most clearly illustrated
by Lenz's recurrent struggle with the concept of free will
and man's simultaneous dependency on nature. The conflict
between freedom and determinism is identified as the overlying
theme of Lenz's dramas by John Osborne.[1] Certainly this is
one of the major existential contradictions which confront
his dramatic characters, but it is not the only one. His
dramatic figures must also contend with a natural inclination
toward friendship, harmony, love, and the desire to act, and
the conflicting actuality of isolation, chaos, alienation
and limitations posed by society and nature.

The paradoxes Lenz identifies to be innate components
of existence are most profoundly expressed through the
dramatis personae he creates; they are, however, also evident
in the structure of his dramas and in his treatment of
language. His portrayal of character, dramatic dialogue,
and episodic structure frequently contradicts the intent
delineated in his theoretical writings. Contradictions,
therefore, do not only exist within his individual works,
but also between his dramatic and theoretical writings.

In the "Anmerkungen," his major theoretical work and
dramatic poetics, Lenz makes it clear that the character
rather than the plot is to be the primary concern of
tragedy, whereas in comedy the events have prominence:
"Meiner Meinung nach wäre immer der Hauptgedanke einer
Komödie eine Sache, einer Tragödie eine Person" (p. 744).[2]
Are we then to conclude that Lenz followed his own advice
and that in the Soldaten and Hofmeister, both of which are
designated as a "comedy," the characters are of secondary
importance? Decidedly not! As is well known, an author's
theory and practice are often contradictory, particularly
an oeuvre which contains as much paradox as that of Lenz.
In addition, Lenz's hesitancy concerning genre is well documented: both dramas were alternately referred to by Lenz
as "Komödie," "Tragödie," and "Schauspiel."[3] There is no
doubt that in both dramas, be they comedies or tragedies,
the characters are of greater interest than the events and
have the obvious attention.of the dramatist.

Lenz demands of the theater "dass [es] uns Menschen
liefert" (Blei, IV, 197). That Lenz succeeded in creating
plausible, multi-dimensional characters is demonstrated by
the figures of Marie and Läuffer who are portrayed as individualized personalities and not as types or the personification of a vice or virtue.

Lenz employs a variety of techniques in order to have
his characters come alive. The monologue, albeit on a
limited basis, and the personal letter, are used in both the

<u>Hofmeister</u> and the <u>Soldaten</u> as a means whereby the central
characters, Läuffer and Marie, reveal their most intimate
selves to the audience. The two monologues occur early in
the plays, and both are crucial to comprehending the complex and chaotic nature of the character's psyche, particularly in the case of Marie. Marie's self-revelation
occurs at the end of the first act. She has just experienced the confusing emotions evoked by Desporte's atten-
tions immediately after she has returned from a visit to
her fiancé Stolzius. After the turbulence of the preceding events, evening comes, and at last she finds herself
alone in her room. Both her words and gestures are highly
revealing: Marie sighs, loosens her clothing and steps to
the window. "Das Herz ist mir so schwer. Ich glaub es
wird gewittern die Nacht. Wenn es einschlüge--"; she then
directs her eyes toward heaven and folds her hands over
her chest: "Gott was hab ich denn Böses getan?--Stolzius--
ich lieb dich ja noch--aber wenn ich nun mein Glück besser
machen kann--und Pappa selber mir den Rat gibt." She then
pulls the curtain and says: "Trifft mich's so trifft
mich's, ich sterb nicht anders als gerne." The scene ends
with the following stage direction: (Löscht ihr Licht
aus).[4]

Marie's brief monologue and accompanying gestures bare
her soul and form the nucleus of her character portrayal,

revealing her sense of fatalism and inner disruption.
Marie's inner uncertainty is signified by her sigh, her
reference to her heavy heart, and the fact that she loosens
her clothing and steps to the window as if to find relief
and solace--from nature perhaps. In addition she is plagued
by feelings of guilt. Her rhetorical question "Gott was hab
ich denn Böses getan?" is a reproach of her conscience. Her
conscience is already punishing her not for what she has
done, but for what she knows she will do. And finally, she
refuses to accept responsibility for her actions blaming
them on economic reality and on her father. She attempts to
shut out the confusing and ambivalent emotions she is
experiencing by the act of resolutely pulling the curtain.
Tranquility eludes her, however, and her final state is
one of resignation: "Trifft mich's so trifft mich's, ich
sterb' nicht anders als gerne." The final direction,
"Löcht ihr Licht aus" is ominous and foreshadows the
events which will engulf her and which are partially the
result of her own ambivalent nature.

Läuffer's monologue (p. 11) opens the Hofmeister. It
is not quite as penetrating as that of Marie, but it also
delineates his reaction toward the situation in which he
finds himself. He expresses repugnance for the Geheimrat,
who is generally interpreted as the voice of rationalism
and reason: "ich weiss nicht, ich scheu ihn ärger als den

Teufel. Der Kerl hat etwas in seinem Gesicht, das mir
unerträglich ist." We learn from Läuffer's words that the
Geheimrat refused him a position at the <u>Stadtschule</u> and
that his conversations with the tutor, whom he always
addresses as "Monsieur Läuffer," are trite.

> Er nennt mich immer nur Monsieur Läuffer, und
> wenn wir von Leipzig sprechen, fragt er nach
> Händels Kuchengarten und Richters Kaffeehaus,
> ich weiss nicht: soll das Satire sein, oder--
> Ich hab ihn doch mit unserm Konkrektor bisweilen
> tiefsinnig genug diskurieren hören; er sieht
> mich vermutlich nicht für voll an. (Titel, II, 11)

Läuffer is expressing his dissatisfaction and discomfiture
with his situation and the people with whom he is confronted. He tries to review his possible choices and finds
that they are extremely limited: "Mein Vater sagt: ich
sei nicht tauglich zum Adjunkt...Zum Pfaffen bin ich auch
zu jung, zu gut gewachsen, habe zu viel Welt gesehn..."
(Titel, II, 11). Some critics view these remarks as a
sign of Läuffer's arrogance, but the young man does not
exhibit an arrogant attitude at any other time throughout
the drama. His observation that he considers himself un-
suitable for the ministerhood must therefore be seen as
merely an explanation for his presence in the household
of Major von Berg. He makes it clear that he feels uncomfortable and dissatisfied with his position, a revela-
tion of his inner state which is expressed through
language at only one other point in the drama--in the

letter he writes to his father. The limitations which
circumstances and his own divided nature are imposing on
him come to light in these words to his father: "Dem
ohngeachtet kann ich dies Haus nicht verlassen, und sollt
es mich Leben und Gesundheit kosten" (p. 31). He sees his
life as inextricably interwoven with that of Gustchen and
her family and has become a prisoner of circumstances and
his own drives.

The characterizations of Läuffer and Marie evolve not
only through self-revelation, but also through description
by other characters. Wesener's impression of his own
daughter is that of a young girl in glowing health:
"Meinem Marieel fehlt doch Gott sei Dank nichts und sie hat
immer rote Backen" (p. 187). Interestingly, Marie does not
share her father's assessment of her: "Ja das lässt sich
der Papa nicht ausreden und ich krieg doch bisweilen so eng
ums Herz, dass ich nicht weiss wo ich vor Angst in der
Stube bleiben soll" (p. 187), a remark which Wesener ig-
nores and a condition which Desportes suggests can be cured
by entertaining diversions. Stolzius characterizes Marie
as "solch ein gutes Herz" (p. 211), while the young count
perceives her to be "ein so leichtes offenes unschuldiges
Herz" (p. 223). In direct opposition to the two preceding
observations, the cold, albeit self-indulgent assessment of
Desportes is: "Wie ich dir sage, es ist eine Hure von

Anfang an gewesen und sie ist mir nur darum gut gewesen
weil ich ihr Präsenten machte" (p. 239), to which the
milder Mary replies: "Sie war doch sehr gut angeschrieben
bei der Gräfin" (p. 240). While no one character's description of Marie is completely reliable or accurate,
each statement represents another segment in the mosaic of
her personality. Lenz uses a similar technique in evolving the characterization of Läuffer, who is referred to as
"ein ganz artiges Männchen" (p. 11) by the Major, while for
the Geheimrat he is a "galonierter Müssiggänger" (p. 13).
The Majorin evaluates him strictly on appearance: "Herr
Läuffer, dass Sie sich in Kleidern sauber halten und unserm
Hause keine Schande machen. Ich weiss, dass Sie Geschmack
haben" (p. 13) and for Wenzeslaus Läuffer becomes "ein
teures, auserwähltes Rüstzeug" (p. 80) who he hopes will
walk the thorny but rewarding path of the ascetic life with
him. And finally, Pastor Läuffer perceives his son to be
"ein sittsamer und geschickter Mensch" (p. 24). The main
character is thus introduced to us from a variety of angles
which reveal the multiple facets of his personality on the
one hand, but also suggest the division of his inner
nature. The supporting characters' diverse and often conflicting descriptions of the main characters assist in
evolving the complex and realistic character portrayals
which were Lenz's aim.

In order to represent the individual in his totality, Lenz depicts his characters in a variety of situations. Marie is seen interacting with her sister, with her father, with Desportes, with Mary, and with the Countess. We find Läuffer in conversations with the Majorin, with Gustchen, with Wenzeslaus, and with Lise. In addition, Lenz uses gestures to characterize Marie and Läuffer, with Läuffer's obsequiousness convincingly illustrated by his movements and Marie's fluctuating confusion and coquetry manifested by tears, attitudes of supplication and flirtatious curtsies. Through the techniques of monologue, commentary by other characters, depiction in various situations and gestures, the characters are presented to the spectator in such a manner that the diverse aspects of their personalities are revealed. Marie and Läuffer emerge as fragmented and divided characters in whom no single trait dominates. They are no longer the potent and eloquent dramatic figures of classical antiquity. Lenzian realism has resulted in a dramatic character whose amorphousness is a fore-runner of the modern anti-hero.

The Lenzian hero lacks concreteness because of his inner fragmentation and psychic diffusion. It is, for example, much less difficult to imagine the presence and appearance of a Minna von Barnhelm or Emilia Galotti than that of Marie or Läuffer. Even Marie's alleged red

cheeks and glowing health are of little help because their
existence is questioned immediately after it has been
asserted. Although no specific trait dominates the Lenzian
dramatic figure, it can be safely said that the overwhelm-
ing impression it conveys is one of inner **disorientation.**
One of the primary techniques Lenz uses to express concretely
the internal chaos of his dramatic characters and their
reaction to what they perceive as a disorderly world is
caricature and the grotesque.

In the "Anmerkungen," Lenz makes a brief reference to
caricature:--"nach meiner Empfindung schätz ich den charak-
teristischen, selbst den Karikaturmaler zehnmal höher als
den idealischen" (p. 728). Literary caricature can be defined as "descriptive writing which seizes upon certain
individual qualities of a person and through exaggeration or
distortion produces a burlesque, ridiculous effect."[5] The
effect produced does not always have to be burlesque or
ridiculous; it can also be grotesque.

Caricature is a favorite tool of the satirist. Lenz
is critical of satire:

> Die Satire pflegt gemeinhin der letzte
> Nachschössling einer absterbenden Sprache,
> das heisst einer Sprache ohne Dichter zu sein.
> Darf ich's sagen, dass nach Boileau und Popen
> sich die Dichtkunst unserer Nachbarn noch kaum
> hat erholen können. Die Satire reduziert die
> Einbildungskraft auf Vernunft, und führt, wenn
> sie übertrieben wird, eine falsche Scham ein,
> die allen freien Gebrauch der Sprache hindert.

> Glückliches Land, wo die Satire nur verdorbene
> Sitten trifft, und falscher Geschmack nur
> durch das ernste Stillschweigen der Weisheit
> zur Selbsterkenntnis gebracht wird! (Titel, I,
> 455)

Nevertheless, he frequently resorts to that literary mode
as evidenced specifically by the sketch _Pandämonium_
Germanicum. In this short play, Lenz also raises the
issue of caricature and the grotesque: "Ach ich nahm mir
vor hinabzugehen und ein Maler der menschlichen Gesellschaft zu werden: aber wer mag da malen wenn lauter solche
Fratzengesichter unten anzutreffen" (p. 260). In a subsequent scene the image of the mirror which Lenz uses repeatedly in his definition of mimesis reappears. The
mirror in question is not clear and crystalline, but we are
confronted with a cylindrical mirror which, of course,
causes distortions and disfigurations. (We recall a remark in the "Anmerkungen": "Aber mit alledem, wenn die
Camera _obscura_ Ritzen hat" p. 723). The characters representing various authors to whom the mirror is shown react
first with shock, but then are able to laugh at their own
grimaces because as the stage directions tell us, they are
reasonable people (p. 263). The consensus is: "So
gefällt's uns doch besser als nach dem Leben" (p. 263).

The use of caricature and its grotesque effect stands
in opposition to Lenz's call for realistic portrayal of
character. A caricature distorts reality and therefore is

inconsistent with the techniques of realistic drama. It can, however, be both a manifestation of a distorted internal reality and an illustration of the disorder perceived in external reality.

Grotesque allusions are found throughout Lenz's dramas. The grotesque is a literary technique which joins dissimilar elements in new and startling combinations. Like caricature, it distorts reality. In the 20th century, the technique has attained moral implications and is regarded as an indication of lack of faith in an existing cosmic order and frustration at the role man is forced to play. The grotesque constitutes a stark contrast to classicism's idealized representation of nature. Both approaches embellish nature, but whereas an idealized reality calms the reader or spectator, the grotesque has a tendency to disturb him or her. This seems to be Lenz's intent, at least in some of the instances in which he makes use of grotesque elements. For our purposes, we shall concentrate on Wenzeslaus and Pätus in the Hofmeister and the figure of the grandmother in the Soldaten.

The caricatured figures of Pätus and Wenzeslaus are not, of course, a manifestation of Läuffer's inner distortions, but they are an embodiment of the discordant world in which all of the characters exist. Thus Pätus, who describes himself as "eine so grosse dicke Bestie" (p. 36) is

mocked by Bollwerk: "Aber hör Pätus, Pätus, Pä Pä Pä
Pätus--Döblin ist angekommen. Hör Pä Pä Pä Pä Pätus, wie
wollen wir das machen? Ich denke, du ziehst deinen
Wolfspelz an und gehst heut abend in die Komödie" (p. 37).
Pätus protests and tells his tormentor that he cannot go to
the theater because he has no proper jacket. But Minna von
Barnhelm proves irresistible, and Jungfer Knicks reports
her reaction to the man who was seen running through the
streets in a wolfskin later in the evening, a scene she
experiences as comical:

> Ich kann's Ihnen vor Lachen nicht erzählen,
> Frau Rätin, ich muss krank vor Lachen werden.
> Stellen Sie sich vor: wir gehen mit Jungfer
> Hamster im Gässchen hier nah bei, so läuft
> uns ein Mensch im Wolfspelz vorbei, als ob er
> durch Spiessruten gejagt würde; drei grosse
> Hunde hinter ihm drein. Jungfer Hamster
> bekam einen Schubb, dass sie mit dem Kopf an
> die Mauer schlug und überlaut schreien musste.
> (p. 39)

The tumult of the scene Jungfer Knicks describes is immediately obvious to the reader--the loud scream of Jungfer
Hamster and the derisive laughter of both women, one in
which the spectator is not sure he should join. Jungfer
Knicks continues to describe the hapless Pätus' discomfort in detail--his flying hair, his red face and open
mouth, and his great effort to escape from the yelping
dogs. The figure of Pätus, the poor and serious young
student, has become a caricature and an object of ridicule.

Henry J. Schmidt in his study of the effect of
caricature in Büchner's dramas, describes caricature as
follows: "A caricature can reflect various levels of
meaning simultaneously, exposing on the surface social
evils of one kind or another, but indicating at the same
time that the roots of disorder lie deep within human
nature itself."[6] Both levels of meaning seem to be at
work in the figure of Pätus. The parsimony of the father
who refuses to offer his son sufficient economic assistance
during his student years comes under attack. In addition,
the malisciousness of Pätus' fellow students and of the
two women is depicted. But a certain disharmony seems
to be present in the character of Pätus himself, who turns
out to be a man who can experience feelings of brotherly
love for Fritz, but who has so little control over his
temperament that he slaps the musician Rehaar, who rightfully accuses him of the attempted seduction of his
daughter.

Similar discrepancies are expressed in the figure of
Wenzeslaus. When the character is first introduced to the
reader he gives the impression of being a relatively satisfied, rational and well-balanced school teacher, who is
happy with his duties, his meal, his pipe and who is kind
enough to give refuge to the pursued Läuffer. As the play
develops, however, Wenzeslaus reveals that he is an obsessed

ascetic in whose tormented soul the battle of the spirit
and the flesh continues to rage and who is convinced he
must smoke a constant pipe in order to subdue his sexual
desires. At this point, Wenzeslaus is no longer able to
express empathy for Läuffer or mankind as a whole and becomes a caricature of a teacher and preacher. The effect
of the twisted figure of the teacher is grotesque, reflecting his inner excesses and imbalances. The concept of
mimesis as applied by Lenz rejects the idealization of
nature in favor of distortion of nature. This technique
illustrates the many ills which Lenz perceived in both
society and the individual.

The spirit of the grotesque is not only expressed by
caricature, but also by specific events and situations.
Läuffer's self-castration must be seen in that light. It
represents the disharmony which exists deep within Läuffer's
own nature and within the social structure. The senselessness of his action and the disjointed world in which
such senselessness could occur is portrayed in a scene in
which Wenzeslaus, suspecting Läuffer of still harboring an
inclination toward the fair sex, chides him for his behavior in church. Wenzeslaus maintains that Läuffer let
his attention wander toward the young woman Lise during his
sermon, but Läuffer attempts to persuade him that he was
led astray by a painting hanging in the church:

> Ich muss bekennen, es hing ein Gemälde dort,
> das mich ganz zerstreut hat. Der Evangelist
> Markus mit einem Gesicht, das um kein Haar
> menschlicher aussah als der Löwe, der bei ihm
> sass, und der Engel beim Evangelisten
> Matthäus eher einer geflügelten Schlange
> ähnlich. (p. 90)

Läuffer is describing a grotesque scene, one in which
nature has been distorted and which he views with apprehension. We are unable to determine from his description if
the faces of the angel and of St. Marc are actually modeled
upon those of animals, but they must contain animalistic
traces if Läuffer perceives them as such. Kayser points
to the ominous aspect of grotesque paintings and ornamen-
tations in which the clear borders between man, animal and
vegetable have been blurred and in which the fixed order of
nature has been dissolved.[7] The faces Läuffer describes
are Lenz's "Fratzengesichter," which here are not limited
to the temporal world but have been extended to include aspects of the divine. The distorted faces of the saint and
the angel become chillingly threatening: not even the
divine, a traditional anchor and source of security, can
be depended on any longer. Kayser describes the effect of
the grotesque as follows: "Das Groteske zerstört grund-
sätzlich die Ordnungen und zieht den Boden fort."[8] He
elaborates on the observer's reaction to the grotesque:

> Mehrere und offensichtlich widersprüchliche
> Empfindungen werden erweckt, ein Lächeln über
> die Deformation, ein Ekel über das Grausige,
> Monströse an sich, als Grundgefühl aber, ...

>   ein Erstaunen, ein Grauen, eine ratlose
>   Beklommenheit, wenn die Welt aus den Fugen
>   Geht und wir keinen Halt mehr finden.[9]

This is what Läuffer experiences, when he perceives the
face of St. Mark as distorted.

A basic technique of the grotesque is the juxtaposition
of disparate elements. The sense of apprehension experienced by the reader of a text or observer of a drama or
painting is evoked by the imbalance and lack of order.
Certainly the pairing of the blooming, healthy Lise, her
yellow hair refusing to stay tucked beneath her red
bonnet, and the involuntary eunuch Läuffer elicit a sensa-
tion of grotesqueness. Their union must remain fruitless
and unnatural, a dissonance which even Wenzeslaus recognizes as fatal. A similar sense of imbalance charged with
ominous overtones is present in a pivotal scene in the
Soldaten (p. 208): Marie has just received a letter from
Stolzius in which he accuses her of unfaithfulness, a
fact which is not stated directly but implied by her reaction: "Sehen Sie nur, was mir der Mensch der Stolzius
schreibt, recht als ob er ein Recht hätte mich auszu-
schelten" (p. 206). She sanctimoniously defends herself,
an endeavor in which she is supported by Desportes and her
father. Her response changes from tears to indignation to
coquetry. The scene degenerates into a playful, if not
riotous shuffle between Desportes and Marie which noisily
continues behind closed doors in an adjoining room. At

this point, Marie's grandmother creeps across the stage
(p. 208). She sits down near the window and begins to
sing with a voice which Lenz describes as óld and rough.
The old woman--glasses perched on her nose, her singing
a croak rather than a melody, relentlessly knitting--is a
caricature which evokes images of the occult and inescapable
fate. There is little that is reassuring about this figure
and her song which ominously prophesies Marie's future and
counterpoints the boisterous frolic in the adjoining room:

> Ein Mädele jung ein Würfel ist
> Wohl auf den Tisch gelegen:
> Das kleine Rösel aus Hennegau
> Wird bald zu Gottes Tisch gehen.
>
> Was lächelst so froh mein liebes Kind
> Dein Kreuz wird dir'n schon kommen
> Wenn's heisst das Rösel aus Hennegau
> Hab nun einen Mann genommen.
>
> O Kindlein mein, wie tut's mir so weh
> Wie dir dein Äugelein lachen
> Und wenn ich die tausend Tränelein seh
> Die werden dein Bäckelein waschen.

The juxtaposition of the old woman's song and the playful
interlude forces the reader to recognize the tragic implications of Desportes' interference in Marie's life. Although Desporte's true nature has not yet been revealed, it
is now obvious that his union with Marie exhibits an inherent disharmony, one which is not only caused by their
difference in social status, but also by their inner dis-
cord. What should be lighthearted gaiety between lovers

acquires grotesque overtones which is described by Lenz
as "Geschrei" and "Gejauchz" (p. 208). These are not the
sounds of harmony and love, but of disorder and isolation.
The entire scene exudes anxiety instead of joy and is designed to instill a sense of apprehension in the spectator.

As has been indicated, the grotesque aspects in Lenz's
dramas which consist of caricature and the juxtaposition
of unrelated elements, underline the disharmony between
the characters' aspirations and their social and psychological reality. They also have another function, however. Because the grotesque consists of unaccustomed and startling
patterns and juxtapositions, it forces the observer to
see in a new and different fashion, a process intended to
discover truth. In that sense the grotesque becomes an
instrument which brings about a more accurate perception of
reality. As used by Lenz, the grotesque becomes both a
means to illustrate disorder and a technique to unmask conventions which veil the truth. In the final analysis,
however, it is the portrayal of reality which Lenz pursued
on the stage. His primary concern was experimentation with
a new dramatic technique, not social criticism and reform
which are often regarded as the primum mobile of Lenz's
oeuvre.[10] Lenz makes the following comment in the second
of his "Briefe über die Moralität der Leiden des jungen
Werthers":

> Man hat mir allerlei moralische Endzwecke und
> philosophische Sätze bei einigen meiner
> Komödien angedichtet, man hat sich den Kopf
> zerbrochen, ob ich wirklich den Hofmeisterstand
> für so gefährlich in der Republik halte, man
> hat nicht bedacht, dass ich nur ein bedingtes
> Gemälde geben wollte von Sachen wie sie da sind
> und die Philosophie des geheimen [sic] Rats nur
> in seiner Individualität ihren Grund hatte.
> (Titel, I, 385)

Of course one could argue that once again Lenz's non-
dramatic observations are in disagreement with his dramatic
practice. It is, however, not just Lenz's comment which
leads one to doubt the apparently reformational theme of
the Soldaten and Hofmeister. An analysis of the figures
of the Gräfin and the Geheimrat, the two characters who
represent "progressive social thought," leads to the conclusion that the viability of their point of view is
questioned by the author.

The Geheimrat is customarily interpreted as the voice
of reason who, in opposition to his volatile and impas-
sioned brother, the Major, attempts to foster order, en-
courage individual freedom and work for the betterment of
society.[11] Curious, then, is Läuffer's impression of the
Geheimrat: "ich weiss nicht, ich scheu ihn ärger als den
Teufel. Der Kerl hat etwas in seinem Gesicht, das mir
unerträglich ist" (p. 11). We also discover that the
Geheimrat has an irritating effect on the Major: "Ich muss
meine Tochter wieder haben, und wenn nicht in diesem Leben,

doch in jener Welt, und da soll mein hochweiser Bruder und mein hochweiseres Weib mich wahrhaftig nicht von abhalten" (p. 67--emphasis mine), and in response to the Geheimrat's advice on the care of Gustchen: "Bekümmert Euch um Euer Fleisch und Bein daheime" (p. 70). In addition, we have discovered from Läuffer's monologue that the Geheimrat refused to employ him in the Stadtschule of which he is the director, and that he does not take Läuffer seriously as an individual. Throughout the drama, the Geheimrat pursues his philosophy with a single-mindedness and determination which suggest that all the world's ills could be resolved if only there were no longer any private tutors! In one of his numerous diatribes, the Geheimrat admits: "Es ist einmal meine üble Gewohnheit, dass ich gleich in Feuer gerate, wenn mir ein Gespräch interessant wird: alles übrige verschwindet mir denn aus dem Gesicht und ich sehe nur den Gegenstand, von dem ich spreche" (p. 28). Not only does the Geheimrat repeatedly interfere in the affairs of others when, in fact, his own family is in need of attention (Fritz's incarceration), but his perception of a problem is narrow, lacking the broad perspective necessary to produce true social betterment. In that sense, he is very much like the Gräfin, who exhibits a similar singleminded determination. Rather than treating Marie as a troubled individual, the Gräfin approaches her as a case

history, as a fallen woman, and envisions herself as her
self-anointed saviour. This is particularly evident in the
Gräfin's analysis of what has gone wrong with Marie's life:

> Ihr einziger Fehler war, dass Sie [Marie] die
> Welt nicht kannten, dass Sie den Unterschied
> nicht kannten, der unter den verschiedenen
> Ständen herrscht, dass Sie die Pamela
> gelesen haben, das gefährlichste Buch das
> eine Person aus Ihrem Stande lesen kann.
> (p. 225)

Marie replies, "Ich kenne das Buch ganz und gar nicht"
(p. 225). The Gräfin does not seem to understand the
multiplicity of the human soul nor does she exhibit any
desire to delve into its intricacies. Her rational explanation that officers are by nature unfaithful does not
assuage the pain of Marie's cry: "Er liebte mich aber"
(p. 227). The Gräfin shows her insensitivity and dis-
interest in Marie as an individual when she adamantly refuses to grant forgiveness after a forbidden rendezvous
with Mary and sends Marie out of the house with the harsh
words: "Ich verzeih es dir niemals wenn du wider dein
eigen Glück handelst. Geh!" (p. 232). Of course Marie
does not perceive her actions to be contrary to her own
happiness at all; they are, however, contrary to what the
Gräfin thinks Marie's happiness should be. Marie's ejec-
tion from the Gräfin's household forces her into the
world and partially contributes to her eventual prostitu-

tion, much like the Geheimrat's refusal to give Läuffer
a position contributes to the necessity of his seeking
employment as a private tutor.

The Geheimrat and the Gräfin are alike in that they
are obsessed by a single idea which dominates all of their
thoughts and actions. Their zeal becomes, in fact, an idée
fixe which is dehumanized and leaves no room for consideration for the individual. Their supposedly enlightened
stance and zest for social reform is so exaggerated that
it becomes caricature. Lenz's criticism here is not
directed so much at the Enlightenment itself, but those
aspects of the Enlightenment which not only disregard the
totality of the human personality, but frequently subju-
gate the individual to the idea. Perhaps the Gräfin un-
wittingly offers an insight into the problem when she says:
"Wenn ich etwas ausfündig machen könnte, ihre Phantasei
mit meiner Klugheit zu vereinigen, ihr Herz, nicht ihren
Verstand zu zwingen mir zu folgen" (p. 232). This remark reflects Lenz's own ambivalent attitude toward the
Enlightenment which is also evinced by the contradictory
nature of his theoretical writings. After she has thrown
Marie out of the house, the Gräfin seems to recognize that
because of man's labyrinthine psyche, an appeal to the
intellect alone is insufficient. Nevertheless, she is incapable of helping Marie and therein lies the irony of her

"enlightened philosophy." Her belated awareness that a
program for social improvement cannot only concern itself
with practical application of ideas, but must also consider
the individual, makes her proposal to provide soldiers with
state supported female companionship all the more absurd:
The complexities of the individual would again be ignored
in such a "solution." Like Desporte's prescription for
pleasure, a brothel for soldiers would not alleviate
Marie's sense of alienation. Lenz seems to have recognized the Gräfin's dubious position in the final scenes
of Act IV, (p. 232).

In the second version of the last scene of Act V,
(p. 245), (both versions depict a conversation between the
Gräfin and Graf von Spannheim), the proposal for the
brothel is no longer formulated by her, but by Graf von
Spannheim with the Gräfin questioning men's capability to
understand the feminine heart. The duplicity of Lenz's
attitude toward the ideals of the Enlightenment are clearly
demonstrated in the figures of the Gräfin and the Geheimrat.

A central thought in Lenz's dramatic theory is the
autonomous hero, the strong, independent and active individual who influences and controls his environment.

> Es ist die Rede von Charakteren, die sich ihre
> Begebenheiten erschaffen, die selbstständig und
> unveränderlich die ganze grosse Maschine selbst

> drehen, ohne die Gottheiten in den Wolken
> anders nötig zu haben, als wenn sie wollen
> zu Zuschauern, nicht von Bildern, von
> Marionettenpuppen--von Menschen.
> ("Anmerkungen," p. 729)

Do Läuffer and Marie fit that description? Are they the
kind of dramatic heroes who leave the spectator with a
sense of awe and move him to exclaim as Lenz suggests:
"das ist ein Kerl," or in the case of Marie, the feminine
version thereof? That is, of course, an absurd suggestion
and the answer is of course not. By no turn of the imagination are Läuffer or Marie a Götz von Berlichingen or a
Karl Moor. However, the terminus "Kerl" does appear in
Lenz's dramas, primarily in the vocabulary of the Major,
who expresses the hope that his son will become a soldier,
"ein Kerl, wie ich gewesen bin; to which the Geheimrat
answers: "Das lass nur weg, lieber Bruder; unsere Kinder
sollen und müssen das nicht werden, was wir waren; die
Zeiten ändern sich, Sitten Umstände, alles..." (p. 12).
To the Major's protestations: "Potz hundert! wenn er
Major wird und ein braver Kerl wie ich und dem König so
redlich dient als ich?" the Geheimrat responds: "Ganz gut,
aber nach fünfzig Jahren haben wir vielleicht einen andern
König und eine andre Art ihm zu dienen" (p. 12). "Kerl" as
it is used in the Hofmeister has acquired a negative connotation and seems to suggest a fellow whose love of system

causes him to act mechanically and blindly even when his
actions may no longer be fruitful or appropriate. Läuffer
does fit into that category, but both he and Marie evoke
pity and not the admiration inherent in the Storm and
Stress application of the term.

Although Läuffer and Marie are not completely passive
individuals--Marie attempts to manipulate her future by
writing letters and maintaining contacts and Läuffer resorts to the tutorship only after his efforts at finding
other employment did not succeed--they both fail miserably
to influence their environment contrary to Lenz's vision
of the autonomous hero. Both become "ein Ball der
Umstände" which, in conjunction with their inner longings,
entangle them in a web of misery which almost proves
fatal. On various occasions throughout the drama where
Marie tries to take control of her destiny, her every
attempt to improve her situation is thwarted. In a series
of events that seem to be orchestrated by an evil spirit,
Marie's situation worsens. Suffering and increasing misfortune is, of course, the central theme of classical
tragedy. The suffering of Marie, however, is not re-
deemed by recognition, nor is the spectator relieved
through catharsis. The harmony which did not exist at
the beginning of the drama cannot be restored at the end.

The Soldaten begins after Marie's return from a

visit to her fiancé and his mother. Although Desportes
has been a visitor in the Wesener household in the past
as Wesener's greeting indicates, Marie has continued her
relationship with Stolzius and is in the process of
writing a letter to him and his mother. She is somewhat
uncertain of her own orthography and syntax, but completes
the letter without her sister's help, a task she cannot
accomplish independently later in the drama. At this
point Desportes appears on the scene (p. 185). Marie
succumbs to his flattery and agrees to disobey her father
and secretly visit the theater with Desportes. The
titles of the two plays to which Desportes invites Marie
are prophetic: La chercheuse d'Esprit and the Deserteur.
Up to this point, Marie has exhibited a degree of autonomy, which she tries to retain even after the appearance
of Desportes. "Wenn Er mich doch nur wollte für mich
selber sorgen lassen. Ich bin doch kein klein Kind mehr"
(p. 189) she tells her father. Her father, however,
representing authority and the patriomonial social order
steps in: "Lass mich nur machen, ich weiss schon was zu
deinem Glück dient...Kannst noch einmal gnädige Frau
werden närrisches Kind. Man kann nicht wissen was einem
manchmal für ein Glück aufgehoben ist" (196-97). However, as subsequent events illustrate, this time father
does not know best!

After Desporte's sudden departure, Marie increasingly
loses control over her life. She continues writing
letters to him, all to no avail (p. 220). Her association
with Mary is primarily motivated by Marie's desire to remain in touch with Desportes. When the Gräfin invites
her to join her household, she reluctantly leaves her own
home and only upon the Gräfin's strong urgings (p. 228).
Marie no longer acts but reacts, and becomes the victim
of not only the events which swirl about her like pulsat-
ing strobe lights, but also of an inner urgency which relentlessly drives her toward her final despair. Surely
she is not an autonomous heroine, but a defeated and
pitiable creature who must suffer the final indignity of
her own father mistaking her for a common woman of the
streets.

Marie's bid for autonomy has ended in failure. Both
her and her father's helplessness and dependency are em-
phasized by the final stage directions: "Eine Menge
Leute versammeln sich um sie und tragen sie fort" (p. 243).
On the other hand, there is a note of hope in the fact
that a forgiving father and his daughter are reunited
and that the crowd takes a concerned interest in their
fate. Marie's future, however, and whether or not a
similar situation could repeat itself, are left open, for
the final scene in which the brothel is proposed does not

really address itself to Marie. Again, the paradoxical
nature of Lenz's oeuvre is demonstrated.

The figure of Läuffer is a far more passive character than that of Marie. When the Hofmeister opens,
Läuffer has forsaken all efforts to influence the course
of his life. His earlier attempts to find a position outside of private tutoring had been unsuccessful. His one
effort to intercede in his own behalf, the letter to his
father requesting him to persuade the Geheimrat to participate in his financial support by permitting him to
teach his son, is a failure. Like Marie, he reacts and
becomes a mere puppet in the hands of a greater power.
He dances upon the command of the Majorin and bows and
scrapes as if manipulated by invisible strings. Läuffer's
discussion about individual freedom with Wenzeslaus,
"Haben Sie nie einen Sklaven im betressten Rock gesehen?
O Freiheit, güldene Freiheit" (p. 57) is purely academic,
for Läuffer would have no more autonomy in the hand of
Wenzeslaus whose expressed intent it is to form him in
his own image. The Geheimrat's observations on personal
freedom have the same ring of histrionics:

> Ohne Freiheit geht das Leben bergab rückwärts,
> Freiheit ist das Element des Menschen wie das
> Wasser des Fisches, und ein Mensch der sich
> der Freiheit begibt, vergiftet die edelsten
> Geister seines Bluts, erstickt seine süssesten
> Freuden des Lebens in der Blüte und ermordet
> sich selbst (p. 25)

for he, like all of the characters, is doomed to
follow the demands of society, his own inner urgings, or
his particular spleen.

In order to illustrate the character's helplessness
in a particular situation or the event's overpowering
effect on the individual, Lenz has his characters fall
down in a faint or swoon. This technique, which he uses
frequently in his dramas, is reminiscent of Kleist. Thus
the Majorin faints after she has discovered Gustchen's
and Läuffer's liaison, (p. 50) and Läuffer himself loses
control of his senses when he recognizes the child carried
by the old woman Marthe as his own, (p. 77). And in Der
neue Menoza one of the central characters, Wilhelmine,
falls into a faint on two occasions, when Prince Tandi
tells the story of his daring jump from the tower and she
realizes that he narrowly escaped death, (p. 109) and when
after their marriage she and Tandi are alleged to be
brother and sister and he attempts to leave (p. 146).
In all instances the characters recognize their total
impotence in the face of a greater power and their complete inability to prevent or alter events. Prinz Tandi's
criticism that all around him he sees the substitution
of "Geschwätz für Handlung" (p. 123) certainly also
applies to the characters in the Hofmeister and the

202

Soldaten.

In depicting his dramatic characters as "Spielbälle der Umstände" Lenz demonstrates his belief that chance plays a major role in the course of human events. In his theoretical writings he had lamented the circumstance that indeed man seems to be at the mercy of capricious fate, (Titel, I, 572) and in his dramas that view is reiterated. The Gräfin most aptly describes Marie's nature which is subject to random influences and directions: "Mädchen du bist wie das Bäumchen hier im Abendwinde, jeder Hauch verändert dich" (p. 232). As an unpredictable and sudden wind assaults a young tree, the chance occurrences in Marie's life tend to dominate her. Fritz, the son of the Geheimrat uses the metaphor of life as a ship at sea to illustrate the role of chance in human events: "Wir sind auf der See, der Wind treibt uns." He proves to be an echo of his father when he adds, "aber die Vernunft muss immer am Steuerruder bleiben" (p. 71). He tries to be true to his word by marrying Gustchen and caring for her illegitimate child, ending the play with the promise that the tutor's son will never be educated by a tutor. In spite of Fritz's intercession in Gustchen's life at this point, the events that occurred are not as Fritz would have planned them; his life, too, is largely determined by circumstance and chance.

The attitude of the Lenzian hero toward any attempt
to achieve autonomy and its continuous frustration by the
reality of his existence is illustrated in the exclamation of Strephon in Die Freunde machen den Philosophen,
"O unerforschlicher Himmel!" (p. 321). Strephon's recognition of the unfathomable nature of the universe is a
direct contrast to Lenz's contention that the dramatic
hero must be a character who controls and creates his own
destiny. It is an admission of man's dependency on nature
and his ensuing frustration, but it is not an admission of
defeat. As Lenz observes in "Über die Natur unsers
Geistes," man's dependency on nature is a fact, but so is
his unease with that dependency, (Titel, I, 572).
Lenz's dramas therefore reflect the paradox of man's condition: his desire to be autonomous but his inability to
achieve that autonomy due to the restraints of circumstances and his own complex nature. The illustration of
that major incongruity of life lends to his dramas the
realistic mode which he advocated.

In the essay "Über Götz von Berlichingen" Lenz describes the biography of an average individual as follows:

Wir werden geboren--unsere Eltern geben uns Brot
und Kleid--unsere Lehrer drücken in unser Hirn
Worte, Sprachen, Wissenschaften--irgend ein
artiges Mädchen drückt in unser Herz den Wunsch
es eigen zu besitzen, es in unsere Arme als unser

> Eigentum zu schliessen, wenn sich nicht gar
> ein tierisch Bedürfnis mit hineinmischt--es
> entsteht eine Lücke in der Republik wo wir
> hineinpassen...und was bleibt nun der Mensch
> noch anders als eine vorzüglichkünstliche
> kleine Maschine. (Titel, I, 378)

The thrust of the essay is an exhortation to rise above the
condition of being "eine vorzüglich-künstliche kleine
Maschine" which fits into "eine Lücke in der Republik."
It is, however, precisely the effort to find "eine Lücke
wo... sie hineinpassen," at least externally, which
occupies both Läuffer and Marie. Their attempt to find
social and personal stability is not successful, however.
Instead both characters suffer increasing alienation, both
from the self and from society.

Marie's growing isolation and alienation from her
family and her social group and the accompanying loss of
identity are poignantly illustrated in the reaction of
Jungfer Zipfersaat (p. 208). Marie adopts the speech she
perceives to be the sophisticated frivolity of the upper
classes and ostentatiously introduces Desportes to her
friend as a baron who has fallen madly in love with the
Jungfer. Marie plays the role of a sophisticate who is
at home in the world of the theater and the company of
aristocrats. Affecting a stance of worldliness, Marie
invites Desportes to offer his declaration of love to
Jungfer Zipfersaat. Jungfer Zipfersaat's reaction is one

of incredulity: "Ich weiss nicht wie du bist, Marieel"
(p. 208) she says in an embarrassed tone. The scene ends
with the grandmother's song accompanying the riotous teas-
ing in the adjoining room. Jungfer Zipfersaat, however,
does not remain in the house, for the directions state:
"Jungfer Zipfersaat geht ganz verdrüsslich fort" (p. 208).

Jungfer Zipfersaat is perceiving her friend as a
stranger who no longer fits the image she has had of her
and whom she no longer recognizes as the Marie she once
knew. Lacking a solid inner core and social bond, Marie
grows increasingly alienated. Finally, her self-identity
is shattered, and when the drama ends, she is only a
shadow of the pretty daughter of a middle-class business
man she once was.

Not only Marie, but all of the characters in the
drama lack a solid bond which unites them in a spirit of
community and cooperation. It becomes immediately obvious, for example, that the relationship between Marie
and her sister Charlotte is founded on disrespect and
competition. Charlotte is portrayed as the brighter, but
uglier of the two sisters, with the father blatantly pre-
ferring the prettier Marie: "Halt's Maul! Marie hat ein
viel zu edles Gemüt als dass sie von dir reden sollte,
aber du schalusierst auf deine eigene Schwester; weil du
nicht so schön bist alls sie, sollst du zum wenigsten

besser denken" (p. 195). Indeed, Charlotte treats her
sister with ascerbic bitterness: "Die gottvergessne
Allerweltshure will honette Mädels in Blame bringen weil
sie so denkt" (p. 195). But the fairytale motif of the
pretty sister marrying the handsome prince in spite of
the ugly sister's jealousy is no longer valid in the
Soldaten, for it is Marie who must suffer.

The relationship between Marie and her apparently
adoring father is also problematical. On the one hand,
Wesener calls her his "einzige Freude" (p. 189) and
thereby explains his extreme concern for her welfare. On
the other hand, his reprimands are devastating: "Ja lüg
nur, lüg nur, lüg nur dem Teufel ein Ohr ab--geh mir aus
den Augen du gottlose Seele" (p. 194). Wesener's manipulations in the Marie-Desportes affair and his expressed
interest in having a "gnädige Frau" in the family are
certainly not only motivated by concern for his daughter,
but also by self-interest. His interaction with Marie
resembles the relationship between the Major and Gustchen.
In a conversation with Läuffer, for example, the Major
complains about his wife's tendency to be a tyrant and
confesses that his daughter is his only consolation:
"das Mädchen ist meines Herzens einziger Trost" (p. 19).
Like Wesener, the Major has ambitious, if not obsessive
plans for his daughter's future. Even after the desperate

events which occurred and almost resulted in Gustchen's
death, the Major has difficulty relinquishing his dream.
When the Geheimrat tells the Major that a husband is
available for Gustchen, he responds: "Doch keiner zu
weit unter ihrem Stande? O sie sollte die erste Partie
im Königreiche werden. Das ist ein vermaledeiter Ge-
danke! wenn ich doch den erst forthätte; er wird mich
noch ins Irrhaus bringen" (p. 101). And his feelings toward his daughter are as ambivalent as those of Wesener.
After he has prevented her death in the pond, his observation is: "O du mein einzig teurester Schatz! Dass ich
dich wieder in meinen Armen tragen kann, gottlose
Kanaille!" (p. 70).

The constellations Marie-Wesener and Gustchen-Major
are reminiscent of the father-daughter relationships in
the bourgeois tragedy. In that drama, the father, as the
authority figure and guardian of social mores and middle
class values attempts to preserve the existing order.
This he accomplishes by guarding the honor of his daughter
and his family and by preventing marriage outside specific
social classes. The father is a homogenous figure whose
devotion to his daughter is unfaltering and who is generally unforgiving if a transgression occurs. An important
difference exists in the characterizations of Wesener and
the Major. They themselves are not unified, holistic

characters, but broken figures whose inner fragmentation
is reflected in the ambivalence of their attitude and reaction to their daughters. They are more forgiving than
their traditional counterparts, but their forgiveness is
tinged with dark undertones. The once cherished orderly
world which is worth preserving no longer exists; they
too are experiencing a disharmony which they hope to
assuage, at least partially, by their daughters' marriages
into the upper class. The conventions of the bourgeois
drama are being replaced with a new orientation. Politically significant is that not the middle class Marie,
but the aristocratic Desportes meets with death at the
hands of a member of the middle class.

The personal isolation and alienation of the Lenzian
characters is also illustrated by the daily behavior and
occupation of the Major. According to the Majorin, he
is "den ganzen ausgeschlagenen Tag auf dem Felde, und
wenn er nach Hause kommt, sitzt er stumm wie ein Stock"
(p. 42). Helmut Arntzen points out the estrangement between the individual and society and within the individual himself expressed in Storm and Stress comedy: "Für
die Komödie des Sturm und Drang ist aber nicht mehr der
Konflikt, sondern bereits die Fremdheit zwischen Gesellschaft und Individuum und beider mit sich selbst Aus-
gangspunkt." [12] He characterizes the Hofmeister as a

comedy of alienation and notes the personal alienation experienced by all characters in the play, those who according to him are "rational" and those who are not.

> Der Komödienkonflikt artikuliert sich nicht
> mehr im Gegensatz des einen Unvernünftigen zu
> der vernünftigen Gesellschaft; die Vernünftigen
> sind so isoliert wie die anderen, und ihre Vernunft
> ist abstrakt und darum wirkungslos für die anderen
> wie für sie selbst.[13]

That isolation and inter-personal alienation experienced by the Lenzian character is poignantly portrayed
in a scene between Läuffer and Gustchen. The scene opens
with Gustchen languishing on her bed and Läuffer sitting
at the bed-side (pp. 40-41). Läuffer is preoccupied with
his grim economic prospects, but soon the dialogue turns
toward their personal situation. It is clear that Gustchen does not recognize Läuffer as an individual, but that
she is playing a role, that of the suffering Juliette with
Läuffer, the stand-in for Fritz, as her Romeo.

> O Romeo! wenn dies deine Hand wäre--Aber so
> verlässest du mich, unedler Romeo! Siehst
> nicht, dass deine Julie für dich stirbt--von der
> ganzen Welt, von ihrer ganzen Familie gehasst,
> verachtet, ausgespien. O unmenschlicher Romeo!
> (p. 41)

Läuffer, who had been absorbed in his own thoughts, is
startled out of his reverie by Gustchen's theatrical
gesture of pressing his hand against her eyes. After
asking the question "Was schwärmst du wieder?" (p. 41),

Läuffer again sinks into his reverie, and Gustchen loudly
speculates about Fritz's lack of correspondence. At this
point Läuffer makes the comment: "Es könnte mir gehen
wie Abälard--" to which Gustchen responds: "Du irrst
dich--Meine Krankheit liegt im Gemüt--Niemand wird dich
mutmassen" (p. 41). Gustchen makes it clear that she does
not accept Läuffer as an individual or as her lover. Her
comment "niemand wird dich mutmassen" reveals her disrespect and an inability to deal with Läuffer as a human being. Both she and Läuffer retreat into role playing--he
sees himself as Abälard--and can only approach each other
on this artificial level. Unlike the historical Abälard,
however, Läuffer feels no genuine passion for Gustchen,
nor does Gustchen experience love for the tutor. Both
Läuffer and Gustchen have hidden and isolated themselves
behind a cardboard persona, a mask, which does not permit
personal communication or involvement. They are solitary
monads trapped in their own circumferences. In "Versuch
über das erste Principium der Moral" Lenz writes "Wir
müssen suchen andere um uns herum glücklich zu machen"
(Titel, I, 496). In the figures of Gustchen and
Läuffer he depicts characters who, estranged from each
other and themselves, are unable to provide each other
with warmth and support. Nevertheless, Lenz's dramas
do not achieve the profound moral nihilism which marks so

much of 20th century literature. For Lenz the individual,
trapped in an incoherent cosmos and plagued by his own
complex nature, can never forget totally that although a
fool, he once believed himself a god--"man...glaubt sich
einen Gott und ist ein Tor" (p. 489). Although Strephon
in Die Freunde machen den Philosophen makes the cynical
observation: "Der Mensch ist so geneigt, sich selber zu
betrügen" (p. 319), the need for human love and contact
remains as Läuffer demonstrates by his admiration of Lise.
Lenz the realist and Lenz the idealist are always in precarious balance--the spark, his faith in the perfectibility of man, never completely dies. The result is a
drama as complex as life itself.

The personal isolation experienced by the individual
characters in Lenz's dramas is also reflected in their
attitude and reaction toward nature. Nature does not
play a major role in the dramas; it does not become a
point of reference or discussion, but several of the
character's primarily unconscious responses to nature are
worth considering.

In most of the scenes in both the Hofmeister and
Soldaten which occur outdoors, nature is purely functional
and serves as a backdrop. This seems to be the case in
the scene depicting Marie's rendezvous with Mary in the
Gräfin's garden. It is noteworthy, however, that the

directions specifically indicate that the color of the garden wall through which Marie hears Mary's seductive words is green (p. 231). "Green" is also the color of Desportes' room (p. 220) in which he writes requesting Marie that she cease further correspondence until she receives a new address, when in fact his real intention is that he does not wish to continue communicating with her. Because Lenz mentions color so seldom in his plays, it seems significant that the color in both of these scenes in which Marie is being deceived is the color of nature. The color green suggests that nature is a silent observer if not collaborator in the web of deception entangling Marie. Indeed, this is the concept of nature which is apparent in the observations about nature by a number of characters. In an evening scene which takes place in the moonlight in the garden, Prinz Tandi is uncertain that his love for Wilhelmine will be reciprocated:

> Ihr Sterne! die ihr fröhlich über meinem
> Schmerz daher tanzt! du allein, mitleidiger
> Mond--bedaure mich nicht. Ich leide willig.
> Ich war nie so glücklich als auf dieser
> Folter. Du unendliches Gewölbe des Himmels!
> du sollst meine Decke diese Nacht sein.
> Noch zu eng für mein banges Herz. (p. 119)

Although the Prinz reveals himself to be a Schwärmer in this passage, his words make it clear that he cannot expect solace from the frivolous stars and unfathomable heavens. Nature is largely depicted as indifferent to human suffering. The moon alone is portrayed as compassionate, but in another play, Die Freunde machen den Philosophen, the moon is personified and acquires the characteristics of a sybarite--lascivious and wanton: "Vorher aber muss ich sie noch einmal sehen, in den Armen ihres Buhlers, vielleicht vom lüsternen Monde beguckt" (p. 323). In this instance, nature becomes an adversary, a participant in the forces which conspire against and seek to overwhelm the individual. A wanton moon is an ugly and disturbing image. It suggests a world in which order and harmony have fled to be replaced by doubt and upheaval, a world in which not even nature can offer a degree of comfort and solace. In such a world the individual feels threatened and vulnerable. "Ich bin verloren! da kommt was die Treppe herauf" (p. 465) Catharina exclaims in the fragment Catharina von Siena, a fear which is echoed by Läuffer: "Ich höre was auf dem Gang nach der Schulstube" (p. 41). The neuter pronoun "was" refers to an unknown--although in Läuffer's case they fear discovery by Gustchen's father also--an ominous, menacing entity which is just as much a part of the character's inner world as it is a physical reality. The anxiety expressed in these two statements foreshadows Woyzeck's "Still, hörst du's Andres, hörst du's? Es geht was!"[14]

214

On the few occasions when Lenz makes a reference to natural phenomena in the <u>Soldaten</u> and the <u>Hofmeister</u>, nature is depicted as violent or hostile. In the crucial scene in which Marie reveals her innermost emotions, she expects it to storm during the night: "Ich glaub es wird gewittern die Nacht, Wenn es einschlüge--" (p. 197). A few scenes later, Stolzius comments: "Es geht ein so scharfer Wind draussen, ich meine wir werden Schnee bekommen" (p. 202). And in one of the play's final scenes, when Stolzius prepares to buy the poison that will kill Desportes, he is pacing back and forth in front of a pharmacy and Lenz tells us that it is raining (p. 238). At no time is nature described as warm and welcoming, as offering cheer or consolation. It is depicted either as indifferent or even as hostile. Unable to find succor, the characters are as alienated from nature as they are from each other and themselves. The painter Rosalbino, afraid that Catharina may have died in the desert, voices the strongest rejection of nature to be found in Lenz's dramas in the fragment <u>Catharina von Siena</u>: "O ich will in der Natur nichts mehr malen. Du hast mich verraten. Ich habe dir alles aufgeopfert, falschste aller Mütter. Du hast mich um alles gebracht" (p. 476).

In his dramatic works, specifically the <u>Hofmeister</u> and <u>Soldaten</u>, Lenz has realized his major dramatic tenet--

the portrayal of man. His characters are not contrived but realistic, yet they are carefully crafted portraits of average individuals whose external and internal conflicts and complexities are manifested through dramatic discourse, gesture, and scene. He has created characters who frequently are at odds with his dramatic theories. The autonomous hero whom Lenz envisions as evolving toward ever greater freedom through active intervention in his destiny is thwarted by circumstances and his own lack of homogeneity. Confronted with the impossibility of decisively altering his environment, he is beset by inertia, alienation and isolation. At times he attempts to act, but his actions are doomed to failure. Yet, the dream of autonomy is never totally absent from his consciousness. It appears again and again in such disparate figures as the Geheimrat, the Hofmeister, and subconsciously even in Marie. The ideals of the Enlightenment are in collision with the reality of a rapidly changing social and economic structure and a different philosophical orientation.

Both of Lenz's major dramas have a peculiarly forced ending, but his characterizations are anything but typical or artificial. Not idealized, they represent a new direction in the German theater, one which is admirably expressed by Prinz Tandi: "ich nehme die Menschen lieber wie sie sind, ohne Grazie, als wie sie aus einem spitzigen Federkiel hervorgehen" (p. 117).

2. Language: The Dialogue of Realism--A Collision
    of Codes.

In a paean to Shakespeare's linguistic sensibility,
Lenz writes the following:

> Seine Sprache ist die Sprache des kühnsten Genius,
> der Erd und Himmel aufwühlt, Ausdruck zu den ihm
> zuströmenden Gedanken zu finden. ...Seine Könige
> und Königinnen schämen sich so wenig als der
> niedrigste Pöbel, warmes Blut im schlagenden
> Herzen zu fühlen, oder kützelnder Galle im
> schalkhaften Scherzen Luft zu machen, denn sie
> sind Menschen. ("Anmerkungen," p. 745) 15

Ostensibly, Lenz recognizes in Shakespeare's dramatic
dialogue a quality he found lacking in the formal language
practiced on the German stage: an ease and naturalness of
discourse which resembles that of everyday speech. By
identifying Shakespeare's kings and queens as "Menschen"
who sometimes do not speak like kings and queens but like
ordinary human beings, in other words, who do not speak a
uniform language, he also recognizes the various spheres
of language which are in operation in drama which attempts
to veer away from the formal discourse dictated by theatrical
convention. Inspired by Shakespeare, Lenz advocates "realism"
on the stage in character portrayal and in dramatic discourse.

Lenz's overt interest in language is not only apparent
in his theoretical writings, in which he expresses the view
that understanding can be achieved by agreeing to a mu-
tually acceptable linguistic code, but his dramatic characters also specifically concern themselves with difficulties
posed by language. The reader joins Marie, for example,

in <u>media</u> <u>res</u> of a baffling orthographic problem. "Schwester

weisst du nicht, wie schreibt man Madam, Ma, ma, t a m m,

tamm, me, me" (p. 183). Marie's confrontation with the

word continues through the drama, particularly when she

is attempting to put her feelings on paper.

> Marie: Indessen müssen nicht alle Ausdrücke
> auf der Waagschale liegen, sondern auf
> das Herz ansehen, das Ihnen--wart wie
> soll ich nun schreiben.

Charlotte: Was weiss ich?

Marie: Sag doch wie heisst das Wort nun? (pp. 214-215)

And in the <u>Hofmeister</u> in a scene which finds Pätus reading

a letter from Seiffenblase, Pätus comments: "Was der Junge

für eine rasende Orthographie hat" (p. 84).

This "metalanguage," conversations about language in

this case concerning its elusiveness and limits particu-

larly in reference to writing, not only reflects the dif-

ficulties in finding accurate expression for an emotion

or even a concept, but is also an indication of the

artist's growing self-consciousness. As the emphasis in

drama is shifting from man's confrontation with the gods

towards an exploration of his inner self, the artist him-

self and the work of art are increasingly becoming the

subject of literature. Marie's struggle with the word

illustrates at the same time the difficulties encountered

by not having mastered a language, and the complex nature

of language itself, which so often refuses to yield the

word which will give a correct expression to the experience. A perhaps unconscious language skepticism seems to be present here.

Related to the search for a new dramatic language is the rejection of classical mythological allusions in favor of biblical references and the use of folk songs and fairy tales in modern drama. According to Volker Klotz, the bible, together with folk tales and songs provides the dramatic character with a world of easily accessible images which function as a linguistic anchor in an alienated world. Klotz assigns that function to the grandmother's song in the Soldaten.[16] The dramatic character's reliance on such images--a dependency which reveals an inability to find appropriate linguistic terms-- in order to give expression to experience is one aspect of their presence in non-Aristotelian drama. It must be remembered, however, that the exponents of Storm and Stress, particularly Herder and Haman, had purposefully advanced a literary usage of the bible, of folk song and of Teutonic mythology. There is no reason to believe that biblical and folkloric motifs are not as much a part of public consciousness and as "natural" to European society as classical mythology had been for the ancients. Their interpolation in modern drama is therefore not so much a "Auftauchen im Unterbewussten gelagerter Bilder, die dem Einsamen [the dramatic character] Bestätigung und Halt in

seiner Lage versprechen,"[17] as a conscious effort by the
dramatist to create a dramatic world which is representative of the modern European and not the classical Greek
age. An example is the folksong offered by the grandmother
in the pivotal <u>Soldaten</u> scene, "Ein Mädele jung ein
Würfel ist"(p. 208). The song is the old woman's only
appearance on stage and it functions as a grotesque commentary on Marie and Desportes' playful yet disconcerting
actions. The role played by chance in the course of life
is illustrated by the comparison between a young girl and
a die, an image which reflects the events of Marie's life
over which she increasingly looses control. And when
Stolzius contemplates revenge, he asks, "Wie heisst's in
dem Liede Mutter, wenn ein Vögelein von einem Berge all
Jahre ein Körnlein wegtrüge, endlich würde es ihm doch
gelingen"(p. 211). Both songs are conscious analogies
constructed by the dramatic character and function primarily as an illumination of the particular scene and of
coming events. They are an extra-linguistic means of
communication, but rather than represent a desperate and
last linguistic resort, they have the same technical function as a universal means of communication in non-Aristotelian drama, as mythological allusions have in classical
drama.

In the essay, "Über die Bearbeitung der deutschen

Sprache" Lenz suggests that misunderstandings can be
alleviated or at least decreased by agreeing to the use
of a standard language. He is concerned here not with
poetic language and its inherent multiple meaning of
words, but with a spoken language which can be used as a
reliable tool for communication by all members of society.
If no linguistic conformity is achieved, Lenz predicts
dire results:

> Treffen wir mit andern in Ansehung unserer
> gemeinschaftlichen Sprache keine Verabredung,
> so vereinzeln wir uns selbst auf die aller-
> grausamste Weise. Sind es gar Leute, mit denen
> wir zu teilen haben, und verstehen nicht alle
> Schattierungen in ihrer Sprache, so entstehen
> daraus unzählige Verwirrungen und Missver-
> ständnisse, die oft mit der Zeit zu Hass,
> Feindseligkeiten, und Untergang ganzer
> Familien, Gesellschaften und Nationen
> Ausschlagen können. (Titel, I, 457)

Lenz's suggestion that communication can be assured simply
by agreeing to use a standard language does not take into
account the background and experience of the individual
who brings to any communicative act a unique frame of
reference which can interfere with true communication in
spite of the use of the same code. Modern communication
theory is not so far different from Lenz's conception of
the communicative process for it posits that "that genuine
communication depends on the capacity of the two (or
more) parties involved in the exchange to employ the same
code"[18] although a more generous version of the theory

"holds it sufficient that the receiver be <u>acquainted</u> with
the sender's code and so be able to decode the message."[19]
What interests us, however, is what happens if individuals
who are not acquainted with each other's "codes" are
forced to interact, a situation which is unavoidable in a
variegated social structure and in realistic drama. How
complex the communicative process actually is, is master-
fully demonstrated by Lenz in the <u>Hofmeister</u> and <u>Soldaten</u>.
The manner in which language functions in these two plays
contradicts the optimism expressed in Lenz's proposal for
a "Klopstockischen Landtag" (Titel, I, 455), which
would resolve linguistic problems by standardizing language.

In his excellent essay of 1962, Walter Höllerer has
identified the various spheres of language effective in the
<u>Soldaten</u>. Specific language codes can be related to the
various figures. However, individual characters change
their manner of speaking, frequently within brief time
lapses. For example, Höllerer distinguishes between five
distinct language spheres utilized by Marie in the brief
scene which begins with Marie's maudlin reaction toward a
letter from Stolzius and ends with her abandoned frolic
with Desportes.[20] Faltering speech and shifting modes of
speaking are seen by some critics as indicative of a
divided personality, but they are also a technique of
realistic character portrayal.[21] There is ample proof that

the individual does not employ the same tone or manner of speaking in all of his daily encounters, and this is what Lenz attempts to reproduce on the stage. In the use of their language, the characters are not typical, but rather individual figures who do not speak a formal stage language nor are they solely characterized by their individualistic speech patterns, but rather they resort to various modes of speaking in response to specific stimuli. This technique is also demonstrated in the <u>Hofmeister</u>.[22]

Läuffer, for example, joins in the affected rococo mannerisms of the Majorin: "o...o...verzeihen Sie dem Entzücken, dem Enthusiasmus, der mich hinreisst" (p. 14), is cast in the role of the supplicant when he asks protection from Wenzeslaus: "Dürft ich mir ein Glas Wasser ausbitten?"(p. 52) and uses the language of reason after he has been wounded by the Major: "Ich bitt Euch, seid ruhig. Ich habe weit weniger bekommen, als meine Taten wert waren. Meister Schöpfsen, ist meine Wunde gefährlich? (p. 67). This is a new dramatic character whose dialogue changes as the situation demands. As we shall see, his linguistic versatility also creates for him problems of identity and alienation, a condition illustrated primarily in the figure of Marie.

In addition to variegated speech patterns of individual figures, separate modes of speaking can be asso-

ciated with specific characters. Höllerer identifies the
following interpersonal spheres of language in the Soldaten: the language of the middle class businessman
practiced by Wesener; the language of sentimentality represented by the Gräfin; the rococo mannerism and exaggerated courtly etiquette of Desportes; Eisenhardt and
Spannheim representing the language of rationalism and its
parody manifested in Pirzel; and finally, the "language
of genius" spoken by the officers. As Höllerer points
out, the various "Stände" and the "geistesgeschichtlichen
Strömungen" of the 18th century are recognizable in the
illustrated modes of speaking.[23] Of primary interest to
our discussion, however, is the question of what happens
when the various language spheres or language codes meet
and collide, and to what extent the characters play
language "games" and use language to dominate and manipulate each other.

The collision of language codes has its most devastating effect on the life of Marie. It is most apparent in
her encounters with Desportes. As a member of the aristocratic class who is avidly pursuing the seduction of
Marie, Desportes goes to great length to flatter her, not
only with presents but also with verbal compliments and
with verses. The following verbal encounter between Marie
and Desportes is typical:

> Desportes: Was machen Sie denn da meine
> göttliche Mademoiselle?
>
> Marie: O nichts, nichts, gnädiger Herr--.
> Ich schreib gar zu gern.
>
> Desportes: Wenn ich nur so glücklich wäre,
> einen von Ihren Briefen, nur eine
> Zeile von Ihrer schönen Hand zu sehen.
>
> Marie: O verzeihen Sie mir, ich schreibe gar
> nicht schön, ich schäme mich von meiner
> Schrift zu weisen. (p. 185)

As the dialogue continues, Marie interjects Desportes'
fawning with the observation that his remarks are superficial: "O Herr Baron, hören Sie auf, ich weiss doch
dass das alles nur Komplimente sein," (sic., p. 185) but
she is not convinced of her own protestations. By the
time she has received a letter from Stolzius in which he
questions her sincerity, Desportes has completely ingra-
tiated himself and turned into her "protector": "Ums
Himmels willen, was ist das für ein Brief der Ihnen
Tränen verursachen kann?" (p. 206). The "göttliche
Mademoiselle" and "goldenes Marieel" (p. 206) has been
beguiled by the exaggerated politeness and manneristic
adulation of Desportes. Marie's easy surrender to
Desportes' flattery has often been interpreted as a sign
of bourgeois ambition to rise in social status. That
ambition, however, is far more pronounced in Wesener
than it is in Marie, and her relationship with Desportes
cannot be seen as her calculated effort to become a member

of the aristocracy. If that were the case, the play
would not have the appeal it has today. As a "Bürgermäd-
chen" she is, of course, flattered by the baron's attention, yet rather than hope to achieve the external trapp-
ings of status, Marie seems to be searching for the solid
center she lacks. She attempts to continue her relationship with Desportes after he has left (pp. 232-234), and
neither Mary nor the young count become the easy substi-
tutes which Läuffer becomes for Gustchen (pp. 40-41).
Until the end Marie insists "Er liebte mich aber" (p. 227).

Revealing of the effect of Desportes mode of language
is Marie's and Wesener's reaction to a "verse" which
Desportes has written for Marie:

> Du höchster Gegenstand von meinen reinen Trieben
> Ich bet dich an, ich will dich ewig lieben.
> Weil die Versicherung von meiner Lieb und Treu
> Du allerschönstes Licht mit jedem Morgen neu.
> (p. 196)

Marie is pleased that a verse has been written in her
honor, and Wesener concludes after rereading "Du höchster
Gegenstand von meinen reinen Trieben," that Desportes' in-
tentions are honorable after all--"Er denkt doch honett
seh ich" (p. 196). Both Wesener and his daughter are
clearly deceived by language with which they are neither
familiar nor comfortable--that of the aristocratic cir-
cles. Today, the formulation "reine Triebe" would repre-

sent an oxymoron, but even in the 18th century sense the
sexual connotation was not absent from it, although the
term also implies a drive toward a goal--according to
Adelung: "Uns alle treibt ein natürlicher Trieb zu dem
Glücke, diesem Ziele unserer Wünsche."[24] Adelung points
out that for convenience's sake, "Triebe" was often used
to rhyme with "Liebe" and it must therefore have had a
less negative connotation than it does today. Nevertheless, both Wesener and Marie clearly mistake Desportes'
stilted and artificial verse for a testimony of true devotion. The noble sentiments which they detect in what
they perceive as elevated language is merely lust veiled
in Lenz's parody of literary convention. The misunderstanding is the result of the collision of two opposed
language codes, the polished and artificial speech of the
courtly cavalier and the faltering speech of Marie.

In one instance Marie tries to copy Desportes'
syntax and vocabulary:

> Junger Zipfersaat hier hab ich die Ehre dir einen
> Baron zu präsentieren der sterblich verliebt in
> dich ist. Hier Herr Baron ist die Jungfer von
> der wir soviel gesprochen haben und in die Sie
> sich neulich in der Komödie so sterblich
> verschameriert haben. (p. 207)

Her speech has the same bewildering effect on her long-
time friend as Desportes mode of speaking has on her. It
is alien to Jungfer Zipfersaat and she can only respond

with: "Ich weiss nicht wie du bist Marieel" (p. 208) and
then leave the friend who has become a stranger to her.
Although theoretically Lenz envisions understanding and
communication through unity of language, his dramas show
that communication, which is difficult enough between
conversational partners who are employing the same linguistic code, is almost an impossibility between members of
dissimilar social groups. While language systems do not
control and imprison the individual, the individual can
become enmeshed in a code in which he feels comfortable,
but which is often not an effective tool for communication.
Reliance on a specific mode of speaking tends to systemize
thinking. Social change cannot occur until conventional
patterns of thinking have been altered, and that cannot
take place until the verbal formulas and platitudes which
define public thinking have been recognized as such.
Lenz's awareness of the major role language plays in
human affairs is unique and is artistically reflected in
his dramas.

Various language codes are also represented in the
Hofmeister which at least contribute to the lack of true
communication and personal alienation in that play. The
Major and Majorin, for example, do not speak the same
language. Her language, which is saturated with French,
is pretentious and superficial: "Aber...aber was sagen

Sie dazu, Herr Graf! Haben Sie in Ihrem Leben eine
ärgere Kollektion von Sottissen gesehen?" (p. 44). This
in response to the Major's lamentation about his daughter's
loss of health and attractiveness for which he partially
holds the Majorin responsible. The Major's language alter-
nates between emotional outbursts and the purposefully
blustering speech of the "Genies." "Lächerlich! Es gibt
keine Familie; wir haben keine Familie. Narrensposssen!
Die Russen sind meine Familie: ich will Griechisch
werden" (p. 62), he tells the Geheimerat after Gustchen's
disappearance. In an earlier scene when he describes his
preferred methods of education for his son to Läuffer, his
tone is boisterous: "So recht; so lieb ich's; hübsch
fleissig--und wenn die Kanaille nicht behalten will, Herr
Läuffer, so schlagen Sie ihm das Buch an den Kopf, dass
er's Aufstehen vergisst..." (p. 16). Physical threats are
also present in his mode of speaking when he talks to his
wife: "Willst du mit der Sprach heraus?--Oder ich dreh dir
den Hals um" (p. 50). The Major and Majorin approach
each other from different linguistic planes which collide.
The Major's exclamatory language fails as a tool for communication because it makes a response impossible. No
wonder the Major finally sits "stumm wie ein Stock"
(p. 42) after returning home from the fields in the evening.

Similarly, communication does not occur between
the Geheimrat and Pastor Läuffer and between Wenzeslaus
and Läuffer. The Geheimrat and Wenzeslaus utilize the
language of rationalism and engage in lengthy diatribes
calculated to persuade the listener by sheer force of
volume. The monosyllabic response of Pastor Läuffer and
particularly that of Läuffer: "Ich bin satt überhörig
(p. 59), "Welche Demütigung," (p. 60) indicate that they
are not equal partners employing the same mode of speech
in the dialogue. Both the Geheimrat's and Wenzeslaus'
apparently rational language is flawed. As indicated,
the Geheimrat admits to an almost irrational fascination
with the subject he is discussing: "ich seh dann nur den
Gegenstand von dem ich spreche" (p. 28). In effect, he
is building verbal constructs to which he has become a
slave. His arguments have become ritualized and systemized
and exist for the sake of themselves, while he has become
ineffective as a catalyst for social change.

Imagery of violence is also present in Wenzeslaus'
discourse and to a lesser degree, in that of the Geheimrat. Wenzeslaus' response to the Major's physical attack
on Läuffer is: "Ich will sie zu Morsch schlagen, die
Hunde--" (p. 67). The Geheimrat uses animal imagery
when he compares a "Meineidigen" to "eine Schlange oder
einem tückischen Hunde" (p. 23). This is no longer the

230

language of reason. It alienates the listener but also
reveals a basic powerlessness and sense of frustration as
part of Wenzeslaus' and the Geheimrat's psyche.

The dogmatism of Wenzeslaus' and the Geheimrat's
speech serves to intimidate and overwhelm rather than
clarify and enlighten. Like the Major's exclamations to
which no response is possible, their lengthy declamations
are linguistic overkill which anesthezises the listener
and does not effectively communicate concepts. Their
elaborately constructed and passionately pursued arguments are in vain. Ronald W. Langacker defines a communicative act as successful if the conceptual picture of
the sender has much in common with that of the receiver.[25]
Not only is this criterion absent in the majority of the
dialogues in the Hofmeister and Soldaten, for the conversational partners approach each other with different expectations, but they also fail to employ linguistic codes
which are familiar to both the sender and receiver. Instead they function within the distinctive language
spheres of varying social classes and philosophical orientations. As a result the "Verwirrungen und Missverständ-
nisse" (Titel, I, 457) and the personal isolation occur
of which Lenz speaks in the essay "Über die Bearbeitung
der deutschen Sprache."

A collision of language codes also occurs within

individual characters. It is particularly noticeable in
the figure of Marie and contributes to her growing personal
isolation and loss of identity. Her affection in adopt-
ing Desportes' speech has already been noted. Marie also
imitates the business style of her father when writing
letters: "Ihro alle die Politessen und Höflichkeit wider
zu erstatten. Weil aber es noch nicht in unsern Kräften
steht, als bitten um fernere Condinuation" (p. 184), a
sentimental style in conversation with the Gräfin:
"(hebt den Kopf rührend aus ihrem Schoss auf) Gnädige
Frau--es ist zu spät" (p. 228), and occasionally speaks
like herself, the middle class daughter of a business man:
"Aber Papa. Was wird der arme Stolzius sagen?" (p. 197).
It is noteworthy that Marie has less control over language
than any of the other characters. She is swayed by and
easily adopts the varying linguistic stimuli with which
she comes in contact. She struggles to find the correct
word and must ask others for help ("Marie: So sag doch
wie heisst das Wort nun" p. 215). Whether her linguistic
uncertainty is the result of her inner disharmony or the
cause of it is a moot question. It is clear, however,
that because of her inarticulacy and lack of personal
style, she is easily manipulated by her environment. Not
only Desportes, but her own sister Charlotte exercises a
certain power over her, because she has better control of

language. Marie, for example, cannot write a letter
without Charlotte's help. In one scene, Marie begins to
cry while composing a letter and Charlotte must complete
the correspondence. Her reaction is one of ridicule:
"Charlotte (sieht sie an und lacht): Na was soll ich ihm
denn schreiben?" (p. 215), to which Marie responds:
"Schreib was du willst" (p. 215). Marie finally tears the
letter to pieces because she recognizes that it is not
truthful but only fabrication. Charlotte's angry reaction,
however, is: "Luder! warum zerreisst du denn, da ich eben
im besten Schreiben bin." (p. 215). Charlotte is not
sympathetic toward Marie's suffering nor does she care
whether her words contain the truth; she is only concerned
with the verbal construct she has created. She is able to
manipulate both the truth and the people around her with
her ability to invent linguistic structures. It is a
power which Marie lacks and which forces her to be dependent upon her sister.

An analogy to the middle class search for its own
linguistic style can be recognized in Marie's struggle to
find her own words and in her easy imitation of the speech
of others. For Marie, the process is a painful one. At
times the language she temporarily adopts alienates her
from her environment and certainly it causes an identity
problem until she finally no longer knows who she is. In

the words of Stolzius after he has received one of her
letters: "Marieel--nein sie ist es nicht mehr, sie ist
nicht dieselbige mehr--" (p. 211).

In his characters' confrontation with language, Lenz
illustrates the potential of language as a tool for wielding power and the need to master language in order to influence one's environment. As discussed in Chapter I,
this is a view of language shared by Gellert. The dogmatism permeating his characters' dialogues, their expressions of violence and the overt examples of manipulation
through language all denote the use of language as an
instrument of domination. Through ritualized argumenta-
tion, violent explosives and better control of language,
the characters intimidate and manipulate others. They do
not achieve communication, which is not their primary
goal, but intimidation through the sheer force of language.

Lenz further illustrates the complexity of the
communicative act by having the conversational partners
engage in a series of language "games." This is evident
for example, in the dialogue between Gustchen and Läuffer
in which she formulates love as tragedy and successfully
precludes communication. The language games always serve
to hide true feelings and emotions. In Gustchen's case,
she alone has escaped into fantasy and adopts language
which excludes Läuffer. However, both partners in a dia-

logue can employ language which masks their true feelings
and conduct an outwardly successful dialogue, as in the
linguistic encounter between Pätus and Frau Blitzer.

As Frau Blitzer enters the room shortly after the
scene has begun with a dialogue between Pätus and Fritz
von Berg, the apparently robust and good-humored landlady
and Pätus engage in good-natured banter. Frau Blitzer is
serving Pätus his afternoon coffee and he greets her with:
"In aller Welt, Mutter! wo bleibst du denn? Das Wetter
soll dich regieren. Ich warte hier schon über eine
Stunde--" (p. 34), to which Frau Blitzer replies: "Was?
Du nichtsnutziger Kerl, was lärmst du? Bist schon wieder
nichts nutz, abgeschabte Laus? Den Augenblick trag ich
meinen Kaffee wieder herunter--" Their dialogue continues
in this jocular mode:

> Frau Blitzer: ...Nu, ist der Kaffee gut? Ist er
> nicht? Gleich sag mir's, oder ich
> reiss Ihm das letzte Haar aus Seinem
> kahlen Kopf heraus.
>
> Pätus (trinkt): Unvergleichlich.--Aye!--Ich hab in
> meinem Leben keinen bessern
> getrunken.
>
> Frau Blitzer: Siehts du Hundejunge! Wenn du die
> Mutter nicht hättest, die sich deiner
> annähme und dir zu essen und zu
> trinken gäbe, du müsstest an der
> Strasse verhungern...(p. 35)

However, serious undertones develop. "Der Kaffee schmeckt
nach Gerste" (p. 35) Fritz von Berg complains like the

child who notes that the Emperor has no clothes. Pätus
tastes the coffee again and throws the coffee pot out of
the window. This gesture does not reflect harmony between Pätus and Frau Blitzer, nor do her suddenly cold
words: "Wie? Was zum Teufel, was ist das? Herr, ist
Er rasend oder plagt Ihn gar der Teufel" (p. 36). The
encounter concludes with Frau Blitzer's threat of legal
action against Pätus because she knows he does not have
the financial resources to pay for the damaged coffee pot.
After Frau Blitzer has left, Pätus turns to Fritz with
the resigned comment: "Was ist zu machen, Bruder! man
muss sie schon ausrasen lassen" to which Fritz responds:
"Aber für dein Geld?" (p. 36).

The apparently harmless verbal fencing match has un-
masked itself as a thin disguise for feelings of frustration and powerlessness harbored by both Pätus and Frau
Blitzer. Pätus' economic plight forces him to remain in
the sub-standard household of Frau Blitzer and she apparently depends on boarders for part of her livelihood. The
persiflage between Pätus and Frau Blitzer veils anger
which both conversational partners fear to express overtly.
When she calls him "Hundejunge" and he retorts with "Das
Wetter soll dich regieren," the critical vocabulary spoken
in jest contains more than a kernel of truth as humor
often does. Both Pätus and Frau Blitzer are using

language to conceal the truth which is revealed only by
Pätus' act of throwing the coffee pot out of the window.

The frequent occurrence of gesture in Non-Aristotelian drama has been noted by critics. According to Crumbach, "Demonstration ist nicht Selbstzweck, sie ist ein
Mittel, die Hauptelemente des Dramas ins Licht zu setzen."[26] In the Hofmeister and Soldaten, gesture is a
means whereby truth which is concealed by language is revealed. As in Ugolino, Lenz's frequent stage directions
primarily refer to gestures. The character's mode of
speaking has a mimetic quality indicated by descriptions
of tone, for example "brüllt mit einer erschröcklichen
Stimme" (p. 202) and "weil in tiefen Gedanken gesessen,
ruft sie ängstlich" (p. 214), and by actions which
visualize the connotation of words: "Charlotte (droht ihr
mit dem Dintenfass): Du--" (p. 215). Theatrical discourse is, of course, by nature mimetic, but gesture for
Lenz becomes a separate language. We find, for example,
that Wesener is overly concerned with Marie's liaison
with Desportes. His warnings and protestations are loud
and constant: "Fort von mir, du Luder--willst die
Mätresse vom Baron werden?" (p. 194) and "Weil er dir ein
paar Schmeicheleien und so und so--Einer ist so gut wie
der andere, lehr du mich die jungen Milizen mit kennen."
(p. 189). However, Wesener's gestures reveal an entirely

different sentiment. When Wesener first enters the scene, he walks up to Desportes and the stage directions tells us "umarmt ihn" (p. 186). Later in the same scene, when he refuses Desportes' present to his daughter and returns it to him, we are informed "gibt sie ihm lächelnd zurück" (p. 188--emphasis mine). This is only one example of how gesture often contradicts and certainly illuminates the words being spoken, as is also the case with Pätus' coffee pot. Gestures are such an inherent element of Lenz's dramas and so often reveal what language conceals that their frequent occurrence is another of the several indications of language skepticism. The recognition of the capriciousness and limitations of language forces the dramatist to search out other means whereby truth can be illustrated. He resorts to gesture to express that which "alienated" man can no longer express linguistically be-cause he does not speak "naively" but hides behind com-plicated language games. Gesture, which has a long theatrical tradition, attains a more complicated func-tion in Non-Aristotelian drama, where it primarily serves to unmask the truth which language veils and which language can no longer convey. His reliance on gesture to reveal the truth because language fails represents a major contradiction of Lenz's enlightened notion that linguistic problems can be resolved by the application of rational principles and that language is reliable as an accurate instrument of communication. Lenz's theoretical writings about language and his treatment of language in his dramas are another example of the profoundly paradoxical nature of his oeuvre.

Unlike classical drama whose convention requires that characters speak a uniform language, the figures in the Soldaten and Hofmeister, which correctly has been identified by Höllerer as the beginning of modern drama, employ a variety of linguistic codes.[27] The failure to achieve communication and its accompanying personal isolation and alienation, a phenomenon absent in classical drama, is at least partially the result of the collision of various language spheres. Language is used by Lenz to mirror the individual psyche and milieu and as a technique of realistic character portrayal. Language skepticism and a recognition of the limitations of language are reflected in the characters' inability to communicate, struggle with the word and the recurrent use of gestures. In the Hofmeister and the Soldaten--a world in which the understanding Lenz thought possible through reformation of language has not occurred--he has created a linguistic tapestry which illustrates the complexity of the communicative act and thereby the complexity of life.

3. Structure--A Montage of Character Constellations

The episodic structure of Lenz's dramas has been often
noted. Although the <u>Hofmeister</u> and the <u>Soldaten</u> retain
the conventional five act division, they are not constructed along the traditional schema of a systematic plot
development. In the "Anmerkungen" Lenz proposes a radically new dramatic structure. No longer is the plot to be
linear and unified, but it is to consist of many single
scenes following each other in rapid succession and is to
be held together by the dramatic hero

> ...bei den alten Griechen wars die Handlung,
> die sich das Volk zu sehen versammlete. Bei
> uns ists die Reihe von Handlungen, die wie
> Donnerschläge aufeinander folgen, eine die
> andere stützen und heben, in ein grosses Ganzes
> zusammenfliessen müssen, das hernach nichts
> mehr und nichts minder ausmacht, als die
> Hauptperson, wie sie in der ganzen Gruppe ihrer
> Mithändler hervorsticht. (p. 731)

Lenz's primary concern is always the dramatic character. The dramatic figure must be seen from a variety of
perspectives and his motives must be explored in great detail. A unified plot which relentlessly strives towards
its climax and denouement gives the dramatist fewer
opportunities to present his characters in their multiple
psychological manifestations. Lenz's aim is to dissect
the individual who is after all a "zusammengesetztes
Wesen" (Titel, I, 484) and to uncover the intricacies

of the human psyche. In other words, Lenz wants to portray man in his "totality" and illuminate his character
from various perspectives so that he and his actions may
be understood better. In order to achieve that, "tausend
grosse Einzelheiten" ("Anmerkungen," p. 732) have to be
depicted and the plot can no longer be a unified whole, but
must consist of multiple actions and many individualized
scenes.

Lenz adheres to his intent in the Hofmeister and
Soldaten. The unities of time and place are disregarded
because the dramatic characters must be seen over a period
of time and events must occur in several locations in
order to develop a comprehensive picture of their circumstances. Thus the action continues over at least three
years in the Hofmeister and over several months in the
Soldaten. The scenes in both dramas change to various
cities tracing the travels of the individual characters.
The Hofmeister consists of thirty-four individual scenes
and the Soldaten of thirty-five. (It is interesting to
note that a modern play like Peter Weiss' Marat Sade
consists of 33 scenes). The scenes do follow each other
in rapid succession and the tempo increases particularly
in the fourth act of the Soldaten where the dizzying
change of extremely brief episodes illustrates the confusion of events which are engulfing Marie. Five changes of

location occur between the fourth and eighth scenes, and each episode is extremely brief. The fifth scene, which is the shortest one Lenz composed, consists of only a few words by Wesener: "Marie fortgelaufen--! Ich bin des Todes" (p. 233). After this utterance Wesener exists and the scene shifts to Mary's apartment.

The individual scenes are open-ended. Since the plot does not follow a linear action, no resolution occurs in individual scenes requiring the characters to execute a specific action. For example, Scene 5 of Act II in the Hofmeister ends with an incomplete dialogue between Läuffer and Gustchen. No understanding has occurred between the two characters, and the status of their relationship remains undetermined. The same is true in the Soldaten. In Scene 3 of Act III for example, Marie has discovered Desportes' sudden departure and attempts to re-establish contact with Stolzius. At the same time Wesener promises to enforce Desportes' "obligations" to Marie. Open-ended scenes suggest that the characters have certain choices available to them. They are not committed to only one course of action which logically arises out of a specific event and leads to the following episode. The diversified and non-finalized scenes also illustrate that the individual exists in a constant state of flux and change, a state of becoming and not of completion.

Ideally, Lenz views man's state as a process of continuous becoming "Wir sollen immer weiter gehen und nie stille stehen" (Titel, I, 489) and his destiny as an "immer-währendes Wachsen, Zunehmen, Forschen und Bemühen (Titel, I, 489). Paradixocally, however, the Lenzian hero who appears to have every opportunity for a choice of action, is also trapped within the sphere of the individual scene. Because a logical thread does not lead from scene to scene and the episodes are not a chain of causes and events as they are in Lessing's dramas, for instance, the character often becomes the helpless victim of the un-forseeable circumstances of the immediate scene. He is not an autonomous individual who holds the scenes to-gether by the sheer force of his personality as Lenz had intended; Läuffer and Marie are not the powerful central characters in whose persona the splintered plot is uni-fied into "ein grosses Ganze." (p. 730). Instead, they frequently do not act at all and are incapable of con-trolling the events in the drama. Lenz's technique of the Einselszenen again illustrates man's paradoxical posi-tion between freedom and determinism and Lenz's oscilla-tion between idealism and realism.

The alienation and isolation experienced by the dramatis personae are also illustrated through the structure of the drama. Characters appear closed off from

each other in separate rooms. Gustchen retreats to her
own room, (p. 40), Marie shuts herself off in her room
after her first encounter with Desportes, (p. 197), and
Läuffer becomes a virtual prisoner in the house of the
Major (pp. 12-51). Windows, a means whereby contact with
the outside world can be established, are mentioned. It
is noted numerous times in the stage directions that
characters position themselves near windows: "Jungfer
Zipfersaat ganz verlegen tritt ans Fenster" (p. 208);
"Geheimrat, Gustchen, Major stehn in ihrem Hause am
Fenster" (p. 83). And in one major scene Marie stand by
a window but closes it and pulls down a curtain to shut
out the storm raging outside suggesting that the desired
contact has not been established. The preponderence of
scenes that are set inside of rooms corresponds all too
well with the protagonists' state of mind; isolated,
incarcerated, alienated. Time also functions to underline
the estrangement and impotence of the dramatic figures.
In the Hofmeister time does not consist of manageable segments but becomes as distended and languorous as Läuffer's
life itself. It is mentioned only in passing: "Major:
Ein ganzes Jahr--Bruder Geheimrat--Ein ganzes Jahr--und
niemand weiss, wohin sie [Gustchen] gestoben oder geflogen
ist" (p. 62). Clearly, the characters have as little
control over time as they have over their own lifes. The

off-handed mention of the passage of years, also in regard
to the length of time Läuffer has spent as a tutor, underlines the passivity and inactivity of Läuffer and the
other characters. Time passes in a somewhat more concen-
trated manner in the Soldaten, but then Marie is a more
active character than Läuffer. As a whole, however, she
too exists in unstructured time. Time attains a universal quality and becomes synonymous with life.

It is frequently asserted that in dramas which follow
an episodic rather than a linear structure, individual
scenes may be interchanged or left out entirely. This is
an assertion which should be approached with caution.
While the scenes in Non-Aristotelian drama do not follow
a linear development of the plot, there certainly is a
logical reason for their existence. Lenz's desire to portray the individual aspects of a character's life and thus
present the dramatic figure in an approximation of its
totality determines his choice of scenes. If a scene were
left out or interchanged, a vital aspect of a character's
psychological portrait and his motivation would become un-
clear. It would therefore be willful tampering with the
unique fabric of a specific drama if individual scenes
were arbitrarily removed or interchanged. Thus the sudden
and apparently arbitrary transformation of scene from
Desportes and Marie at the end of Act I to the romp in the

house of Aaron with which Act II begins (p. 197) appears
to be irrelevant. Viewed in the entirety of the drama,
however, it provides an important signal of the frivolous
nature of Desportes' character because he is, after all,
one of the officers. The officers' behavior reiterates
the ominous prophecy of the grandmother's song which
immediately precedes the scene and increases the spectators apprehension and concern for Marie. This is only one
example of a non sequitur scene which nevertheless has a
vital function in the development and exposition of the
individual characters. Each scene functions like a segment in a mosaic, and their totality represents the multicolored portrait of the characters' psyche and the society
in which they "exist."

Läuffer and Marie, the central characters in the
Hofmeister and Soldaten, are not autonomous figures. They
do not dominate the action and do not cause the series of
episodes to come together into a homogenous whole. The
characters as a whole do dominate the dramas however, and
the scenes are bound together by virtue of the dramatic
figures' participation in them. Essentially, the dramatis personae give the two plays the structural unity without which any work of art would be an impossibility. We
must keep in mind Shaftesbury's "inner form"--a structural
technique which develops organically out of the content of

the drama and is not externally superimposed upon it. We
are partially indebted for the following insights to
Edward P. Harris. Harris sees a basic unity of theme,
plot and characterization in the Hofmeister in the functional interrelationships of groupings of dramatic persons. According to Harris, the Hofmeister is a Familienstück in which stable groups of positive relationships have
been disrupted and are restored. The dramatic conflict
is contained in the "force field" of a triangular structure.[28]

    While we disagree with Harris' conclusion that the
Hofmeister "is concerned with the story of the disruption
and ultimate reestablishment of a positive familial
unit,"[29] and do not follow the character relationships he
has determined, we find his approach of seeking unity
within the schema of characterizations useful. It reflects Lenz's aim to achieve unity through character,
albeit by virtue of the central character ("Anmerkungen,"
p. 730).

    In both the Soldaten and the Hofmeister, three major
character constellations exist which absorb the dynamics
of the many diverse scenes. In the Hofmeister we find
the following three primary groups of characters: 1) the
Berg family, which includes Läuffer not as an integral
part of the family (but then, the family is not an inte-

grated unit anyway) but as a member of a group of characters involved in specific situations and events; 2) Wenzeslaus, who is later joined by Läuffer; and 3) the students Fritz and Pätus, with Fritz of course also belonging
to the Berg family. It is already apparent that individual characters shift from one character constellation to
another and thereby provide necessary connections between
characters, situations and events. Both Läuffer and Fritz
are included in the character constellations of the Berg
household; Fritz later branches out and provides the link
to the episodes depicting the student life in Leipzig and
Läuffer represents the connection between Wenzeslaus and
the milieu of the public school. It is important to note
that the dramatic conflict does not extend across the
entirety of the play as is characteristic of Aristotelian
drama, but that conflict and resulting tension are contained within individual scenes. In Non-Aristotelian
drama the antagonist is less clearly defined than in
classical drama. In classical drama the gods are unquestionably the antagonists of the dramatic hero. In the
bourgeois drama of the 18th century and much of 19th
century drama, the conflict is primarily enacted between
the individual and society. In many 20th century dramas, however, the conflict is played out _within_ the individual
and life itself becomes the adversary. Büchner's Woyzek

and Danton are examples of this latter kind of dramatic
hero. Inner conflict already plays a major role in Lenz's
dramas and accounts for the self-contained tension of the
dramatic episodes.

Most of the first act of the Hofmeister takes place in
the household of Major Berg and introduces all of the members of the primary character configuration--that of the
Berg family. The spectator witnesses encounters between
the Geheimrat and the Major, the Majorin and Läuffer,
Läuffer and the Major, and finally Fritz, Gustchen and the
Geheimrat. Läuffer is the central figure in the first
act, and his precarious and uncomfortable position in the
Berg household is established. A potential complication
arising out of Fritz's and Gustchen's separation is
brought to the attention of the audience. The second act
elaborates the complications which are implied in the first
act. Transition is provided by the figure of the Geheimrat who is depicted in a dialogue with Läuffer's
father (pp. 25-31). Later in the act, (p. 33), the
second primary character constellation, that of the students in Leipzig, is introduced. Again structural unity
is achieved through the presence of a dramatic character--
Fritz von Berg who originally belonged to and has become
separated from the primary character constellation. The
spectator follows Fritz to Leipzig in order to observe

the life of a student and thereby become acquainted with
an additional facet of a character's composition. That
Fritz is not malicious or unfaithful to Gustchen is
visually demonstrated, a technique which is more effective
than a mere narration of his reliability and loyalty would
be.

The third major character constellation, that of
Wenzeslaus-Läuffer (and later Lise), comes into play in
the third act. This time the structural link is provided by Läuffer's presence. Act III consists of only
four scenes alternating between members of the Berg con-
figuration and the Läuffer-Wenzeslaus constellation.
After Act III and the introduction of all three character
constellations, the scenes alternate much more rapidly
among the three groups of characters. Act IV complicates
the picture because Gustchen has left the Berg constellation and acts on her own, although she is soon joined by
her father and is absent from her primary character
group during only one scene, (p. 64). In Act V, which is
the longest act, the focus switches rapidly from one
character constellation to another. The rapid transition
among the three character constellations suggests the
cinematic or montage technique of many current novels and plays
plays. Groups of characters are briefly illuminated and
disappear again in the darkness while the spotlight shifts

to another character constellation or to an individual
character. A similar technique is evident in the final
act of the Soldaten. For maximum effect the scenes must
occur in extremely rapid succession, a situation that is
best achieved through modern stage lighting techniques.
Montage, of course, is related to cinematography. Wilpert defines montage as follows:

> Die schon im Drehbuch vorgesehene
> künstlerische Aneinanderfügung einzelner
> Bildfolgen und Szenen in räumlich und
> zeitlich verschiedenen Situationen, die
> nicht sachlich-handlungsmässig oder
> gedanklich verbunden sind, durch die
> Assoziationsfügung einzelner konkreter
> Gegenstände.[30]

The fragmentary "Einzelszenen" of Lenz's dramas which do
not exhibit thematic unity anticipate the modern montage
technique.[31] Lenz's Hofmeister is not a play in which a
temporarily disrupted world order is re-established. The
existing world order is questioned throughout both the
Hofmeister and the Soldaten and unity of theme and character do not exist in these two diversified and paradoxical dramas. But structural unity, which is a dramaturgi-
cal and not a philosophical problem, does exist and is
provided by the dramatis personae themselves.

   We have already noted that a tripartite division into character constellations may also be observed in the

Soldaten. The three major groups which concern us here
are 1) Marie and the Wesener family; 2) Desportes and the
group of officers surrounding him; and 3) the Gräfin and
her household. We must not forget Stolzius, but because
of his initial link with Marie he can be incorporated into
the milieu of the Wesener family, whereas later he joins
the group of the soldiers although he is at no time an
integral part of that group. The dramatic figures do not
serve as links among the three character configurations
in the same manner in which they sustain a unifying function in the Hofmeister. Instead a definite rhythm develops
in the Soldaten as the result of the character constellation's sequential appearance on stage. The first and
second acts alternate scenes focusing on the Wesener
household with episodes depicting the milieu of the
soldiers. A brief scene depicting Stolzius and his
mother is interjected in the first act, (p. 184). Toward the end of the second act, (pp. 206-221) and well into the third act a pattern develops consisting of a
Wesener-Soldaten-Stolzius sequence, a composition which is
interrupted by the entrance of the Gräfin, (p. 221). The
remainder of the fourth act and the fifth act, (pp. 221-
247), repeates the Wesener-Soldaten alternation for the
most part with one scene in each act reserved for the

additional development of the Gräfin and her milieu
(p. 231 and p. 243).

As in the <u>Hofmeister</u>, the various strands of action
in the <u>Soldaten</u> intensely affect the central character,
but do not converge in her persona. The drama has an
open ending which leaves Marie's future in serious doubt.
Her inner conflict has not been resolved and the play
does not represent a harmonious whole. Structural unity,
however, has been achieved to a large degree by the rhyth-
mic reappearance of specific character configurations.

Lenz's contemporaries were rightfully perturbed by
the fragmented nature of the <u>Hofmeister</u> and the <u>Soldaten</u>,
for neither play adheres to the traditional structural
principles familiar to 18th century German dramatists and
theoreticians. The splintered action which so consistently characterizes Lenz's plays is already evident in
Gerstenberg's <u>Ugolino</u>, for example, a drama which also
baffled his contemporaries. Although outwardly a model
of Aristotelian dramatic structure, the play's depiction
of the characters' psychological deterioration does not
systematically develop a conflict. As a result the action is fragmented; however, structural unity is attained
and the play is held together primarily by the characters
themselves. This is also the case in Lenz's plays.

<u>Der</u> <u>Hofmeister</u> and <u>Die</u> <u>Soldaten</u> are two plays which

cannot be easily categorized. Karl S. Guthke notes that
even their author was uncertain whether the plays should
be known as "comedies," "tragedies," or neither of the
two. He traces the history of Lenz's hesitancy in identifying his dramas: Although Lenz originally identified
the Soldaten as a comedy, he later observed in a letter
that the play would better be called a Schauspiel. The
Hofmeister also shared the title of comedy, but in
several letters Lenz refers to it as a Trauerspiel.[32]

Lenz's indecisiveness is the result of the enigmatic
quality of his two major dramas, which do not comfortably
fit into either genre but hover in a sphere between the
tragic and the comic. His original designation of the
two dramas as comedy reflects the traditional genre division which requires that tragedy concern itself only
with important events and persons of significance and
comedy be confined to depicting the lower classes. In his
theoretical writings, however, Lenz had already noted
that today's dramatist must write tragedy and comedy
simultaneously.

> Komödie ist Gemälde der menschlichen Gesellschaft,
> und wenn die ernsthaft wird, kann das Gemälde
> nicht lachend werden. ...Daher müssen unsere
> deutschen Komödienschreiber komisch und tragisch
> zugleich schreiben...(Titel, I, 419)

And indeed, Lenz's Hofmeister and Soldaten are not comedies
in the traditional style, but they are dramas which have

the propensity to move the spectator to laughter and
tears simultaneously. The evocation of pity or empathy
with the dramatic hero is an Aristotelian concept which
is elicited by the Non-Aristotelian Lenz. The Lenzian
spectator is moved by the protagonist's psychological
fragmentation and societal alienation.

One solution to the genre problem is to identify
those dramas which contain both tragic and comic elements
as "tragicomedies." Tragicomedy as a genre has a history
which dates back to Euripides, Plautus, Marlow, Shakespeare,
Molière and the medieval mystery plays.[33] In a major study,
Geschichte und Poetik der deutschen Tragikomödie, and in a
subsequent article dealing specifically with the Hofmeister
and Soldaten, Guthke identifies the two plays as tragicomedies.
Guthke is concerned with establishing a universally valid
structural pinciple for tragicomedy and notes a synthesis
rather than a coexistence of tragic and comic elements in
Lenz's plays. Characteristic of Lenz's tragicomic
structure is the incongruence of character and situation,
a structural principle which Lenz originates.[34] Guthke's
interpretation of Lenz's plays as tragicomedies is rejected by Eric Oehlenschläger, who considers the terminus "tragicomedy" too innocuous to encompass the
complexity of Lenz's dramas. In Oehlenschläger's words:

> Er [Lenz] hat es auf die volle Spannweite dramatischer Wirkungsmöglichkeiten überhaupt abgesehen. Das 'Schröckliche,' üblicherweise in der Tragödie ressortiert, holt Lenz dabei noch in den Spielraum der Komödie ein, nun aber--das ist das Ausschlaggebende--nicht unter dem Signum tragischer Notwendigkeit, sondern als Moment im 'Zusammenlauf zufälliger Ursachen.' Die Komödie wird auf diese Weise bis zum Zerreissen beansprucht, vielleicht überschritten hin auf etwas, das nicht mehr exakt gattungstheoretisch lokalisierbar ist, das aber jedenfalls nicht durch die Bezeichnung 'Tragikomödie' verharmlost werden sollte.[35]

I agree with those critics who are uncomfortable with Guthke's analysis. J. L. Styan notes in his study _The Dark Comedy_ that "the term 'tragicomedy' was equivocal enough in the past," but that it is not appropriate for the new serious drama which concerns us now.[36] Styan's work concentrates on 20th century dramatists. He begins his treatise with the following quotation attributed to García Lorca: "If in certain scenes the audience doesn't know what to do, whether to laugh or to cry, that will be a success for me." Styan holds that "such a statement by a playwright could not easily have been made in any century but our own."[37] But of course a similar statement was made by Lenz a playwright of the 18th century, although he seems to express apprehension about the inevitable coexistence of tragedy and comedy and is not as comfortable with the phenomenon as Lorca. Writing in the epistolary novel _Der Waldbruder_, the character Honesta notes:

> Kein Zustand der Seele ist mir fataler als wenn
> ich lachen und weinen zugleich muss, Sie wissen
> ich will alles ganz haben, entweder erhabene
> Melancholie oder ausgelassene Lustigkeit--
> indessen ist es nun einmal so und ich kann mir
> Nicht helfen. (Titel, I, 308)

A subsequent letter by the same character contains the
following observation: "Ich fürchte sehr, das Stück
könne eher tragisch als komisch endigen" (Titel, I,
310). The tragicomic sense seems to be a troublesome
but dominant factor in Lenz's perception of life and conception of dramatic art. It reflects the stance of the
disillusioned idealist, who has chosen to laugh through
his tears at the human comedy. Lenz's observations anticipate the duplistic nature of many 20th century dramas.
His own plays have a greater affinity with the comic-
serious dramas of our century than they do with the more
conventional plays of the past which occasionally mix
tragic and comic elements. The nature of his dramas is
therefore better understood by looking forward to 20th century
playwrights, than by relating the plays to past dramatic
traditions. Der Hofmeister and Die Soldaten cannot comfortably be called tragicomedies because they do not
satisfy certain basic criteria. Both tragedy and comedy
require faith in an imperturbable world order which is
temporarily disrupted but re-established. In Guthke's
words:

> Und zwar handelt es sich in beiden Gattungen
> [comedy and tragedy] um die Störung einer
> solchen normhaften Ordnung durch ein Ungewöhnliches,
> oft durch den zentralen Helden, der sich in
> Auflehnung oder im Ausweichen über sie hinweg-
> setzen möchte; und hier wie dort behauptet sich
> schliesslich die Ordnung als unerschütterliches
> Weltgesetz.38

Guthke is correct when he includes tragicomedy in this
criteria: "Lässt man das Spannungsverhältnis zur Ordnung,
zum Rahmen, den Widerspruch als Grundform der Tragik wie
der Komik gelten, so ist nicht einzusehen, warum der Konflikt nicht auch von beiden Seiten zugleich zu betrachten
sein soll.39 In other words, tragicomedy like tragedy and
comedy requires faith in a cosmos.

The troubled drama of Weiss and Dürrenmatt
and that of their predecessors Wedekind, Büchner and
Lenz, however, does not originate with faith in an un-
shakeable world order. Harmony is _not_ restored in the
final acts of these plays because it does not exist in
the beginning. The spectator does _not_ experience
catharsis, which is another criterion of tragicomedy. The
16th century Italian dramatist Giambattista Guarini defines the nature and effect of tragicomedy as follows:

> ...an action that is feigned and in which are
> mingled all the tragic and comic parts that
> can coexist in verisimilitude and decorum,
> properly arranged in a single dramatic form
> with the end of purging with pleasure the
> sadness of the hearers. (emphasis mine)40

Tragicomedy requires that the spectator leaves the
theater with the conviction that the problems which have
been raised have also been resolved. The modern plays
which Lenz's dramas anticipate leave the spectator with
feelings of uneasiness and apprehension. And they leave
the critic with the problem of how to fit these mavericks
which presume to dominate the modern stage into the existing dramatic tradition.

As has been noted, it is tempting to link Lenz's
plays with the dramatic forms extant in the 18th century,
a solution which is always unsatisfactory. Undoubtedly,
elements of various dramatic trends are present in Lenz's
plays, for a work of art does not exist in a vacuum.
Thus influences of the Saxon comedy and the commedia
dell'arte are identified by Guthke in the Hofmeister,[41]
and certain aspects of the "bürgerliche Trauerspiel" are
evident in the Soldaten and the Hofmeister. But to
suggest that the Hofmeister is a Familienstück in which
unity and harmony prevail at the beginning, are disrupted
by the intrusion of Läuffer and are restored before the
final curtain falls, as Harris does, represents an attempt
to force the play into the mold of 18th century bourgeois drama. Even if one regards Läuffer, whose monologue
begins the play, as an unreliable commentator, it is
made clear in the first act that the Berg family does not

enjoy a harmonious familial relationship. From the
beginning, the Major and the Geheimrat disagree concerning
their philosophy of education. Dissonance is expressed
between the Major and the Majorin, the Majorin and
Gustchen, and the Major and Leopold. And as has been
shown, the characters themselves are not harmonious individuals, but inwardly discordant personalities. Finally,
the last scene (p. 100), which does depict the reunited
family, is at best bittersweet. The exaggerated artificiality of the final tableau, which includes Pätus'
father and his previously neglected grandmother, must be
seen as a parody of familial relationships rather than a
celebration of the harmonious family unit.

Andreas Huyssen also relates the <u>Hofmeister</u> to the
"bürgerliche Trauerspiel" of the Enlightenment, but notes
that the optimism of the Enlightenment has been replaced
by an all pervasive pessimism.[42] For Huyssen the question
of genre is "ein politisches und sozialgeschichtliches
Problem erster Ordnung."[43] Lenz's intensive concern with
dramatic form in his theoretical writings, however, makes
it clear that for him the problem was primarily an
<u>aesthetic</u> one. Lenz consciously struggled to evolve a new
dramatic form, a quest which is obvious in the "Anmerkungen," in "Rezensionen des Neuen Menoza, von dem Verfasser selbst aufgesetzt," and in "über die Veränderung

des Theaters im Shakespear." In one of his letters, the
following revealing remark appears: "Wer auf dem
gebahnten Wege forttrabt, mit dem halt ich's keine
Viertelstunde aus."[44] Lenz purposefully experimented with
a new dramatic structure. The Non-Aristotelian drama he
advocates took its inspiration from Shakespeare and is
glimpsed in the theories of Bodmer and Breitinger and the
other dramatists preceding Lenz who attempted to formulate
a dramatic theory and practice independent of classical
drama. With the _Hofmeister_ and the _Soldaten_ Lenz succeeded
in creating a new drama which is the beginning of a group
of dramas representative of our times. As yet,
these plays defy categorization, but they have one primary
characteristic in common: they reflect a certain ambivalence, a juxtaposition of dark and light elements which
leaves the audience uncertain as to whether it should
laught or cry. Lenz's dramas probably have a greater
affinity with those of Dürrenmatt than they do with 18th
century drama. For Dürrenmatt, as for Lenz, character
is the primary concern, and he too endeavors to depict
the multiplicity of the world.[45] Most intensely of all,
however, they share a view of life and theater as being
simultaneously tragic and comic. For Dürrenmatt tragedy
is no longer possible, and he calls his dramas comedies,
but they are _dark comedies_ in which tragedy is contained.

> Doch ist das Tragische immer noch möglich,
> auch wenn die reine Tragödie nicht mehr möglich
> ist. Wir können das Tragische aus der Komödie
> heraus erzielen, hervorbringen als einen
> schrecklichen Moment, als einen sich öffnenden
> Abgrund, so sind ja schon viele Tragödien
> Shakespeares Komödien, aus denen heraus das
> Tragische aufsteigt.46

The serious-comical drama which mixes the
traditionally separated high and low style and contains
both tragic and comic elements seems to have taken the
place of classical tragedy and comedy. Lenz's <u>Hofmeister</u>
and <u>Soldaten</u> are the first of a series of plays which we
now identify as "dark comedies." These new dramas are
not like ancient tragedy, because modern man has become
too analytical. In Lenz's words: "Was ehmals grausen
macht, das soll uns lächeln machen" (Titel, II, 275).
But neither are the new dramas comedies in which man's
follies are ridiculed. Whether "das Schröckliche" is all
pervasive and engendered by tragic necessity, as it is in
antique tragedy, or appears as a brief moment in comedy
as the result of chance, the pain man experiences in his
relentless struggle against an implacable universe cannot
be minimized. Classical tragedy seems to be an impossibility in our age. But the plays which we today term
"dark comedies" retain the tragic sense.

In the "Anmerkungen" Lenz redefines the nature of
tragedy and comedy: "Meiner Meinung nach wäre immer der

Hauptgedanke einer Komödie eine Sache, einer Tragödie
eine Person" (p. 744--emphasis mine). According to his
theory the events should be of greater importance in his
comedies than the characters. This is not the case, however,
for the characters, rather than the events, are of primary
concern in the Hofmeister and the Soldaten. Paradox, which
is a consistent characteristic of Lenz's oeuvre, is also
apparent in the structure of his dramas. The dramatic hero
does not dominate events as Lenz's theory claims they must.
He becomes the victim of circumstances and unity of action
is not attained through his persona, although structural
unity is achieved through interlinking character constellations.
The open-ended structure of individualized scenes allows
the dramatic figures a choice of action. At the same time,
however, they become prisoners of individual scenes and of
themselves. The all pervasive contradictions within Lenz's
dramas have a striking affinity with the theater of today.

CHAPTER VI

CONCLUSION

"Mein Glück in meinem Vaterlande ist verdorben, weil
es bekannt ist, dass ich Komödien geschrieben," Lenz
writes in a letter to Gotter in August of 1775.[1] In
another letter to the same addressee dated two years
earlier, Lenz had expressed the sincere hope that his
critic Wieland would retract the ascerbic dismissal of
his Menoza as a Mischspiel,[2] which Wieland did not do.
These are only two examples of the many times Lenz found
himself in the position of having to defend his plays
against those theoreticians and critics who continued to
uphold the norms of the classicistic tradition.

Theory and practice were, as is frequently the case,
at odds. In spite of Gottsched's "reform" of the German
theater and recurrent efforts by his and other dramatists
to establish a solid classicistic tradition on the German
stage, the classicistic drama never did enjoy the whole-
hearted support in Germany which it commanded in France.
Opposition to Gottched was swift and forceful, and the
resulting aesthetic debate converging on the Aristotelian
principle of art as mimesis continued the "battle of the
ancients and the moderns"[3] which had emerged in France

264

during the 17th century. It was again at a high pitch when Lenz published his major plays Der neue Menoza and Der Hofmeister in 1774 and Die Soldaten in 1776.

According to August Wilhelm Schlegel, Non-Aristotelian or "romantic" drama has its origin in the medieval morality play which flourished in England and to some degree in Germany in the 15th century.[4] Certainly the drama of the 17th century was Non-Aristotelian, and in its more debased forms it evoked Gottsched's outrage and Lessing's disdain. While in its early manifestation the new "formless" drama which so vigorously demanded attention did not command the critics' respect or admiration, it seems to have coexisted, at least in seminal form, along with its more reputable brother, the classical drama of the ancients.

In his Vorlesungen über dramatische Kunst und Literatur (1809-11), a series of lectures which attempts to define the nature of Non-Aristotelian drama, August Wilhelm Schlegel notes the modern's delight in the mixture of disparate elements counterpointing the classicist's vigorous separation of things dissimilar.[5] A. W. Schlegel has identified a fundamental characteristic of the new drama, one which was also recognized by the earlier 18th century Non-Aristotelians. His uncle, Johann Elias Schlegel, had already suggested the possibility of a union between laughter

and tears, between tragedy and comedy. The most profound
sense of the tragicomic, however, is exhibited in the
dramatic theories and practice of J. M. R. Lenz.

Lenz's theory and practice represent a confrontation
between the ideals of the German Enlightenment--faith in
the perfectability of man and the resolution of social and
personal problems by the application of reason--and subsequent disillusionment and existential doubt when man,
viewed realistically and in historical perspective, emerges
as an irrational being who shows little interest in attaining
a state of perfection. Lenz's theory of the drama and
philosophical stance, hovering between idealism and realism,
are neither an extension of the Enlightenment nor a complete
rejection thereof, but a new vision of the drama and the
society it portrays, one which has its roots in the writings
of Bodmer and Breitinger and the other 18th century dramatists
who did not fully accept Aristotelian dramatic principles.
The resulting tragic-comic, often grotesque drama of Lenz
has a singualr appeal to the contemporary reader, for in
its contradictory nature he recognizes a kindred spirit.
Lenz's dramatic reforms, startling to an 18th century
audience, have become accepted practice today. The disturbing
and troubling plays which Lenz introduced continue to be
written by 20th century dramatists.

NOTES

Chapter 1

1
Theodor Friedrich, Die Anmerkungen übers Theater des Dichters J. M. R. Lenz (Leipzig: Voigtländer, 1909), p. 2.

2
Ibid., p. 3. Italics mine.

3
Ibid., p. 4.

4
Ibid., p. 4. Also see Friedrich Nicolai, Leiden und Freuden Werthers des Mannes (1775); rpt. (München: Fink, 1972), p. 55.

5
Ibid., p. 4.

6
Curt Hohoff, J. M. R. Lenz (Reinbek: Rowohlt, 1977), p. 45.

7
John Osborne, J. M. R. Lenz: The Renunciation of Heroism (Göttingen: Vandenhoeck & Ruprecht, 1975), p. 23.

8
Bertolt Brecht adapted Der Hofmeister for the German stage in 1950 and Heinar Kipphardt did the same with Die Soldaten in 1968. For an analysis of the adaptions see: Laurence P. A. Kitching, Der Hofmeister. A Critical Analysis of Bertolt Brecht's Adaption of J. M. R. Lenz's Drama (München: Fink, 1976) and Karl H. Schoeps, "Zwei Moderne Lenz-Bearbeitungen," Montashefte, 67 (1975), pp. 437-51.

9
Jakob Michael Reinhold Lenz, Werke und Schriften, ed. Britta Titel and Hellmut Haug (Stuttgart: Goverts, 1966), I, 572.

Chapter II

1
Hermann Hettner, Geschichte der deutschen Literatur
im achtzehnten Jahrhundert (Braunschweig: Vieweg & Sohn,
1849), III, 328.

2
Ibid., p. 328.

3
Jakob Immanuel Pyra, Erweis, dass die Gottschedianische Sekte den Geschmack Verderbe/Fortsetzung des
Erweises (1743-1744), rpt. (Hildesheim/New York: Olms,
1974), p. 23.

4
It is incorrect to assume, however, that Gottsched
completely eliminated the marvelous from poetry. Franz
Servaes in "Die Poetik Gottscheds und der Schweizer,"
in Quellen und Forschungen zur Sprach- und Cultur-
geschichte der Germanischen Völker, ed. Bernhard Ten
Brink, Ernst Martin and Erich Schmidt (Strassburg:
Trübner, 1887), p. 29, explains Gottsched's position:
Gottsched hatte also von vornherein dem Wunderbaren
gegenüber eine gewisse feindselige Stellung eingenommen.
Trotzdem aber konnte er ihm die Aufnahme in seine Poetik
nicht versagen. Es hatte sich durch Boileaus Longin-
Übersetzung, die sich als ein 'Traité sublime our du
merveilleux' ankündigte und durch den vielzitierten le
Bossu, der dem 'Admirable' im Epos ein besonderes Kapitel
(III 8) gewidmet hatte, bereits eine zu feste und allgemein
anerkannte Stellung erworben, als dass Gottsched es hätte
auf sich nehmen mögen, demselben offen den Krieg zu er-
klären.

5
Servaes, p. 151.

6
Ibid., p. 163.

268

7
   Johann Jacob Breitinger, <u>Critische</u> <u>Dichtkunst</u> (1740);
rpt. (Stuttgart: Metzler, 1966), p. 53. All subsequent
references are placed in the text.

8
   Pyra, p. 6.

9
   Servaes, pp. 135-36.

10
   Johann Jacob Bodmer, <u>Critische Betrachtungen über</u>
<u>die Poetischen Gemälde der Dichter mit einer Vorrede</u>
<u>von Johann Jacob Breitinger</u> (Zürich: Orell, 1741), p. 391.

11
   See Servaes, pp. 131-43.

12
   Johann Jakob Bodmer, Johann Jakob Breitinger,
<u>Critische Briefe</u> (1746);rpt. (Hildesheim: Olms, 1969),
p. 9.

13
   The words <u>Sitten</u> and <u>Sittenmalerei</u> used by Bodmer
and Calepio (<u>Critische Briefe, p. 47</u>) are synonymous to
Charakter and Charakterschilderung in the 18th century.
See Friedrich Braitmaier, <u>Geschichte der Poetischen</u>
<u>Theorie und Kritik</u> (Frauenfeld: Hubers, 1888), p. 26.

14
   According to Braitmaier, Bodmer was influenced by
Pemberton's <u>Observations on Poetry</u>, in which he argues the
superiority of character over action. See Braitmaier, p.
195.

15
   Johann Jakob Bodmer and Johann Jakob Breitinger,
<u>Die Discourse der Mahlern</u> (1721); rpt. (Hildesheim: Olms,
1969), p. 46. Subsequent references are placed in the text.

16
   Karl August Schleiden, <u>Klopstock's Dichtungstheorie</u>
<u>als Beitrag zur Geschichte der deutschen Poetik</u>
(Saarbrücken: West-Ost, 1954), p. 14.

17
    Gerhard Kozielek, "Klopstocks 'Gelehrtenrepublik'
in der zeitgenössischen Kritik," in Friedrich Gottlieb
Klopstock. Werk und Wirkung (Berlin: Akademie, 1978),
p. 56.

18
    Georg Gottfried Gervinus, Geschicte der deutschen
Dichtung, ed. Karl Bartsch (Leipzig: Engelmann, 1874),
V, 29.

19
    Friedrich Gottlieb Klopstock,"Die deutsche Gelehrten-
republik, ihre Einrichtung, ihre Gesetze, Geschichte des
letzten Landtags," in Klopstocks sämtliche Werke (Leipzig:
Göschen, 1823), XII, 117. Subsequent references are placed
in the text.

20
    Friedrich Gottlieb Klopstock, Werke in einem Band
(München: Hanser, n. d.), p. 356. Subsequent references
are placed in the text.

21
    Briefwechsel zwischen Klopstock und den Grafen Christian
und Friedrich Leopold zu Stolberg, ed. Jürgen Behrens
(Neumünster: Wachholtz, 1964), p. 63.

22
    Gerhard Kaiser, Klopstock, Religion und Dichtung
(Gütersloh: Mohn, 1963), p. 268.

23
    Friedrich Gottlieb Klopstock, "David," Sämmtliche
Werke (Leipzig: Göschen, 1823), p. 149.

24
    Anna Tumarkin, Der Ästhetiker Johann Georg Sulzer
(Frauenfeld/Leipzig: Huber, 1933), p. 13.

25
    Armand Nivelle, Kunst- und Dichtungstheorien zwischen
Aufklärung und Klassik (Berlin: Gruyter, 1960), pp. 47-48.

26
Johann Georg Sulzer, Allgemeine Theorie der schönen Künste, 2nd. ed. (Leipzig: Weidman, 1793), III, 487. Subsequent references are placed in the text.

27
Robert Sommer, Grundzüge einer Geschichte der deutschen Psychologie und Aesthetik von Wolff-Baumgarten bis Kant-Schiller (Würzburg: Stahel, 1892), p. 213.

28
See Erich Auerbach, Mimesis--The Representation of Reality in Western Literature (Princeton: Princeton Univ. Press, 1968), pp. 1-23.

29
Elizabeth M. Wilkinson, Johann Elias Schlegel, a German Pioneer in Aesthetics (Oxford: Blackwell, 1945), p. 6 ff.

30
Ibid., p. 48.

31
Johann Elias Schlegel, Aesthetische und dramaturgische Schriften, ed. Johann von Antoniewicz (Heilbronn: Henninger, 1887), p. 9. Subsequent references are placed in the text.

32
An additional step was taken by Schlegel's brother, Johann Adolph, who denies that mimesis is the highest principle of art. He argues that certain poetic genres, in particular the ode and the "Lehrgedicht," are not based on imitation, and that therefore the principle of mimesis cannot be valid for all art. In a disputation with Batteaux, whose translator he was, Schlegel attempts to formulate a new theory of art, and in particular, of poetry. In an essay entitled "Von dem höchsten und allgemeinsten Grundsatze der Poesie," J. A. Schlegel defines poetry as follows: "Die Poesie ist demnach der sinnlichste Ausdruck des Schönen oder des Guten, oder des Schönen und Guten zugleich durch die Sprache." Poetic language and aesthetic considerations are becoming more important than verisimilitude.

33
The essay is titled "Auszug eines Briefs, welcher
einige kritische Anmerkungen über die Trauerspiele der
Alten und Neuern enthält."

34
Johann Elias Schlegel, Ausgewählte Werke (Weimar:
Arion, 1963).

35
Poetische Gemälde, p. 411.

36
Johann Jakob Bodmer, Von dem Einfluss und Gebrauche
der Einbildungskrafft: Zur Ausbesserung des Geschmackes:
Oder Genaue Untersuchung Aller Arten Beschreibungen,
Worinne die Auserlesensten Stellen der berühmtesten Poeten
dieser Zeit mit gründlicher Freyheit beurtheilt werden
(Franckfurt/Leipzig: no publisher, 1727), p. 28. Cited
by Servaes, pp. 85-86.

37
Schlegel, Ausgewählte Werke, pp. 285-309.

38
Peter Wolf, Die Dramen Johann Elias Schlegels,
Zürcher Beiträge zur deutschen Literatur- und
Geistesgeschichte, 22, ed. Emil Staiger (Zürich: Atlantis,
1964), p. 218.

39
Schlegel, Ausgewählte Werke, p. 301.

40
Modern scholarship is attempting to revaluate
Gellert's oeuvre. Carsten Schlingmann's Gellert--Eine
literarhistorische Revision (Bad Homburg/Berlin/Zürich:
Gehlen, 1967) refutes Kurt May's thesis that Gellert's
major contribution lies in the fact that he lead his con-
temporaries toward a new cultural epoch, in spite of his
general mediocrity as an artist. Schlingmann stresses
Gellert's wit and use of irony, refers to his elegant
"Sprachkunst in Vers und Reim," (p. 180) and concludes:
In einem Zeitalter, das auf dem Gebiet der Innenarchitektur,

272

der Illustrationskunde, der Miniaturen (z. B. auf Porzellan)
oder der Tafelmusik--um nur einiges zu nennen--Unvergleich-
liches in Fülle geleistet hat, steht Gellert in der Tat als
der Meister einer geistreich-sinnlichen poetischen Klein-
kunst da. Doch hier gilt es dem Missverständnis vorzubeugen,
als sei damit gar nicht wirkliche Kunst, sondern nur etwas
Kunstgewerbliches gemeint. Nein, Gellert ist vielleicht
gegenüber einem Zeitgenossen wie Klopstock, wenn auch nicht
der kühnere und mächtigere Geist, so doch der grössere 'Meister
der Feder,' vielleicht sogar der grössere Künstler der klei-
neren Form gewesen" (p. 188). An attempt at rescue, perhaps,
but no enshrinement in the pantheon!

41
Hettner, I, 371.

42
Braitmaier, p. 312.

43
Christian Fürchtegott Gellert, Sämmtliche Schriften,
p. 278. Subsequent references are placed in the text.

44
"Des Herrn Professor Gellerts Abhandlung für das
rührende Lustspiel, translated by Lessing, in Gotthold
Ephraim Lessing, Theatralische Bibliothek (n. p., n. d.).

45
Before Gellert, Adam Daniel Richter had differen-
tiated between two types of comedy, the lasterhafte and
the tugendhafte comedy, in his "Regeln und Anmerkungen der
lustigen Schaubühne." See Johannes Coym, Gellerts Lustspiele, Palaestra (Berlin: Mayer & Müller, 1899), II, 2.

46
Gotthold Ephraim Lessing, Werke (München: Hanser,
1973), IV, 330.

47
Christian Fürchtegott Gellert, Lustpiele, Faksimile-
druck nach der Ausgabe von 1747, ed. Horst Steinmetz, Deutsche
Nachdrucke. Texte des 18. Jahrhunderts (Stuttgart: Metzler,
1966), p. 5. Subsequent references are placed in the text.

48
   Coym, p. 23.

49
   See Gottfried F. Merkel, "Gellerts Stellung in der
deutschen Sprachgeschichte," Beiträge zur Geschichte der
deutschen Sprache und Literatur, Sonderheft (Halle: Niemeyer,
1961), LXXXII, 400-01.

50
   Cited by Gottfried Honnefelder in "Christian
Fürchtegott Gellert," Deutsche Dichter des 18. Jahrhunderts,
ed. Benno von Wiese (Berlin: Schmidt, 1977), p. 131.

Chapter III

1
Gerstenberg is portrayed as a transitional figure by
A. M. Wagner, Heinrich Wilhelm von Gerstenberg und der
Sturm und Drang (Heidelberg: Winter, 1924), and by Pierre
Grappin, "Gerstenberg, critique d'Homère et de Shakespeare,"
Etudes germaniques, 6 (1951), pp. 81-92, while Gerth sees
him as one of the founders of Storm and Stress. See Klaus
Gerth, Studien zu Gerstenbergs Poetik (Göttingen: Vanden-
hoeck & Ruprecht, 1960). Gerth's work is a systematic and
detailed compilation of the individual aspects of Gersten-
berg's poetics within an historical context.

2
For comprehensive studies of Shakespeare's impact
on the German drama see Friedrich Gundolf, Shakespeare
und der deutsche Geist (Berlin: Bondi, 1911) and Marie
Joachimi-Dege, Deutsche Shakespeare-Probleme im 18. Jahrhundert und im Zeitalter der Romantik (Leipzig: Haessel,
1907).

3
Wagner, p. 113. Also see Karl S. Guthke, "Gerstenberg und die Shakespearedeutung der deutschen Klassik und
Romantik," Journal of English and German Philology, 58
(1959), pp. 91-108.

4
Hettner, p. 292.

5
Gerth, p. 19. Subsequent references are placed in the
text.

6
Wagner, p. 6.

7
Heinrich Wilhelm von Gerstenberg, Rezensionen in
der Hamburgischen Neuen Zeitung, ed. O. Fischer (Berlin:

Behr, 1904), p. 11. Subsequent references are placed in
the text.

8
    Klaus Gerth, "Heinrich Wilhelm von Gerstenberg,"
Deutsche Dichter des 18. Jahrhunderts, ed. Benno von
Wiese (Berlin: Schmidt, 1977), p. 395.

9
    Heinrich Wilhelm von Gerstenberg, Briefe über die
Merkwürdigkeiten der Literatur, Deutsche Literaturdenkmale
des 18. und 19. Jahrhunderts in Neudrucken, ed. Bernhard
Seuffert (Stuttgart: Göschen, 1890), p. 112.

10
    Guthke, p. 93.

11
    K. W. Ramler, Einleitung in die schönen Wissen-
schaften nach dem Französischen des Herrn Batteux mit
Zusätzen vermehret (Leipzig: Weidmann & Reich, 1756-58),
I, 203.

12
    Johann Georg Hamann, Kreuzzüge des Philologen,
Sturm und Drang--Kritische Schriften (Heidelberg: Schneider,
1972), p. 110.

13
    Ibid, p. 123.

14
    Johann Gottfried Herder, Sämmtliche Werke, ed.
Bernhard Suphan (Berlin: Weidmann, 1878), III, 135.

15
    As a case in point: early structuralist poetics
"envisaged a literary system which would assign a
structural description to each text" (Culler, p. 242).
Later reception theory maintains that the text has a
plurality of meaning because it actively involves the
reader in the process of producing meaning, a concept
which Gerstenberg's emotional involvement of the reader
suggests. This view stresses, of course, the elusiveness
of the linguistic sign and the historical forces affecting
the reader. Jonathan Culler arges that the reader cannot

approach the text in a state of tabula rasa, but "must
bring to it an implicit understanding of the operations of
literary discourse which tells one what to look for"
(Culler, p. 114). Culler sets his sight not on the individual text, but on a "poetics" which strives to define the
conditions of meaning. Terence Hawkes notes that "the key
concept of the proposed poetics is a concern not with content,
but with the process by which content is formulated (Hawkes,
p. 158). In other words, a model that would define what
Culler calls "literary competence." This, however, would
still not resolve the problem of the elusiveness of the
individual linguistic sign. See Jonathan Culler, Structuralist Poetics (Ithaca: Cornell Univ. Press, 1976), pp.
113-30 and 241-54,and Terence Hawkes, Structuralism and
Semiotics (Berkeley: Univ. of California Press, 1977), pp.
151-60.

16
       Wagner, p. 287.

17
       Mark O. Kistler, Drama of the Storm and Stress
(New York: Twayne, 1969), p. 21.

18
       Fritz Martini, Deutsche Literaturgeschichte, 17th ed.
(Stuttgart: Kroner, 1977), p. 217.

19
       See Henry J. Schmidt, "The Language of Confinement.
Gerstenberg's Ugolino and Klinger's Sturm und Drang," Lessing
Yearbook, 11 (München: Huber, 1979), pp. 165-97, and Bruce
Duncan, "'Ich Platze!' Gerstenberg's Ugolino and the Mid-
Life Crisis," Germanic Review, 53 (1978), pp. 13-19.

20
       Werner Kliess, Sturm und Drang (Velber: Friedrich,
1966), p. 29.

21
       Wagner, pp. 333-35.

22
       Heinrich Wilhelm von Gerstenberg, "Ugolino," Sturm
und Drang--Dramatische Schriften (Heidelberg: Schneider,
1972), p. 54. Subsequent references are placed in the text.

23
William H. Rey, <u>Die Poesie der Antipoesie</u> (Heidelberg: Stiem, 1978), p. 35.

24
Wagner, p. 344.

25
Schmidt, p. 194.

Chapter IV

1
Wagner, p. 38.

2
Gundolf, p. 257.

3
Martini, pp. 221-23,

4
Hohoff, p. 45.

5
Jon San-Giorgiu, Sebastien Merciers Dramaturgische
Ideen im Sturm und Drang (Basel: Hirzen, 1921), pp. 62-63.

6
J. M. R. Lenz, "Anmerkungen übers Theater," Sturm und
Drang--Kritische Schriften (Heidelberg: Schneider, 1972)
p. 729. Subsequent references are placed in the text.

7
Friedrich, pp. 19-25.

8
See Gertrude Joyce Hallamore, Das Bild Laurence Sternes
in Deutschland von der Aufklärung bis zur Romantik (Berlin:
Ebering, 1936, and Harvey Waterman Thayer, Laurence Sterne
in Germany (New York: Columbia Univ. Press, 1905).

9
Among the imitators of Sterne, Thayer (see note 8 above)
lists Johann Georg Jacobi, Johann Gottlieb Schummel, Johann
Christian Bock and others, pp. 112-55.

10
According to Martini, "Die 'Anmerkungen' enthalten
nicht Resultate, sie sind vielmehr eine Sprache des Suchens,

der noch unklaren und unvollkommenen Entstehung von Gedanken."
Fritz Martini, "J. M. R. Lenz' Anmerkungen übers Theater,"
Jahrbuch der deutschen Schillergesellschaft, 14 (1970), p.
163. Martini sees the essay primarily as a search for a new
poetics. The danger in too great of an emphasis on the process
is that results are diminished, whereas the "Anmerkungen"
clearly contain a proposal for a new dramatic poetics. The
style can thus be seen as a provocation for the reader, not
as an indication of a lack of alternatives.

11
    Ivo Brak, Poetik in Stichworten, 5th ed. (Kiel:
Hirt, 1969), p. 41.

12
    Hans Georg Gadamer, Wahrheit und Methode (Tübingen:
Mohr, 1960), p. 365.

13
    Hans Robert Jauss, "Literary History as a Challenge
to Literary Theory," New Directions in Literary History,
ed. Ralph Cohen (Baltimore: Johns Hopkins Univ. Press, 1974),
p. 12.

14
    Aristotle, Poetics, trans. Kenneth Telford, "Analysis,"
(South Bend: Gateway, 1961), p. 29.

15
    See Servaes, p. 85.

16
    J. M. R. Lenz, Werke und Schriften, ed. Britta Titel &
Hellmut Haug (Stuttgart: Goverts, 1966), I, 486.

17
    The information in the above paragraph is augmented
by material from Arthur Wald, The Aesthetic Theories of
the German Storm and Stress Movement (Chicago: Univ. of Chicago
Libraries, 1924), pp. 25-29.

18
    J. W. Goethe, Der junge Goethe, ed. Michael Bernays
(Leipzig: Hirzel, 1875), p. 473.

19
    Karl Eibl defines literary realism in "'Realismus' als Widerlegung von Literatur," Poetica, 6 (1974), pp. 456-67. Starting from Popper's view of reality as "diejenige Instanz, deren Widerständigkeit uns zur Revision unserer Erwartungen zwingt," he condludes that literary realism has the same basic structure as the epistemelogical concept of reality. According to Eibl, literary realism manifests itself as a refutation of existing literary conventions. It seems that in this definition, any new approach could be defined as "realism." Furthermore, applying Popper's concept of reality to literary realism, does not adequately separate the phenomenon from literary idealism and surrealism.

20
    Ottomar Rudolf, J. M. R. Lenz. Moralist und Aufklärer (Berlin: Gehlen, 1970), p. 159.

21
    J. M. R. Lenz, Gesammelte Schriften, ed. Franz Blei (München: Müller, 1910), IV, 23. Subsequent references are placed in the text.

22
    For a current analysis of Lenz's relationship to Shakespeare see Hans-Günther Schwarz, "Lenz und Shakespeare," Shakespeare Jahrbuch (1971), pp. 85-96.

23
    In his Shakespeare essay, Herder makes the following comment: "Wie sich alles in der Welt ändert, so musste sich auch die Natur ändern, die eigentlich das griechische Drama schuf." According to Herder, Shakespeare is a great poet because he remains faithful to his historical period: "Da ist nun Shakespeare der grösste Meister, eben weil er nur und immer Diener der Natur ist." Johann Gottfried Herder, "Shakespeare," Sturm und Drang--Kritische Schriften (Heidelberg: Schneider, 1972), pp. 561-70.

24
    Gustav Freytag, Die Technik des Dramas (Leipzig: Hirzel, 1890), p. 222.

25
    Ibid, p. 219.

26
Eckart Oehlenschläger, "Jacob Michael Reinhold Lenz,"
Deutsche Dichter des 18. Jahrhunderts, ed. Benno von Wiese
(Berlin: Schmidt, 1977, pp. 256-57.

27
Paul Böckmann, Formgeschichte der deutschen Dichtung
(Hamburg: Hoffmann & Campe, 1949), I, 655.

28
Eric Blackall, "The Language of Sturm und Drang,"
Stil-und Formprobleme in der Literatur, ed. Paul Böckmann
(Heidelberg: Winter, 1959), pp. 282-83.

29
Ibid., p. 279.

30
Poetics, p. 17.

31
Ibid., p. 16.

Chapter V

1

Osborne, p. 39.

2

For an historical study of Lenz's theory of comedy
see Roger Bauer, "Die Komödientheorie von Jakob Michael
Reinhold Lenz, die älteren Plautus-Kommentare und das
Problem der 'dritten' Gattung," Aspekte der Goethezeit,
ed. Stanley A. Corngold, Michael Curschmann & Theodore
Z. Ziolkowski (Göttingen: Vandenhoeck & Ruprecht, 1977),
pp. 11-37. Also see Bruce Duncan, "A 'Cool Medium' as
Social Corrective: J. M. R. Lenz's Concept of Comedy,"
Colloquia Germanica (1975), pp. 232-45.

3

Karl S. Guthke, "Lenzens Hofmeister und Soldaten--
Ein neuer Formtypus in der Geschichte des deutschen
Dramas," Wirkendes Wort, 10 (1960), p. 274.

4

J. M. R. Lenz, Werke und Schriften, II, 197. Subsequent references are placed in the text. Titel uses the name
"Mariane" for the central character in the Soldaten. It has
been changed to Marie to conform to current usage.

5

C. Hugh Holman, A Handbook to Literature, 3rd. ed.
(New York: Odyssey, 1972), p. 81.

6

Henry J. Schmidt, Satire, Caricature and Perspectivism in the Works of Georg Büchner (The Hague: Mouton,
1970), p. 40.

7

Wolfgang Kayser, Das Groteske (Oldenburg: Stalling,
1957), p. 21.

8

Ibid., p. 61.

9
Ibid., p. 32.

10
An example is Ottomar Rudolf's Jacob Michael Reinhold Lenz. Moralist und Aufklärer. See note 20, chapter IV.

11
Helmut Arntzen, Die ernste Komödie (München: Nymphenburger, 1968), p. 88.

12
Ibid., p. 85.

13
Ibid., p. 89.

14
Georg Büchner, Woyzeck (Stuttgart: Reclam, 1971), p. 6.

15
Allan Blunden, "Lenz, Language, and Love's Labour's Lost," Colloquia Germanica (1974), pp. 252-74.

16
Volker Klotz, Geschlossene und offene Form im Drama (London: Hanser, 1960), p. 201.

17
Ibid., p. 209.

18
Keir Elam, The Semiotics of Theatre and Drama (London: Methuen, 1980), p. 178.

19
Ibid., p. 34.

20
Walter Höllerer, "Lenz. Die Soldaten," Das deutsche Drama vom Barock bis zur Gegenwart, ed. Benno von Wiese (Düsseldorf: Bagel, 1962), pp. 132-33.

21
According to Franz Hubert Crumbach, who characterizes epic drama as a drama of contrasts, the dialogue of

epic drama reflects the contrasts and divisions of the
dramatis personae. See Die Struktur des Epischen Theaters:
Dramaturgie der Kontraste (Braunschweig: Waisenhaus, 1960),
pp. 334-35.

22
Critics disagree concerning whether Lenz uses language
to stereotype characters. Gert Mattenklott sees linguistic
sterotypes in the Hofmeister. See Melancholie in der Dramatik
des Sturm und Drang (Stuttgart: Metzler, 1968), pp. 145-46.
However Titel, in "Nachahmung der Natur als Prinzip dramatischer Gestaltung bei Jakob Michael Reinhold Lenz," Diss.
Frankfurt, 1961, denies the existence of linguistic stereo-
types. I agree with Titel.

23
Höllerer, pp. 132-35.

24
Johann Christoph Adelung, Versuch eines vollständigen
grammatisch-kritischen Wörterbuches der Hochdeutschen Mundart
(Leipzig: Breitkopf, 1780), VI, 1059.

25
Ronald W. Langacker, Language and its Structure,
2nd ed. (New York: Harcourt, Brace, 1973), p. 91.

26
Crumbach, p. 286.

27
Höllerer, p. 130.

28
Edward P. Harris, "Structural Unity in J. M. R. Lenz's
Der Hofmeister: A Revaluation," Seminar 8 (1972), pp. 80-81.

29
Ibid., p. 87.

30
Gero von Wilpert, Sachwörterbuch der Literatur
(Stuttgart: Kröner, 1969), p. 495.

31
Gert Mattenklott describes Lenz's structural technique
as a filmatic technique, p. 131. See note 22 above.

32
Guthke, p. 274. See note 3.

33
J. L. Styan, The Dark Comedy (Cambridge: Cambridge
Univ. Press, 1968), pp. 7-30.

34
Karl S. Guthke, Geschichte und Poetik der deutschen
Tragikomödie (Göttingen: Vandenhoeck & Ruprecht, 1961),
p. 64.

35
Oehlenschläger, p. 764.

36
Styan, p. 1.

37
Ibid., p. 1.

38
Guthke, Geschichte und Poetik, p. 13.

39
Ibid., p. 15.

40
Giambattista Guarini, "The Compendium of Tragicomic
Poetry," Literary Criticsim: Plato to Dryden, ed. Allan
H. Gilbert (Detroit: Wayne State Univ. Press, 1962), p. 524.

41
Guthke, Geschichte und Poetik, p. 123.

42
Andreas Huyssen, "Gesellschaftsgeschichte und
literarische Form: J. M. R. Lenz's Komödie Der Hofmeister,"
Monatshefte, 71 (1979), pp. 142-43.

43
Ibid., p. 134.

44
Briefe von und an J. M. R. Lenz, ed. Karl Freye &
Wolfgang Stammler (Leipzig: Wolff, 1918), I, 191.

45
    Friedrich Dürrenmatt, "Theaterprobleme," Theater-
schriften und Reden (Zürich: Verlag der Arche, 1966)
pp. 93 & 108.

46
    Ibid., p. 108.

Chapter VI

1
  Blei, V, 375.

2
  Ibid., 374.

3
  The battle between the ancients and the moderns, classicism and modernity, or a newly emerging "realism," had
preoccupied literary critics and poets for some time. In
Spain Cervantes had opted for classical drama, but the
mixed style of Lope de Vega's tragicomedies conquered the
Spanish stage. In England, John Dryden's "An Essay of
Dramatic Poesy" (1668) voices some opposition to the classicistic doctrine. And in France, modernity challenged antiquity
in the views of Perrault in his Parallel d'ancients et de
moderne versus Boileau's L'art poétique (1674).

4
  A. W. Schlegel, Vorlesungen über dramatische Kunst
und Literatur (Stuttgart: Kohlhammer, 1967), II, 32.

5
  Ibid., pp. 111-12.

WORKS CONSULTED

Adelung, Johann Christoph. Versuch eines vollständigen grammatisch-kritischen Wörterbuches der hochdeutschen Mundart. Leipzig: Breitkopf, 1780. Vol. IV.

Aristotle. Poetics. Trans. Kenneth Telford. South Bend: Gateway, 1961.

Arntzen, Helmut. Die ernste Komödie. München: Nymphenburg, 1968.

Auerbach, Erich. Mimesis--The Representation of Reality in Western Literature. Princeton: Princeton Univ. Press, 1953.

Bauer, Roger. "Die Komödientheorie von Jakob Michael Reinhold Lenz, die älteren Plautus-Kommentare und das Problem der 'dritten' Gattung." Aspekte der Goethezeit. Ed. Stanley A. Corngold, Michael Curschmann & Z. Ziolkowski. Göttingen: Vandenhoeck & Ruprecht, 1977.

Benseler, David P. "J. M. R. Lenz: An Indexed Bibliography with an Introduction on the History of the Manuscripts and Editions." Diss. Univ. of Oregon, 1971.

Blackall, Eric. "The Language of Sturm und Drang." Stil- und Formprobleme in der Literatur. Ed. Paul Böckmann. Heidelberg: Winter, 1959.

Blunden, Allan. "Lenz, Language, and Love's Labour's Lost." Colloquia Germanica (1974), pp. 252-74.

Böckmann, Paul. Formgeshichte der deutschen Dichtung. Hamburg: Hoffmann & Campe, 1949. Vol. I.

Bodmer, Johann Jakob. Critische Betrachtungen über die Poetischen Gemälde der Dichter mit einer Vorrede von Johann Jakob Breitinger. Zürich: Orell, 1741.

----------. Von dem Einfluss und Gebrauche der Einbildungs-krafft: Zur Ausbesserung des Geschmackes: Oder Genaue Untersuchung Aller Arten Beschreibungen, Worinne die

Auserlesensten Stellen der Berühmtesten Poeten Dieser
    Zeit mit gründtlicher Freyheit beurtheilt werden.
    Franckfurt/Leipzig: (no publisher), 1727.

Bodmer, Johann Jakob and Breitinger, Johann Jakob. Critische
    Briefe (1746); rpt. Hildesheim: Olms, 1969.

_____. Die Discourse der Mahlern (1721); rpt. Hildesheim:
    Olms, 1969.

Braitmaier, Friedrich. Geschichte der Poetischen Theorie
    und Kritik von den Diskursen der Maler bis auf Lessing.
    Frauenfeld: Hubers, 1888.

Brak, Ivo. Poetik in Stichworten. 5th ed. Kiel: Hirt, 1969.

Breitinger, Johann Jakob. Critische Dichtkunst (1740); rpt.
    Stuttgart: Metzler, 1966.

Briefe von und an J. M. R. Lenz. Ed. Karl Freye & Wolfgang
    Stammler. Leipzig: Wolff, 1918.

Briefwechsel zwischen Klopstock und den Grafen Christian
    und Friedrich Leopold zu Stolberg. Ed. Jürgen
    Behrens. Neumünster: Wachholtz: 1964.

Bruford. W. H. Germany in the 18th Century: The Social
    Background of the Literary Revival. Cambridge:
    Cambridge Univ. Press, 1935.

Büchner, Georg. Woyzeck. Stuttgart: Reclam, 1971.

Burger, Heinz O. "J. M. R. Lenz: Der Hofmeister."
    Das deutsche Lustspiel. Ed. H. Steffen. Göttingen:
    Vandenhoeck & Ruprecht, 1968.

Coym, Johannes. Gellerts Lustspiele. Palaestra II.
    Berlin: Mayer & Müller, 1899.

Crumbach, Franz Hubert. Die Struktur des Epischen Theaters:
    Dramaturgie der Kontraste. Braunschweig: Waisenhaus,
    1960.

Culler, Jonathan. Structuralist Poetics. Ithaca: Cornell
    Univ. Press, 1975.

290

Dosenheimer, Elise. Das deutsche soziale Drama von Lessing
    bis Sternheim. Konstanz: Südverlag, 1949.

Duncan, Bruce. "A 'Cool Medium' as Social Corrective: J.
    M. R. Lenz's Concept of Comedy." Colloquia Germanica
    (1975), pp. 232-45.

----------. "'Ich Platze!' Gerstenberg's Ugolino and the
    Mid-Life Crisis." Germanic Review, 53 (1978), 13-18.

Dürrenmatt, Friedrich. Theaterschriften und Reden. Zürich:
    Verlag der Arche, 1966.

Eibl, Karl. "'Realismus' als Widerlegung von Literatur."
    Poetica, 6 (1974), 456-67.

Elam, Keir. The Semiotics of Theatre and Drama. London:
    Methuen, 1980.

Freytag, Gustav. Die Technik des Dramas. Leipzig:
    Hirzel, 1890.

Friedrich, Theodor. Die Anmerkungen übers Theater des
    Dichters J. M. R. Lenz. Leipzig: Voigtlander, 1909.

Gadamer, Hans Georg. Wahrheit und Methode. Tübingen:
    Mohr, 1960.

Gellert, Christian Fürchtegott. Lustspiele. Faksimile-
    druck nach der Ausgabe von 1747. Ed. Horst Steinmetz.
    Deutsche Nachdrucke. Texte des 18. Jahrhunderts.

----------. Sämmtliche Schriften. Leipzig: Wiedmann &
    Fritsch, 1769.

Genton, Elisabeth. Jakob Michael Reinhold Lenz et la
    scène Allemande. Paris: Didier, 1966.

Gerstenberg, Heinrich Wilhelm von. Briefe über die Merk-
    würdigkeiten der Literatur. Deutsche Literaturdenkmale
    des 18. und 19. Jahrhunderts in Neudrucken. Ed. Bernhard
    Seuffert. Stuttgart: Goschen, 1890.

----------. Rezensionen in der Hamburgischen Neuen Zeitung,
    Ed. O. Fischer. Berlin: Behr, 1904.

----------. "Ugolino." Sturm und Drang--Dramatische Schriften.
Heidelberg: Schneider, 1972, Vol. I.

Gerth, Klaus. "Heinrich Wilhelm von Gerstenberg." Deutsche
Dichter des 18. Jahrhunderts. Ed. Benno von Wiese.
Berlin: Schmidt, 1977.

----------. Studien zu Gerstenbergs Poetik. Göttingen:
Vandenhoeck & Ruprecht, 1960.

Gervinus, Georg Gottfried. Geschichte der deutschen Dichtung.
Ed. Karl Bartsch. Leipzig: Engelmann, 1874, Vol. V.

Girard, René. J. M. R. Lenz 1751-1792: Genèse d'une dramaturgie
du tragi-comique. Paris: Klincksieck, 1968.

Goethe, J. W. Der junge Goethe. Ed. Michael Bernays. Leipzig:
Hirzel, 1875.

Grappin, Pierre. "Gerstenberg, critique d'Homère et de
Shakespeare," Etudes germaniques, 6 (1951), 81-92.

Guarini, Giambattista. "The Compendium of Tragicomic
Poetry." Literary Criticism: Plato to Dryden.
Ed. Allan H. Gilbert. Detroit: Wayne State Univ.
Press, 1962.

Gundolf, Friedrich. Shakespeare und der deutsche Geist.
Berlin: Bondi, 1911.

Guthke, Karl S. Geschichte und Poetik der deutschen Tragikomödie. Göttingen: Vandenhoeck & Ruprecht, 1961.

----------. "Lenzens Hofmeister und Soldaten--Ein neuer
Formtypus in der Geschichte des deutschen Dramas,"
Wirkendes Wort, 10 (1960), 274-286.

----------. "Gerstenberg und die Shakespearedeutung der
deutschen Klassik und Romantik," Journal of English
and German Philology, 58 (1959), 91-108.

Hallamore, Joyce. Das Bild Laurence Sternes in Deutschland
von der Aufklärung bis zur Romantik. Berlin: Ebering,
1936.

Hamann, Johann Georg. "Kreuzzüge des Philologen." Sturm
    und Drang--Kritische Schriften. Heidelberg: Schneider,
    1972.

Harris, Edward P. "Structural Unity in J. M. R. Lenz's
    Hofmeister: A Revaluation." Seminar, 8 (1972), 77-87.

Hawkes, Terence. Structuralism and Semiotics. Berkeley:
    Univ. of California Press, 1977.

Herder, Johann Gottfried. "Shakespeare." Sturm und Drang--
    Kritische Schriften. Heidelberg: Schneider, 1972.

----------. Sämmtliche Werke. Ed. Bernhard Suphan. Berlin:
    Weidmann, 1878. Vol. III.

Hettner, Hermann. Geschichte der deutschen Literatur im
    18. Jahrhundert. 4th ed. Braunschweig: Vieweg, 1893.
    Vol. I.

Hinderer, Walter. "Lenz--Der Hofmeister." Die deutsche
    Komödie. Ed. Walter Hinck. Düsseldorf: Bagel, 1977.

Hohoff, Curt. J. M. R. Lenz. Reinbek: Rowohlt, 1977.

Höllerer, Walter. "Lenz. Die Soldaten." Das deutsche Drama
    vom Barock bis zur Gegenwart. Ed. Benno von Wiese.
    Düsseldorf: Bagel, 1962.

Holman, C. Hugh. A Handbook to Literature. 3rd ed. New
    York: Odyssey, 1972.

Honnefelder, Gottfried. "Christian Fürchtegott Gellert."
    Deutsche Dichter des 18. Jahrhunderts. Ed. Benno
    von Wiese. Berlin: Schmidt, 1977.

Huyssen, Andreas. "Gesellschaftsgeschichte und literarische
    Form: J. M. R. Lenz' Komödie Der Hofmeister. Monats-
    hefte, 71 (1978), 131-44.

Inbar, Eva Maria. "Goethes Lenz-Porträt." Wirkendes Wort,
    28 (1978), 422-29.

Jauss, Hans Robert. "Literary History as a Challenge to
    Literary Theory." New Directions in Literary History.
    Ed. Ralph Cohen. Baltimore: Johns Hopkins Univ.
    Press, 1974.

Joachimi-Dege, Marie. Deutsche Shakespeare-Probleme im 18. Jahrhundert und im Zeitalter der Romantik. Leipzig: Haessel, 1907.

Kaiser, Gerhard. Aufklärung--Empfindsamkeit--Sturm und Drang. München: Francke, 1976.

----------. Klopstock. Religion und Dichtung. Gütersloh: Mohn, 1963.

Kayser, Wolfgang. Das Groteske. Oldenburg: Stalling, 1957.

Kistler, Mark O. Drama of the Storm and Stress. New York: Twayne, 1969.

Kitsching, Laurence P. A. Der Hofmeister. A Critical Analysis of Bertolt Brecht's Adaption of Jacob Michael Reinhold Lenz's Drama. München: Fink, 1976.

Kliess, Werner. Sturm und Drang. Velber: Friedrich, 1966.

Klopstock, Friedrich Gottlieb. Sämmtliche Werke. Leipzig: Goschen, 1823.

----------. Werke in einem Band. München: Hanser, n. d.

Klotz, Volker. Geschlossene und offene Form im Drama. München: Hanser, 1960.

Kozielek, Gerhard. "Klopstocks 'Gelehrtenrepublik' in der zeitgenössischen Kritik." Friedrich Gottlieb Klopstocks Werk und Wirkung. Berlin: Akademie-Verlag, 1978.

Langacker, Ronald W. Language and its Structure. New York: Harcourt, Brace, 1973.

Langen, August. "Klopstocks sprachgeschichtliche Bedeutung." Wirkendes Wort, 3 (1952-3), 330-46.

Lenz, J. M. R. Gesammelte Schriften. Ed. Franz Blei. München: Müller, 1910.

----------. Werke und Schriften. Ed. Britta Titel & Hellmut Haug. 2 vols. Stuttgart: Goverts, 1966.

----------. "Anmerkungen übers Theater." Sturm und Drang--
    Kritische Schriften. Heidelberg: Schneider, 1972.

Lessing, Gotthold Ephraim. Werke. München: Hanser, 1973.
    Vol. IV.

Liebman, Parrinello Giuli. Morale e società nell' opera
    di J. M. R. Lenz. Napoli: Istituto Universitario
    Orientale, 1976.

Martin, G. M. "A Note on the Major Plays of J. M. R. Lenz."
    German Life and Letters, 31 (1977-78), 78-87.

Martini, Fritz. "J. M. R. Lenz' Anmerkungen übers Theater."
    Jahrbuch der deutschen Schillergesellschaft, 14 (1970),
    159-182.

----------. Deutsche Literaturgeschichte. 17th ed. Stutt-
    gart: Kroner, 1977.

----------. "Die stumme Schönheit, Spiel und Sprache im
    deutschen Lustspiel." Deutschunterricht, 15 (1963),
    7-32.

Mattenklott, Gert. Melancholie in der Dramatik des Sturm
    und Drang. Stuttgart: Metzler, 1968.

Melchinger, Siegfried. Dramaturgie des Sturms und Drangs.
    Gotta: Klotz, 1929.

Merkel, Gottfried F. "Gellerts Stellung in der deutschen
    Sprachgeschichte." Beiträge zur Geschichte der
    deutschen Sprache und Literatur. Sonderband. Halle:
    Niemeyer, 1961. Vol. LXXXII.

Nicolai, Friedrich. Leiden und Freuden Werthers des Mannes
    (1775), rpt. München: Fink, 1972.

Nivelle, Armand. Kunst-und Dichtungstheorie zwischen Auf-
    klärung und Klassik. Berlin: de Gruyter, 1960.

Oehlenschläger, Eckart. "Jacob Michael Reinhold Lenz."
    Deutsche Dichter des 18. Jahrhunderts. Ed. Benno
    von Wiese. Berlin: Schmidt, 1977.

Osborne, John. J. M. R. Lenz: The Renunciation of Heroism.
    Palaestra, 262. Göttingen: Vandenhoeck & Ruprecht, 1975.

Parkes, Ford Briton. Epische Elemente in Jakob Michael Reinhold Lenzens Drama Der Hofmeister. Göttingen: Kummerle, 1973.

Pascal, Roy. The German Sturm und Drang. New York: Philosophical Library, 1953.

Pyra, Jakob Immanuel. Erweis, dass die Gottschedianische Sekte den Geschmack Verderbe/Fortsetzung des Erweises (1743-44) rpt. Hildesheim/New York: Olms, 1974.

Ramler, K. W. Einleitung in die schönen Wissenschaften nach dem Französischen des Herrn Batteux mit Zusätzen vermehret. Leipzig: Weidmann & Reich, 1756-68.

Rey, William H. Die Poesie der Antipoesie. Heidelberg: Stiem, 1978.

Rieck, Werner. "Das Pandaemonium germanicum von J. M. R. Lenz als poetischer Kommentar zur Literaturprogrammatik des frühen Sturm und Drang." Kwartalnik Neofilologiczny, 26 (1979), 235-58.

Rudolf, Ottomar. Jacob Michael Reinhold Lenz. Moralist und Aufklärer. Berlin: Gehlen, 1970.

San-Giorgiu, Jon. Sebastien Merciers Dramaturgische Ideen im Sturm und Drang. Basel: Hirzen, 1921.

Schlegel, A. W. Vorlesungen über dramatische Kunst und Literatur. Stuttgart: Kohlhammer, 1967. Vols. I and II.

Schlegel, Johann Elias. Aesthetische und Dramaturgische Schriften. Ed. Johann von Antoniewicz. Heilbronn: Henninger, 1887.

----------. Ausgewählte Werke. Weimar: Arion, 1963.

Schleiden, Karl August. Klopstocks Dichtungstheorie als Beitrag zur Geschichte der deutschen Poetik. Saarbrücken: West-Ost, 1954.

Schlingmann, Carsten. Gellert: Eine Literarhistorische Revision. Bad Homburg/Berlin/Zürich: Gehlen, 1967.

Schmidt, Henry J. "Gerstenberg's Ugolino and Klinger's Sturm und Drang." Lessing Yearbook, 11. München: Huber, 1979, pp. 165-97.

----------. Satire, Caricature and Perspectivism in the Works of Georg Büchner. The Hague: Mouton, 1970.

Schoeps, Karl H. "Zwei moderne Lenz-Bearbeitungen." Monatshefte, 67 (1975), pp. 437-51.

Schwarz, Hans-Günther. "Lenz und Shakespeare." Shakespeare Jahrbuch (1971), pp. 85-96.

Servaes, Franz. "Die Poetik Gottscheds und der Schweizer." Quellen und Forschungen zur Sprach- und Culturgeschichte der Germanischen Völker. Ed. Bernhard Ten Brink, Ernst Martin & Erich Schmidt. Strassburg: Trübner, 1887.

Sommer, Robert. Grundzüge einer Geschichte der deutschen Psychologie und Aesthetik von Wolff-Baumgarten bis Kant-Schiller. Würzburg: Stahel, 1892.

Styan, J. L. The Dark Comedy. Cambridge: Univ. Press, 1968.

Sulzer, Johann Georg. Allgemeine Theorie der schönen Künste. 2nd ed. Leipzig: Weidmann, 1793.

Thayer, Harvey Waterman. Laurence Sterne in Germany. New York: Columbia Univ. Press, 1905.

Titel, Britta. "Nachahmung der Natur als Prinzip dramatischer Gestaltung bei Jakob Michael Reinhold Lenz." Diss. Frankfurt, 1961.

Tumarkin, Anna. Der Ästhetiker Johann Georg Sulzer. Frauenfeld/Leipzig: Huber, 1933.

Wagner, A. M. Heinrich Wilhelm von Gerstenberg und der Sturm und Drang. Heidelberg: Winter, 1924.

Wald, Arthur. The Aesthetic Theories of the German Storm and Stress Movement. Chicago: The Univ. of Chicago Libraries, 1924.

Wilkinson, Elizabeth M. Johann Elias Schlegel, a German Pioneer in Aesthetics. Oxford: Blackwell, 1945.

Wilpert, Gero. Sachwörterbuch der Literatur. Stuttgart: Kroner, 1969.

Wolf, Peter. Die Dramen Johann Elias Schlegels. Zürcher Beiträge zur deutschen Literatur-und Geistesgeschichte, 22. Ed. Emil Staiger. Zürich: Atlantis, 1964.